Golden Tongue:
The Innocent Man that Killed Her?

◆━━◆

by Richard Bailey

The contents of this work, including, but not limited to, the accuracy of events, people, and places depicted; opinions expressed; permission to use previously published materials included; and any advice given or actions advocated are solely the responsibility of the author, who assumes all liability for said work and indemnifies the publisher against any claims stemming from publication of the work.

All Rights Reserved
Copyright © 2022 by Richard Bailey

No part of this book may be reproduced or transmitted, downloaded, distributed, reverse engineered, or stored in or introduced into any information storage and retrieval system, in any form or by any means, including photocopying and recording, whether electronic or mechanical, now known or hereinafter invented without permission in writing from the publisher.

Dorrance Publishing Co
585 Alpha Drive
Suite 103
Pittsburgh, PA 15238
Visit our website at www.dorrancebookstore.com

ISBN: 978-1-6366-1294-2
eISBN: 978-1-6366-1880-7

RICHARD ROLAND BAILEY
From Childhood Until Today: 1929-2012

- CADDIED at Bloomington Country Club, made enough money to buy a bicycle and sell newspapers
- SOLD *LOOK* Magazine door to door after school
- RAISED PIGEONS and sold babies (scabs) to Mr. Goodspeed
- SOLD SNAKES to a scientist. My dog Bob and I would hunt garter snakes water moccasins in a special pasture with a creek.
- WORKED ON PIG FARM, chicken farm, and dairy farm
- PASSED OUT PAMPHLETS and collected alms for brother Tom, a preacher for his tabernacle
- WENT INTO PRODUCE BUSINESS after the Air Force
- GOT INTO COSMETICS BUSINESS with a product known as Satin Leg Shaving Solution. At a franchise show in Las Vegas, sold business to customer for $250, 000
- STARTED A BALLOON GIFT-WRAPPING BUSINESS
- OPENED DRIVER EDUCATION SCHOOLS in Illinois and California with over seventy instructors. Built from the ground up in California on a choice piece of property
- TOOK OVER MEDICAL CLINICS at 500 North Michigan Avenue and the Oak Brook Professional Building in Chicago
- BOUGHT A FIFTY-SEVEN-UNIT APARTMENT BUILDING on a $3 million unsecured note. All condos sold out within a few weeks
- HAD A LEASE OPTION ON A 207-ACRE FARM in Antioch, Illinois
- PROVIDED WORLD CLASS SALES AND MARKETING to independent inventors and entrepreneurs, trademarking, or patenting their ideas
- TAKING OVER BUSINESSES FOR TWENTY YEARS, such as Allied Laboratory, World Class Sales and Marketing for 10 percent of the gross on a five-year agreement.

Golden Tongue

There has been volumes of news media including television, radio, books, magazines, and other print media about Richard Bailey recently.

GOLDEN TONGUE. Prosecutors used this term to imply that I was very persuasive and convincing in what I would tell people, particularly ladies.

GALLOPING GIGILO was used by the national news media based on comments by a person in the courtroom told saying that he saw Helen Brach and myself riding the horse trails.

RAKISH ROMEO was the Brainchild of *People* Magazine's "Romance" Editor.

NUMBER ONE CON-MAN IN THE WORLD was the input from *World News*.

SILKEN ROMEO was the creation of the noted *Chicago Magazine*.

NATURAL BORN CON-MAN is attributable to author Ken Glade in his book titled *Hot Blood*.

POLISHED COUNTRY BOY came into being after I sold a horse to Kit Moss, a Harvard Business Graduate who employs a thousand in her sales and marketing business. She even dated that "polished country boy" for a few years… Hmm?

THE GENIUS. This Richard Bailey comments Perry Snyderman, a top real estate attorney at Rudnick and Wolf Law Firm in Chicago, to this day at the successful conclusion of negotiations to purchase a $3 million condominium property (fifty-five units) on Lake Shore Drive in Chicago. Funding was guaranteed to RICHARD BAILEY on an unsecured NOTE through Paul Jones, through GLENVIEW BANK.

Both Mr. Snyderman and Mr. Jones boarded horses at Bailey's Stables and were considered Mr. Bailey's good friends.

Further, Mr. Jones and Mr. Bailey went fox hunting together in Trion, North Carolina, each January.

Kitt Moss, Perry Snyderman, and Paul Jones are only a very few of the myriad friends of Richard Bailey.

Richard's first grade teacher told his mother, Margaret Self Bailey, Jewish, that she believed Richard belonged in a school for "retarded youngsters."

Other hand, Richard's mother believed in her son and knew he would become a polished, suave entrepreneur.

WORLD NEWS and KEN GLAD will both be proven that I am NOT a "CONMAN from CHILDHOOD."

LT. DAVID HAMM
CONNECTION BETWEEN NOTORIOUS SILAS JAYNE

Introduction

Why did Helen Brach invite me to be with her in New York on New Year's Eve?

A few days before New Year's Eve 1976, I was in my office at Bailey's stables in Morton Grove, Illinois, when I received a call from Helen Brach. She told me that she missed me and was madly in love with me. She said, "I'll send you a ticket, and pay for everything if you will just be with me on New Year's Eve." She had previously told me several times that she had never met anyone that she would rather be with than me. Now, she made me a believer—I accepted the invitation.

I would always have one of Helen's favorite selections a bottle of Rothschild red wine, or Dom Perignon champagne—on ice, ready at the table with one glass—our "love cup."

I would sit right next to her, hold one of her hands lightly, take the glass of wine and give her the first sip, along with a little kiss. Helen thought this to be very romantic, so I would continue to da it throughout the evening. Lamb chops for dinner, always the chivalrous gentleman, I would rise upon her entering or leaving, and assist her with being seated in an animated, obsequious manner. Helen told me that she had never felt so good, so loved, and so much in love in her life.

Richard Bailey

Helen loved to dance, especially with me. Because when we took to the floor everyone would stand back and watch in amazement as we artfully executed fantastic dance steps from my inventory of Arthur Murray styles.

Helen absolutely loved to dance, especially the tango and the waltz. She often told me that she had never danced with anyone who could dance like I did. She never knew that I was once the #1 dance instructor at Arthur Murray before I met her. Well, we had a ball dancing the night away to the melodic strains of the Guy Lombardo band.

The next day we were to be on our way back to our respective destinations—she to Miami, me to Chicago. But prior to our leaving, Helen expressed her strong desire to have me move in

H E L E N, I didn't forget you and I never will…

This is what Richard Bailey will do for Helen Brach. The pattern started to fall into place after having been in prison for nineteen years. The "mob" exposure, the fortune, all the connections are there.

This tragic puzzle will be put to an end and unraveled after all of these years.

Richard Bailey has followed the money… There will be a billion-dollar lawsuit against Animal Protections Institute and its president, Belton Mouras. His association with the "mob" will be revealed. This will open up a can of worms bigger than the moon, Spilotro Brothers who used to run Las Vegas. They had to know about the fortune for the mob to kill them. The way the mob set up the Brach Murder, no one would have ever suspected.

After all of this is exposed, a new Animal Protection Society will be opened with no connection to the ones responsible for what happened in the past. It will be connected only to Richard Bailey and Helen Brach.

Helen Brach had been donating $1 million per year to the Animal Protection Society. When Joe Plemmons finally CONFESSED to killing Ms. Brach and the "mob" involvement was discovered, the estate's annual contribution increased to $187 million.

There will be a book written and a movie deal negotiated, both of which will be hits; the book becoming a best seller.

There will be other lawsuits such as one against Lt. David Hamm, the captain of the ship in the courtroom, and the family vendetta with the Baileys who was connected to the notorious Silas Jayne Horse Mafia in Chicago.

In 1995, Pat Tuite was the Attorney-of-Record for Richard Bailey. Prosecutor, Steve Miller, had Attorney Tuite in his "Back Pocket."

"BRIBERY is the way the government does business," Miller admitted on NBC *DATELINE* in 1996. THIS IS JUST THE BEGINNING of an ongoing saga.

PROCEEDS MADE FROM THE *GOLDEN TONGUE Volumes I, II, III*, and *IV* will be donated to a MEMORIAL to HELEN BRACH in two funds, the first to be dedicated to the preservation of Wild Life around the world. The second to be dedicated to non-denominational Christian organizations spreading the Gospel of Jesus Christ. Both were fundamentally important goals in the life of HELEN BRACH 'CANDY' HEIRESS, "The TRUE LIFE AND DEATH OF ONE OF THE RICHEST LADIES in the world in her time, and one of the most misunderstood…"

I, RICHARD BAILEY, had four years with this wonderful lady as the "Love of My Life." Knowing her so well that after all this time and knowing that she would want the ANIMALS to benefit from the world's loss of this tremendously caring individual, I know that she would want the proceeds from "The Truth Being Told" in THE GOLDEN TONGUE book collection, written by the only person THAT KNOWS THE REAL HELEN BRACH and the TRUTH.

I, RICHARD BAILEY, believe that Helen would want to leave behind a legacy of Assistance for the Animals that are endangered.

The Picture of the Eagle will stand for the strength of a lady whose life was cut short by greed and an insidious World of Business that she really only wanted to be LOVED and LOVE the WORLD of ANIMALS…

Told by RICHARD BAILEY

THE INNOCENT MAN THAT KILLED HER? (This story is being told by the man that has been sentenced to a death penalty by his age and by his health... a man that has proven the "facts" that should have released him, and the facts could only be told after LOVING this LADY.)

RICHARD BAILEY...GUT FEELINGS WHAT HAPPENED TO "CANDY HEIRESS," HELEN BRACH, "LOVE OF MY LIFE..."

From 1977, the year I was waiting for Helen Brach in Palm Beach, Florida, and Helen never showed up. I have had sleepless nights doing a lot of thinking about Helen and what really happened to her. Horse mafia Frank Jayne, Jack Matlick, Lee Rider, and the Spilotro Bros. knew I was in Palm Beach waiting for Helen. I bought Frank Jayn'es plane ticket from him to Palm Beach. Frank insisted I buy his ticket. I told him I'll buy my own. The price was right, so I bought Frank's ticket to Palm Beach. They knew I was going to marry Helen. From the New Year's party, we spent together in New York at the Waldorf Astoria, dancing the night away while the Guy Lombardo Band was playing, Helen and I dated for a few years. The Horse mafia Frank Jayne Jr. hired Larry Salvaggio to kill me by placing a bomb in my car at Belmont Harbor in Chicago. They envied me before ever meet Helen Brach. Now they figure out just what to do with Helen while I am down in Palm Beach waiting for her. This would be the perfect time to take Helen out of Bailey's life, and get all her bonds, money, jewelry, etc. to square up Jack Matlick's debt. Bailey will never know what happened to his beautiful lady, Helen.

After November 13 and 14, 2003, When the conversation that took place at Coleman, Florida in the R. D. office and the Captain's office, while I was thinking about "Helen Brach," on CNN at 7:30 A. M. , on February 2, 2006, the host, Miles, had Dr. Helen Fisher on his program, Dr. Fisher was talking about (murder). Here are a few things she was talking about: Gut Feelings, Intuition Feelings, being Perceptive and following Hunches are important. I realized at that time it was my Gut Feelings that told me this is the way everything took place. This is the way it went. When two detectives left the stables I called Jack Matlick. I said Jack what's up? detectives were at my house asking questions about Helen. Jack you were with her in the house all the time. You must know what happened to her. Mr. Bailey it should have never happened. Jack sounded very nervous and depressed. I said Jack why don't you meet me at the Holiday Inn, Edens and Lake Cook Rd. in about twenty minutes. He agreed. Jack showed up looking very depressed and like he hadn't slept for a while. Jack said I knew Helen was planning on spending the winter with you in Florida. She was going to sell the farm and the house in Glenview. Then I would be out in the cold. I owed big gambling debts to the mob, Spilotro Bros. Also, the Horse mafia Frank Jayne. So, I made a deal with them to come by Thursday around 1:00 P. M. and take whatever they needed to clear up my debts. I told them they had to be out by 4:00 P. M. They said that would be plenty of time. I figured this would work out perfect. Helen would walk in the house with me and the house would be cleaned out while I was gone for the afternoon and picking up Helen from the airport. Then I would have had everything covered. Unfortunately, we walked in around 5:00 P. M. , and they were still there. When Helen saw her house was in shambles and torn up, she ran for the phone and said she was calling the police. At that time Frank and the Spilotro Bros. grabbed her and ended her life. We had no choice. That was horrible how could you ever do something like this? If we hadn't done that, the mob would have killed all of us. Jack what did you do with the body? It was buried in concrete just like Jimmy Hoffa. Jack, meet me at N. W. stable, let's talk to Frank about this. I waited for Jack and we walked in together. He was talking with Lee Rider. Frank said what's up with you and Jack? Frank, you know what's up. You, Jack, and the Spilotro bros. killed Helen. Frank said we had no choice—either that or the mob would have killed all of us. Well, it is too bad they didn't kill you cold blooded killers. Frank, if Jack would have told Helen he owed you and the Spilotro Bros. big bucks, she would have paid it off. Helen was a very liberal person. When I was with Helen in Miami, at the Doral Hotel in the sky dome on top of the hotel having dinner and dancing, a friend of Helen's showed up with his wife to join us. At the end of dinner, Helen took out her checkbook and wrote her husband a check for $100, 000, handed it to him, and said, "I hope this will get you back on your feet." Well, it is too late to do anything now. Frank, where's Helen's body? It is buried in concrete just like Jimmy Hoffa was. You are all a bunch of cold-blooded killers. I am getting out of here. Bailey, before you leave make sure you say nothing to no one, or I will kill you myself. This time it will happen. The state's attorney lawyer was there at this meeting Tom Biesley, John A. T. F. person and John O'Connell from the state's attorney office on November 13 and 14, 2003.

Then (2005) Joe Plemmons admitted he killed Helen Brach. Horse Mafia Frank Jayne, Jack Matlick, Lee Rider and Spilotro Bros. were involved and others. I realize my story is a little different then Joe Plemmons. But the most important part of Joe Plemmons' confession is that he named the same Horse Mafia Frank Jayne, Lee Rider, Jack Matlick and Spilotro Bros. as I did. Plus, I would say this one had to come from Joe's "heart." This was not a "bribe" like in my case. Joe was paid big money, released from prison in California with his girlfriend. Steve Miller admitted on NBC *Dateline* it was a "bribe." When Dennis Murphy confronted Miller, then Miller said that is the way the government does business.

There has never been any connection between Richard Bailey and Joe Plemmons for at least fifteen years. That was when Joe and his brother dropped off a horse on consignment at Bailey's stable in Morton Grove, IL.

Even though they say Joe Plemmons' story is not credible, my Gut Feelings tell me Joe Plemmons' story is Full Proof and 100 percent true. Because the same cold-blooded killers I mentioned in our meeting (2003) when Tom Biesley, John A. T. F. and John O'Connell, an investigator, were at Coleman, Florida. These cold-blooded killers should have to pay for what they have done to Helen Brach.

FRANK JAYNE, insisted that I, RICHARD BAILEY, purchase his one-way ticket for $20 to Palm Beach, Florida.

I used his ticket for my travel to Palm Beach, FRANK, insisted on it. I never understood why, until later.

This transaction took place at the same as the issues with the threat on my life. The immediate question that comes to my mind now is: Why would he even have a need for a one-way ticket to PALM BEACH, FLORIDA?

It is obvious now… why FRANK JAYNE was so insistent that I buy his one-way ticket to PALM BEACH, FLORIDA, I finally figured things out. He had to have, everything all set, to conduct the murder of HELEN BRACH. The ticket would show FRANK went to PALM BEACH if there would have been a problem.

Chapter 1

It was April 1, 1994, and ironically, Good Friday, as well. I was a highly respected, hardworking, surgeon who had put in a difficult week and was very much looking forward to my T. G. I. F. cocktail at The Waterfront. My favorite seafood haunt was just two blocks from my office on West Oak Street in Chicago, and everyday, I stopped by the eatery to slowly, unwind from tensions of the week.

Once inside, the familiar decor of ship models in glass cases, the nautical theme bar and live lobsters in green sea water tanks had a pleasurable calming effect. I pushed my way through the crowd, took a seat at the bar and ordered my customary single drink, a Chablis. He was sitting there too, an attractive stranger wearing a blue suit with an open-collared shirt, his eyes flashing in the room like beacons over a shoal. He didn't say anything right away, yet I immediately felt drawn to this handsome man with curly, blonde shoulder-length hair, a dark tan, and warm brown eyes. Although he was seated a few bar stools away, his big confident smile seemed to fill the restaurant and pulled me out of the gloom into his own special and peaceful pool of light. I returned his smile and suddenly felt safely distanced from a nearby group of bar sharks idling their afternoon away.

The good-looking newcomer didn't remain a stranger for long. He moved to the seat next to mine and struck up a conversation, telling me his name was

Richard. My first impression was that he was extremely cheerful and self assured. His spellbinding voice made him seem almost magical. It was as if I had been sitting alone in a dark quiet room all my life, then this man showed up and turned on the lights, bringing with him the cast of *South Pacific* (my all-time favorite musical!) and a Dixieland band. In a matter of minutes, I was quickly beyond merely interested in getting to know him better.

I was intrigued.

And as impossible as it might seem, in fifteen minutes, I sensed a stirring of feelings I had not felt in twenty years.

Love?

Maybe.

But things like that don't happen in real life, I chided myself, especially not in cynical Chicago. They only happen in the movies like… well… *South Pacific*. As I continued to stare into the stranger's eyes, all the long-ago images flashed through my head: Bloody Mary singing about Bali Hai, selling her native wares to gullible sailors, the Seabees bemoaning the fact that their movies and free advice from Tokyo Rose couldn't make up for their lack of dames; and of course, Nellie Forbush, the navy nurse who fell in love with the dashing French planter. What was his name? Emile something. Oh, yes, Emile De Becque! How different they were, yet how perfect their love. I smiled to myself, remembering, "Some Enchanted Evening… you will meet a stranger…"

A stranger!

Surely this could not be happening to me!

I pushed away the old romantic images and decided a denial of my impulsive feelings was the best way to keep the situation from getting out of hand. What I needed to do was to focus on enjoying the moment. Nothing more. I could then wait and see what, if anything, developed. Most of all, I didn't want to get hurt again. A man this charismatic had to have more than a few girlfriends.

As the conversation continued to flow between us, I quickly discovered that aside from being congenial, Richard was also a funny man. I was surprised to hear myself laughing out loud from time to time. It had been a while…a long while since I felt so happy.

I was experiencing a "down" period in my life. True, my professional self was prospering, but the emotional side of me was withering. To put it simply, I was lonely. There had been no one special in my life for years. Because I was considered something of a V. I. P. in the Chicago area, men tended to be intimidated by me. The stranger who seemed so interested in me now… would he, too, be put off by my vitae? I hoped not… but I couldn't be certain.

Months ago, the day had finally arrived (as it does in most single professionals' lives), when I realized I was not going to meet "Mr. Right" among my clientele. Because I was really ready to get married again, I had joined a dating service and asked God to help me find a lifelong companion.

Now I wondered. Perhaps this man I had met by chance could be a far better mate than anyone the service could possibly offer. I had not seen Richard's pedigrees, but I had certainly experienced his class. Even so, I needed to move slowly as well as carefully. Loneliness was a trap easily baited.

The afternoon at the Waterfront moved effortlessly into evening, and Richard and I ended up having dinner together. Later, when we walked out of the restaurant. a sprinkle of rain announced the beginning of an April shower. As the valets brought our cars around, I noticed we were both driving a Mercedes Benz: his, a flashy red sports convertible with a license plate that ordered, "SHAVE IT!" and mine, a sedate black sedan. We chuckled at this coincidence, but I quickly realized the cars were metaphors for the two of us. Like his sports car, Richard was jaunty, colorful, ready to compete, while I was the sedan, steady, dependable, the quiet utilitarian.

I lacked pizzazz!

Not only was there no Dixieland band in my life before Richard showed up, but I had even forgotten such a band existed! I found myself secretly wishing that I owned the sports coupe with the enigmatic license plate.

"Richard," I said playfully, pointing at his car, "tell me that license plate is not some risqué double-entendre."

He chuckled. "No. I have a company that makes a special depilatory cream for ladies' legs." He paused, winked, and added, "Of course, the boys in the expressway toll booths have other theories."

I could not suppress a chuckle of my own.

When I started to get in my car, Richard asked if I would see him again on Sunday. Easter Sunday, I remembered. A family time. A special time. The expectant, trusting faces of my two children raced through my mind and although I was smiling, I shook my head no. "I plan to go to church with my family in the morning," I said, "and after the service, I'll be spending the day with them."

Richard looked terribly disappointed. Then, although it was out of character for me, I said, "Sunday evening I'm free."

Richard smiled broadly showing the most perfect, white teeth I had ever seen, and for a moment I could feel the wind in my hair.

Before he could speak, I added coyly, "I'd look forward to seeing you then."

Richard flashed another smile, nodded quickly, then at my request, followed me home so he would know where to pick me up on Sunday. When we arrived, I once again stepped out of character, inviting him inside where we chatted briefly before calling it a night.

Richard was so different from the lime, my/mine men I knew that even after I had opened the door and let him out, the warmth of his presence seemed to linger in the room. I glanced in the foyer mirror and saw I was now wearing his infectious grin! I couldn't have been more pleased. The evening had been uplifting and unusual. Somehow, I didn't want it to end.

I walked upstairs, draped a half bottle of soap bubbles into my tub, turned on the faucet, and in a few minutes, was completely relaxed, my body hidden under a mountain of lacy froth.

"Explain what happened tonight," I said out loud to the smiling face in the floor-to-ceiling mirror beside the tub. "Did someone play an April Fools' joke on you…or could Richard have been sent by God?" (I had not forgotten it was Good Friday!)

The response came immediately. "Who can explain it… Who can tell you why, fools give you reasons, wise men never try…?"

I laughed and the soap bubbles before me parted into a wide smile. As far as I was concerned, that was as good an answer as any.

Chapter 2

On Easter Sunday, Richard arrived promptly at 6:00 P. M as we stood in the foyer, I noticed be was even more tastefully dressed than before, this time in a deep blue jacket with contrasting, light blue trousers, and a white silk, breast pocket handkerchief. There was a hint of muscle playing underneath his clothes, and the warm engaging smile was once again in place.

Here is a tranquilizer for the soul, I thought, as he took both my hands in his, kissed me on the cheek and said, "Your Cartier earrings are exquisitely crafted. I especially like the delicate way the little curves and swirls enhance the design." He smiled shyly then added, "They're perfect… just like your ears."

I could feel myself blushing, but Richard stepped back, looked me up and down and went on, "I also like how your suit fits tightly but not too tight, very complimentary for such an unbelievably tiny waist, and of course, Dior uses the very best models."

He smiled so sincerely discarded my first thought, which was, "Blarney!"

He went down the list. He noticed my dimple, a particular arch of my eyebrow, the shape of my lips and even the color of my dark pink lipstick. I had taken a great deal of time to match my lip color to my suit, a little thing woman does by reflex to enhance her appearance, but something most men never notice, and if they do, they are hesitant to mention.

Thankfully, Richard had none of these hang-ups. He was, by any definition, the consummate Renaissance Man: courtly manners, eclectic interests, and enough coiled energy emanating from his presence that one knew instantly here was a man who could take care of himself… and his woman… but he didn't have to grunt, lift weights or be rude to get the message across.

He also had a way about him that exuded a sense of decency, as well. His speech was soft, and he treated waiters and bartenders with mutual respect. I would come to appreciate all these facets of the man in the days ahead and inexplicably, I knew this would be true with the certainty of a seer.

We dined at the Ritz Carlton that evening and our animated conversation jumped from one subject to another. I told him about my work, that it was my passion, that if I had another life, I'd go back to medical school and become a plastic surgeon all over again. When I told him I had arrived in this country from South Africa with an M. D. behind my name and only $27 in my pocket, he became the complete audience. He listened as no man ever had, nodding, agreeing, patting my hands when I mentioned the sad parts of my family history.

Richard told me story after story about adventure, misadventures, coups, and mistakes in the world of business, especially in the horse business, and I learned that Richard had been the owner of Blue Ribbon, Midwest Northwestern, and Bailey's Stables in the Chicago suburbs. One of my favorites stories was about a prospective horse buyer who was also a retired major. Richard made the sale and called the man a colonel ever after. I suspected he was making some of the story up, but I smiled, chuckled and once again, found myself laughing out loud.

The evening ended with a long, long hug and a chaste kiss in front of my home and as I stepped into the foyer, I was greeted by another stranger, my own smiling self in the hall mirror! I blushed. Forget Nellie Forbush! I felt deep inside me beat the heart of a beautiful young woman. "Younger than springtime," I whispered.

Good things were happening!

Amazing, magical, positive things!

The next day, Richard called me two or three times, "just to make certain that I was alright," he said. His standard opening sentence was always a warm, seductive, "Hey, hey, my beautiful doll …" Each and every time I heard his voice tinkling over the wire, I had to smile.

I also had to ask myself who exactly was this attractive man who had come into my life. He was the epitome of charm, a cavalier with a touch of the swashbuckling adventurer tossed in. I had come to treasure our chance encounter and the moments since and now looked forward to seeing him again on Tuesday evening.

Would the schoolgirl feelings I had for Richard still be there when I saw him once more? The realist in me said this bliss could not go on forever, that I was too old to be infatuated for any length of time no matter who the man was. But I also realized I was over my head in the deep end of the pool with this fascinating new addition to my life.

I wondered where Richard and I would go on our third date and was surprised to find myself in the Pump Room, a fancy and popular local club with above average food and entertainment. I figured we would have dinner, then take a couple of turns around the dance floor under the glittering chandeliers, swaying to the predictably mellow efforts of the piano player and torch singer.

I couldn't have been more wrong.

That night the piano player became a pianist and the singer metamorphosized into a vocalist whose range and vibrancy immediately imparted a big band ambiance to the elegance of the room. Tommy Dorsey's orchestra played in my mind and our two turns around the floor became an evening of ballroom dancing, me playing Ginger Rogers to Richard's Fred Astaire.

It was heaven!

We danced, DANCED, DANCED!

Sultry sambas, wild mambos, sensual lambadas (!), erotic twists and stately waltzes where my feet seemed to never touch the floor. We were lyrical in movement, and somewhere I just knew that Terpsichore was watching and smiling with the same, perfectly symmetrical smile my partner wore. As I spun around in the center of the glittering room, people stopped dancing and eating to watch. I had an audience! In my heart, I was once again the aspiring prima ballerina I had been in my youth in South Africa. But unlike my career as a ballet professional, Richard's and my pas de deux would hopefully never end. This man was not only my perfect emotional Doppelganger, but he could also dance!

Suddenly my future was not only warm and fuzzy, but it was also exciting!

More importantly, it was here!

And the lyrics just kept getting better!

I was soon to learn that simple things like drinking a glass of wine would suddenly become an extremely poignant, romantic experience. Richard would select a wine from a proffered list, order, sniff the cork. The waiter would pour, then slurp up the expected compliment on Richard's selection. Routine stuffed shirt protocols designed, I have always believed, to give men a chance to show off in front of their dates.

But then the mundane would become the magnificent.

Not all at once, however.

As I sipped my wine that Tuesday evening, I noticed that Richard's glass sat untouched between us. He sat erect, attentive, smiling, the smile that reminded me of The Joker from the Batman movie, flat on the top, turned up and pointed at the ends. He appeared to be waiting for something. What was happening here?

I finally decided that Richard was playing some sort of game with the wine, a practical joke hadn't picked up on. After all, if he didn't want the wine, he certainly wouldn't have ordered it. I felt a sudden chill and found myself waiting for him to call out, "Ha, ha! Joke's on you! Joke's on you! I'm really a professional actor! Your best friend Marian hired me to play the perfect companion and to brighten up your dull life!"

Yes, I thought, maybe he's an actor.

Or Don Juan or Fred Astaire or Ronald Coleman or The Joker or Emile De Becque, that good looking French planter from South Pacific or… or who?

I had no idea, but whoever Richard was, he was truly the ultimate in a romantic date.

I reined in my thoughts and stared at Richard's wine. It was still untouched. Finally, I couldn't stand his indifference any longer. "Are you going to drink that?" I asked, pointing at his wine glass.

"Not alone," he said, eyes twinkling. "This is our loving cup, and it holds our love. We are going to share it." And for the rest of the evening, we drank from that single glass. I had been wrong in my suspicions about Richard being an actor, and I was more than a little thankful I had kept my fears to myself.

That evening, I literally danced the night away in Richard's rock-hard arms, yet I felt no fatigue. I would soon learn I simply could not be tired, bored, hungry, or thirsty when I was with this man. My chronic pains became comic pains, the worries that plagued me during the day all vanished in the night.

Inexorably, I was being reborn, and I was thankful for the gift of light that was Richard.

Chapter 3

When the phone rang Wednesday afternoon in my private office, I found myself waiting to hear the now familiar, deep booming voice, "Hey, hey, my beautiful doll…" I had known Richard for only five days, but I could not deny that I was totally smitten. I was in love and had been for days.

One enchanted evening, in the blink of an eye, I fell in love with an attractive stranger (like the young naive nurse with her French planter). Such a powerful attraction, I thought, was not man-made. I was never happier, never felt more alive than when I was in Richard's company. He was like a river that had come to a dry place, and if the fates continued to smile, maybe, just maybe, in a year or so, he would be mine.

That afternoon on the phone, Richard's voice was filled with excitement and mystery. My first thought was that he sounded like a little kid with a humongous secret. "Come join me for a weekend in Las Vegas," he pleaded.

I must admit I was more than a little surprised by his sudden invitation. "Richard," I said softly, "you're moving too fast for me." Yes, I was in love, but I was also a highly moral person. Aside from myself, I had my children to consider. Then, too, I didn't want or need an outbreak of gossip in my professional circles.

Richard went on chatting, making me laugh time and again (like always). My rejection of his offer did not seem to faze him in the least. After we hung up, I knew I had made the right decision. My only fear was that perhaps I had offended him. Maybe held never call again.

But if Richard chose to avoid me because I refused to join him on an out-of-town date, then I knew I was just a passing fancy. Whatever the future held for me, I realized it was better to have it out in the open so I could deal with the problem and go on with my life.

Richard called me in my private office. The Vegas offer was still on the table and just like before, he was charmingly insistent. This time he made it perfectly clear (as if I had not already said no) that there would be nothing for me to worry about in Las Vegas, that I would be his "guest."

"After all," he said laughing, "we're just going to visit my money!"

Although I didn't want to say yes, I could feel myself weakening and reluctantly giving M. Finally, I teasingly asked, "If I went with you, would you promise to be a good boy?"

"I give you my word I'll be a perfect gentleman" was Richard's immediate reply.

Like always, I thought. In the end, I felt I had no real reason not to go. It was just a date with wings, and there was plenty of rooms in Vegas so there would be no reason to double up. It's not like you're flying off to Nevada to have a wild affair, I told myself.

That Saturday morning, I chose a silver silk jump suit for the trip and Richard showed up in tastefully coordinated sports clothes, this time, an olive-greencoat and pants. I definitely approved.

The flight out was an event, though uneventful. We held hands and kissed all the way there! Richard's attentiveness made the hours pass like minutes. When we landed in Vegas, a shiny black limousine was already waiting for us, and at that point, I immediately suspected Richard had a reputation for being a "high roller," a big gambler the hotel casinos spoiled with limos and other complimentary offerings, some less socially acceptable than others.

Even before the driver opened the car door, I could see an ocean of exquisite white roses filling the car, at least twelve dozen, maybe more! I was astonished! This was no gaudy casino proffer; the roses were Richard's! I was thrilled by the flowers, thrilled I had come! Why had I hesitated? This was a man like no other I had ever met. And most importantly, he seemed to genuinely care for me. We made a place for ourselves in between the flowers, Richard ordered the driver to proceed, and we were off into the fantasy land of monopoly money and the gauche of Glitter Gulch!

As we sped out of the airport, it occurred to me that unlike other men I had dated, I rarely heard Richard use the word, "L." Attentive, selfless, charming. Fun with a capital "F." The points stacked up in his favor.

Richard had told me on the plane we were staying at the MGM Grand Hotel, and so I was surprised when the driver steered the car past the Greer Glosh. When I pointed this out to Richard, he smiled a knowing smile, held my hand tighter and said, "I know, sweets, trust me on this one." I thought it was a prank a surprise. I felt no anxiety.

I fell silent, closed my eyes, and enjoyed the fragrance of so many beautiful roses. I had expected a long drive to wherever we were going, but in a matter of minutes, the limo pulled up in front of a building bearing a sign announcing, "Marriage License Bureau."

I looked over at Richard. He was smiling his Joker's smile.

"County courthouse," he said matter-of-factly.

My mouth must have been open in a wide "O," but I didn't care. There was no way to conceal my surprise that we had stopped at the Marriage License Bureau. Here I was blissfully riding along in a limousine with a man whose adoration kept bubbling up to me through a sea of roses. There had been no proposal, just that wistful yet wicked smile. Again, I had to ask myself, what is going on? Although I felt happy, the initial worries about coming on the trip began to resurface.

Perhaps I was the victim of some sort of prank, I thought once again. In my search for the progenitor of this huge practical joke, I again marked down my friend Marian as the prime suspect. A minute later, I discarded the idea.

Our stopping at the courthouse and Marriage License Bureau had to be some kind of an unusual stunt, but no matter how hard I tried to come up with an explanation for Richard's behavior, I came up empty. Surely the answer was hidden somewhere in his smile. It was a mystery, but one I was enjoying, and I didn't want to disappoint him. He'd obviously gone to a lot of trouble.

Just then the chauffer opened the door, Richard helped me out, and with an expectant grin, I walked inside the building. My heart was pounding with excitement. With Richard looking over my shoulder, I quickly filled out a marriage application. Why not? I thought. It would make a great souvenir.

I was thinking what a memorable gag this was going to be (when I found out what it was). All I knew for certain was that I had never, never in my life, done anything even remotely similar to buying a wedding license for a weekend, nor did I even know anyone with enough imagination to have come up with such an incredible plan. This was a setup pure and simple, I decided, and gave Richard high marks for the feigned innocence of his performance.

The next thing I knew we were back in the rose-scented limo. Like before, Richard was holding my hand and smiling, and in minutes, the driver was parking in front of a marriage chapel.

A marriage chapel!

Only then did I realize that Richard was taking this stunt too far. I could end up getting hurt, something I had tried to avoid from the very first night.

But maybe I was making the same mistake twice.

I had once thought Richard didn't care and it turned out he did, very much; his loving cup was an innocent part of his romantic nature. He had been affectionate but serious with the wine sharing.

My God, what if he were serious now?

The answer came quickly.

He had to be.

Why else would we be here?

I had to put a stop to it.

"Richard," I said firmly. "Enough. There's no way I can marry you IF that's what you intend. Why, we hardly know each other!"

He said nothing, but there was a strange gleam in his eye and the mysterious smile was still playing over his lips. I couldn't stand to be in limbo anymore. "What is going on, Richard?" I asked. "This is a prank… right?"

He kissed me softly on the lips, looked into my eyes, and said, "All you need to know is that I am very, very much in love with you, and I will truly care for you forever." His eyes were warm, his voice sincere. I believed what he was saying. Who would not? He was Mr. Perfect, and he was there!

Although I was caught up in the moment and wanted with all my heart to marry Richard, there was another consideration that now began to break my train of thought like a warning siren in a city night.

Could I possibly be a target?

After all, I was a woman of some obvious means, and Richard had proposed marriage in a matter of days.

I brought the subject up, but Richard gave me a litany of reassuring statements about his financial situation that obviated my concerns. He pointed out that he owned four stables, a driving school and a company that was a depilatory franchise. Then he provided the clincher, "I give you my solemn promise that after we get back to Chicago, we will set up a post nuptial agreement in which each of us takes nothing from the other in the event of the marriage's failure."

Fine, I thought, quickly brushing aside all other concerns. People will find the entire arrangement really bizarre, but eventually, eventually, it will all work out.

Once again, the limo driver opened the car door. Richard took my arm, and I seemed to float inside to the matrimonial factory, a small box draped in peppermint-pink satin. Smooth and slick to ease you in and out quickly, I thought. Commercial? Definitely… but easy on the eyes.

When the ceremony was over, my new husband kissed me passionately and aside from feeling absolutely wonderful, I also felt somehow relieved. This was meant to happen, I told myself. Why else would I have even noticed the smiling stranger out of all those people last Friday night at the Waterfront?

Back in the limo, I said, "Lucky, lucky me!" but Richard didn't know what I was talking about, thought I wanted to be embraced once more and kissed me again, even longer than he did after the ceremony. I adored his kiss… I adored my new husband! Everything was so perfect! I had a guardian angel who was looking out for me. I just knew it!

I asked Richard to stop at a pay phone and called my friend Marian back in Chicago. I was so excited my sentences weren't making too much sense, but after I shouted into the receiver that I was married, she was so stunned, all she could manage was a weak, "Oh, well…" I figured that would be the reaction of most people I knew. Total disbelief.

At that moment, I could have cared less.

I was fifty-two years old and had been married before, but I felt happier than I could ever recall. I thought Richard was absolutely wonderful. Every time he showed up at my door, it was like opening a Victorian Valentine. I adored his "old-time," European charm and the way he made me laugh; his romantic ways drew me to him like powerful magnets. All my fears, I realized at that moment, had been groundless. I had made the right decision. I had no doubts whatsoever.

What woman alive could doubt a man like Richard? He was the magician of my emotions, the prestidigitator of my intellect, the grateful keeper of my heart.

On the way to the MGM, Richard had the limo driver stop again and buy a bottle of my favorite, Mum's Extra Dry champagne, and a single glass; then, surrounded by the cloying smell of roses, we kissed each other and sipped champagne from Richard's loving cup, the cup of love. We were a deliriously happy couple.

I was certainly pleased with my impetuous decision because a future with this man promised me everything I had ever wished for: warmth, passion, contentment, exhilarating surprises, dancing, travel, the sharing of experiences new and old, all with me at the centerpiece of his life.

Added to all this was a spicy sense of mystery, the exotic, the faraway and dreamy. I closed my eyes for a moment and saw images of waterfalls cascading down lush tropical greenery, pristine white beaches kissed by rolling waves, palm trees swaying against hot pink sunsets and Richard and I, together, embracing it all. Bali Hai, a most special island!

My marriage to this wonderful man was almost too much to hope for and yet it had happened! Richard loved me and there was no question that I loved him back with a love I wouldn't have thought possible a week before.

A week?

Yes… yes…

Chapter 4

Our Loving Cup

On the evening of Easter Sunday, Richard arrived promptly at my home. It had been a beautiful day, and it was still light outside. As we stood in the foyer, I noticed he was as tastefully dressed as was the case on Friday and Saturday evenings. This time, in a deep blue jacket with contrasting, light blue trousers, and a white silk handkerchief in his breast pocket. There was a hint of muscle playing underneath his clothes, and the warm engaging smile was once again in place.

Here is a tranquilizer for the soul! Taking both my hands in his, he kissed me on the cheek. "Your earrings are beautiful. I especially like the delicate little swirls." With that, he stepped backward to admire the earrings. Then he added, "They're perfect… just like your ears."

I could feel myself blushing as Richard proceeded to look me up and down before rendering a final judgment. "I also like how your suit fits tightly but not too tight, very complimentary for such an unbelievably tiny waist. You and Dior were made for each other."

"Oh, Richard, I appreciate it, but…"

"But nothing. You are a beautiful woman, and you need to know that."

He seemed sincerely interested in my appearance, even noticing a particular arch of my eyebrows and subtle depth of my eyes. I had taken a great deal of time to match my lip color to my suit, a little thing a woman does by reflex to enhance her appearance. Impulsively, I asked Richard, "Do you not hie my lipstick? It's a brand-new shade for spring."

Richard replied simply, "It's you."

I had to admit that Richard was, by any definition, the consummate Renaissance Man. With courtly manners, he was every bit a man's man and yet a woman's man at heart. On this Easter Sunday evening, my spirits had definitely risen.

Richard suggested we dine at the Ritz Carlton that evening. My favorite piano player was playing a medley of romantic tunes. We ordered surf and turf. As we waited for our dinner to arrive, our animated conversation jumped from one subject to another. I discussed my work, and the wide variety of patients I came into contact with. "Richard, plastic surgery is my passion. If I had another life, I'd go back to medical school and become a plastic surgeon all over again." Richard said he appreciated women who not only had beauty, but depth. He asked me if I were born in America, When I told him I had arrived in this country from South Africa with an M. D. behind my name, and with little money in my pocket, he became the complete audience. He listened as no man ever had, nodding, agreeing, and patting my hands when I mentioned the sad parts of my family history—in South Africa parents are distant. I was pressured to be a little adult at all times. "But, even then," I said by way of explanation, "I was never a conformist."

Then it was Richard's turn. His story was one of adventure, misadventures, coups, and mistakes in the world of business and, especially, in the horse business. Even though I had ridden horses as a teenager, I had no idea what the horse business in America was all about. Richard said it wasn't the pristine business one would think from the festive horse shows and top thoroughbred horses that competed. In fact, he said that his introduction into the buying and selling of horses was a lesson he dearly paid for. He bought a thoroughbred only to discover that he had paid many times over what the horse was actually worth. He said he considered this as tuition in the school of hard knocks. He saw the experience as an opportunity in disguise and decided he ought to become a seller rather than a buyer of horses.

After making a few connections in the horse world, Richard earned his spurs and graduated to stable ownership. He was owner of Midwest Stables, part owner of Blue Ribbon Stables, and then he owned Bailey's Stables and Northwestern Stables in the Chicago suburbs. One of my favorite stories was about a prospective horse buyer who had an engaging presence and spoke with the voice of authority. Richard made the sale and called the man a colonel ever after. I found myself laughing out loud. I asked if the Colonel had ever been in the military and Richard said that was beside the point. He had a commanding attitude. For some reason, I asked what his real name was, and Richard replied, "Harold Pick."

"What a small world," I said, genuinely surprised. I had met him at a charity ball. "He's an antique appraiser."

Richard laughed. "Well, he's certainly no horse appraiser. He made quite a few bad buys."

The evening ended with a long, long hug and a chaste kiss in front of my home. Stepping into the foyer, I was greeted by a stranger—my own smiling self reflected in the hall mirror! I approved. Somewhere underneath the layers and layers of professional surgeon, there was still the spirit of the ballerina, ever open to beauty and the effervescent light of new experience. That evening when I spoke with my older daughter, Yvette, she commented that I seemed happier.

The following day, Richard phoned me two or three times, saying he wanted to make certain that I was all right. His standard opening sentence was always a warm, seductive, "Hey, hey, my beautiful doll…" Each and every time I heard his cheerful voice over the wire, I had to smile.

Yet, I also had to ask myself who exactly was this attractive man who had come into my life? He was the epitome of charm, with a cavalier touch. Although I had to remind myself to be cautious, I had come to treasure our chance encounter. Would the schoolgirl feelings I had for Richard be there when we met for our third date? The realist in me said this bliss could not go on forever, that I was too old to be infatuated for any length of time no matter who the man was. When Marian called to apologize for having canceled our dinner date, I told her that when one door closes, another opens, and I proceeded to gush about the newly found man in my life. Marian listened well, as always.

Then she said, "That's what happens whenever I leave you alone—you get into trouble."

I laughed. No matter how Marian tried to slow me down, I realized I was over my head in the deep end of the pool with this fascinating new addition to my life.

Suddenly, my future was exciting! Under Richard's tutelage, I was soon to learn that simple things like drinking a glass of wine would suddenly become poignant. Richard would select a fine wine and sniff the cork before the waiter poured a small portion into Richard's glass. The waiters seemed to appreciate his selections. Our regular dating night became Tuesday night. This particular Tuesday, I was to meet Richard at Nick's Fishmarket in the heart of the Loop. Descending the stairs to the restaurant, I caught a glimpse of Richard. My heart skipped a beat, knowing that this handsome man was waiting for me and for me alone. As I rounded the corner, he did not immediately notice me, and my friendly greeting startled him. "As usual, my dear Richard, you are punctual, have you had a trying day?"

He seemed to force a smile as he invited me to sit next to him I felt I had to lead the conversation. Richard perked up when the waiter came to take our drink order. waited for him to explain the source of his unease, but no explanation was offered. Richard's glass of wine set untouched. Richard sat attentively. He appeared to be waiting for something.

I decided that Richard was playing some sort of game with the wine, a practical joke I hadn't picked up on. After all, if he didn't want the wine, he certainly wouldn't have ordered it. I felt a sudden chill and found myself waiting for him to call out, "Ha, Ha! Joke's on you! Joke's on you! Joke's on you! I'm really a professional actor! Your best friend, Marian, hired me to plan the perfect companion and to brighten up your dull life!"

I reined in my lack of self-confidence and, instead, sat quietly staring at Richard's wine. It was still untouched. Pointing to his wine glass, I asked, "Are you going to drink that?"

"Not alone," he replied. "This is our loving cup, and it holds our love. We are going to share it." And for the rest of the evening, we drank from that single glass. I had been wrong in my suspicions about Richard's being an actor, and I was more than a little thankful I had kept my fears to myself: I decided to put a brake on the reservations I had about letting a new man into my life. I decided that if I continued to watch my feet while dancing, I would surely trip.

That evening, I literally danced the night away in Richard's rock-hard arms, yet I felt no fatigue. I would soon learn I simply could not be tired, bored, hungry, or thirsty when I was with this man. My chronic pains became comic pains; the worries that plagued me during the day all vanished in the night.

I was thankful for the gift of light that was Richard.

Chapter 5

I started calling people at eight-thirty that morning. Most of them were still asleep, but I was too excited to wait until later to share the good news... that I was madly in love and was now a married lady!

But the truth was I was really two ladies. One was the glowing, dreamy female, head over heels in love with a dynamic, attractive man (albeit a stranger!). The other was the quintessential professional surgeon, the independent, analytical woman who relied on impeccable and accurate details to excel in her profession. My problem was those necessary details with regard to Richard were conspicuous by their absence.

A small cloud of doubt, once a mere wisp of concern, now blossomed like a thunderhead in a Midwestern summer sky. Without knowing the commotion this doubt was to cause, I seeded that storm cloud with a few pellets of logic and came up with a downpour of distrust. I couldn't help it. There were just too many unanswered questions.

On the way into my office, I faced the fact that the man I loved was a work of fiction... probably his own, and the man I married might be something far less, or worse, than the cavalier who swept me into the little pink chapel in Vegas.

My more pragmatic self also demanded that the emotional me garner some discipline regarding Richard. I would, therefore, proceed with my investigations.

If I were wrong, the worst that could happen was there could be some gotten this far without incident validation of the commitment Richard and I had made to each other. Relieved that the space age computer inside my brain had completely overcome the sixties sweet music in the jukebox of my heart, I took the first, uncertain step to discovery.

In between seeing patients, I picked up the phone and dialed the office of Nancy Lewis, a generally trustworthy and ethical private investigator I knew in Chicago.

"Hello, Nancy," I said brightly, "Guess what? I just married a wonderful man named Richard Bailey!" I announced this bit of news as though I had just won the lottery. To my dismay, I was rewarded with a pregnant pause, third trimester, viable.

"Richard Bailey!" Nancy finally shrieked, making my husband sound like Bluebeard instead of Prince Charming. My heart skipped a beat, but I couldn't give up. When I placed the call, I wanted answers... now I needed answers.

"Well, uh... yes... and I want you to do a background on him." Traitor, I heard in my head, but I Couldn't abandon what I had come to call my business moxie. Ever since a former employee was caught stealing from me, I always ran a thorough check on any person I was considering for employment. Why not investigate the man who was going to enter my inner sanctum?

"Wait a minute!" Nancy exclaimed. She was shouting so loudly I thought she might choke. "You mean you have actually married Richard Bailey?" A low whistle, another pregnant pause, then she said, "Of course I'll do the B. G. for you, Doc, but I don't think you'll like it when you read it."

I chuckled nervously. "Come now, he can't be all that bad."

"Oh no? Wait until you've finished reading his file!" Nancy retorted. "It will be rather lengthy, by the way... But as soon as I compile it, I'll fax it over to you. We need to get your eyes open in a hurry!"

"But... but..."

"Just give me his social security number or the number off his driver's license."

I promptly gave her all the numbers I had written down from Richard's driver's license the night he was so ill in Vegas. I apologized for the paucity of information, but Nancy was impressed with my amateur detective work.

"By the way, Doc, have you two had sex?" Nancy asked suddenly.

I was happy she couldn't see my blush. "A bit personal, aren't we?"

"Yes, it might seem so, but it's extremely important."

"Actually, we didn't," I replied, wondering if I should make some excuse for that now serendipitous deficiency in our marriage.

"Thank God for small favors," Nancy said, obviously relieved. "My advice is to slow down. Whatever you do, please don't get yourself in a compromising position."

I couldn't help but think how Victorian Nancy suddenly sounded, but I knew better. But not having sex, it would leave the marriage open to annulment. "Let me hear from you ASAP," I said, then hung up.

Tense. I was very tense. I calmed myself down by remembering something one of my teachers had told me years ago. "Don't act until you have all the facts because without those facts, you're walking around blind."

Could I have been wearing blinders each and every time I went out with Richard?

If so, heaven help me!

But I had no time to wait on heaven... this time I had to help myself.

I picked up the phone, asked the operator for a number then just sat there, holding the receiver in my hand, afraid to place the call.

I hadn't forgotten that Richard had dropped the name Harold Pick, "Colonel" Harold Pick, one evening at dinner. Richard had been in the Thoroughbred and show horse business and I remembered this man Pick also owned horses. Maybe the "Colonel" could help shed some light on Richard. The problem was I didn't know exactly how much light I could handle. In the end, I forced myself to dial the number, dreading all the while what I might hear! next.

"Colonel Pick," a flat metallic, New York-ish accent announced sharply.

I decided to resort to a minor subterfuge the moment I heard that snobby voice.

"Hello," I said, giving him my name. "I'm trying to locate a horse dealer named Richard Bailey. Someone told me you would know where to find him?"

"Find **HIM**? Find **HIM**? Everybody wants to find **him**! He's a bad guy! A swindler! A liar! Let me tell you a few thousand ugly things about Richard Bailey!" His voice could not have been more cold or angry.

"You don't understand," I broke in. "I'm just trying to locate him." I was making a valiant effort to sound coy.

"Well, when you find him, you'll find a double dealing, swindling S. O. B. who makes a living bilking women out of their money."

"Are we talking about the same Richard Bailey?"

"We most certainly are! Oh, wait a minute… You're one of them, aren't you?"

"I beg your pardon?"

"One of them; you're a mark, right?"

"What's a mark?" I asked weakly.

"Jesus Christ, lady! A mark… a pigeon… a victim in a confidence game. You know—a vic, a patsy, an LOL with bucks!"

"LOL?"

"Little Old Lady! Richard's specialty! You wouldn't be a lonely widow by any chance?"

"I may be a widow, but I can assure you I am no little old lady!" I snapped, completely unmasking my attempted ruse. "And I'm not sure I believe you…"

"You don't have to believe me; read the damn book!"

"What book?"

"*Thin Air*!" Colonel Pick said with a triumphant chuckle.

"*Thin Air*? What's that about?"

"Oh, Richard Bailey and the disappearance of Helen Vorhees Brach. He's the guy who romanced the Brach candy heiress twenty years ago and then she suddenly vanished without a trace. I've got a copy right here in my office … out of print now."

What was he saying?

My Richard… a… a… murderer?

I couldn't speak and nearly fainted. The silence stretched out and then "Colonel" Pick added, "Yes, it's that Richard Bailey." He then gave me a tinny laugh that sounded like a villain in the old movies, "Heh hehheh."

My hand was shaking so badly that I don't know how I held up the receiver, but I couldn't hang up. If the book was out of print, I needed to borrow it from this man, no matter what I thought of him.

"If you don't mind, I'll send a messenger to pick up the book right away," I said trying to sound calm but not carrying it off. "But just because I'm borrowing the book, it doesn't mean that I believe you... about Richard that is..."

"Then don't! But don't forget to send a deposit for the loan of the book." He hung up without warning, leaving me listening to the sound of my own rapid breathing in the receiver.

After speaking with "Colonel" Pick, I found myself staring into space. I was afraid and felt very alone. On the plus side, I would soon be dealing with cold hard facts instead of mere fantasies, and I was quite at home with facts, having built a career on them. Once I had all these details, I told myself, I would know how to proceed. In the meantime, there was nothing left to do but to wait for the arrival of Nancy's investigation file and "Colonel" Pick's book.

Thin Air.

One thought haunted me.

I've lust launched my life into thin air!

Or worse...

Yes, as they said in the old melodramas.

WORSE!

I could not help but think I was married to a man who was involved in a murder... or worse.

Had there been worse?

Rape?

Torture?

What?

By drawing on the inner reservoir of strength that came from so many hard lessons in life, I managed to get through the long hours at work and take partial control over my fears. My secret? I put aside my own life and focused completely on my patients, but I was badly shaken. That day I felt as if as if something very important marched out on my life without saying goodbye.

When Richard showed up that evening, I gave him no hint of the tornado beginning to shape up just over the horizon and prepared a very nice dinner for two, poached fish, asparagus, and a salad. Like an atavistic urge, I had been pushed by stress into falling back into the role of Hausfrau, a part I had abandoned many years ago when my faith and trust in life had taken a protracted vacation without providing notice.

After dinner, I kept hearing Nancy Lewis' voice in my head advising me to put off making love. At that point, I certainly didn't think the avoidance would be a hardship. I was too terribly confused and hurt by Richard's seemingly endless deceptions to even want to have sex. Without saying anything to him about what I had learned from my phone calls earlier, I decided to follow Nancy's advice to the letter.

No sex.

Impossible to imagine just a few days ago. Given the opportunity, we would have made love. I was grateful that we had not and stepped into my abstinence role for the night. Strangely enough, the evening turned out to be one of the most wonderful and enchanted nights of my life. Once I gave out the signals that I wasn't interested in making love, Richard and I cuddled, cuddled, and cuddled some more. He did not push me, and once again, I believed it was because he was so finely tuned to my psyche that he was the perfect soulmate.

That night, I felt very comforted in being held. And once again, I also felt that my very presence was important, even essential, to this man. As the hours passed, I could not believe that this warm, caring person could ever harm anyone physically or, for that matter, steal money. The only thing he had stolen from me was my heart.

I discovered I was still madly in love but scared, oddly not terrified, and in fact, more uncertain than frightened of Richard. Who could blame me? Loving Richard was an exercise in cognitive dissonance, like standing under a bright sunny sky and being hit by hail the size of coconuts.

Sleep was impossible that night. Curled up next to Richard, my thoughts kept returning to two little words.

Thin Air.

When I sensed the first light streaming through the window, I saw in my mind's eye the pained face of the French planter from South Pacific. He was standing next to Nellie Forbush and although I couldn't remember the exact words, he was telling her something about being a fugitive from France because he had killed a man there.

Chapter 6

On the way out the door the following morning, Richard told me he had business to attend to and would be back home around 5:00 P. M. that evening. For a brief flicker, I felt like a Judas once again for not believing in my new husband, or, more importantly, for not sharing my secret thoughts. His demeanor was so trusting, so supportive. I had to assume he still knew nothing about any of my calls to check him out.

Later that morning, Nancy Lewis called me at my office, said the fax was on its way and that she had contacted Ernie Rizzo, an ex-Franklin Park policeman now possibly a private detective, who had confirmed her suspicions that my life as well as my assets made might well be at risk. What Nancy didn't tell me about Mr. Rizzo was that he was most famous in the Chicago area for his artesian fountain of theories regarding the probable Helen Brach murder, and that he was addicted to hearing himself expound those theories on various local talk shows. But since I did not know this self-aggrandizing egocentric at the time, I lent green credibility to the fact that Rizzo confirmed Nancy's opinion that I was in a potentially dangerous situation.

Nancy ended our conversation by calling Richard a cad, a gigolo, a gold digger, even a con artist. She would have gone on with more derogatory remarks, but I cut her off. I had heard just about all the bad news I could take for one morning. It was hearsay without concrete evidence applying to me and I desperately wanted to believe my negatives about him.

After I hung up the phone, all I could do was shake my head at the disaster my heart had gotten me into. I had never thought of myself as a weak person, but I had to admit I was more than a Little depressed. All I could think of was Nancy's fax and what action would I take after I read it.

When the report arrived later that morning, I realized Nancy had just been warming up with her earlier comments about Richard. Detailed in the lengthy fax was a litany of charges against Richard (Richard Bailey, my husband!). In essence, the document said that he did not have bad credit, he simply had no credit. Even Shave It! , Richard's franchise company he had told me so much about, was not his any longer and his business was not even recognized as a legally incorporated entity in the State of Illinois.

I was also amazed to learn that Richard had filed for bankruptcy once before but, subsequently had it reversed. he had it reversed.

Bankrupt!

Richard was bankrupt!

That was why he didn't have any credit cards in Las Vegas! I flashed back to the look of innocent puzzlement on his face at the check-in desk at the MGM Grand.

What an act.

Or was it?

The file also revealed that Richard knew the civil court system inside and out; he'd been sued for fraud in multiple cases related to his horse sales. Then it hit me. Richard was a swindler! No wonder he was such a dynamic and smooth conversationalist!

Just when I finished reading the fax, the phone jingled, and Nancy was on the line again with the ultimate clincher. She had just found out from one of her sources that Richard took money from every vulnerable lady he met, usually widows who were lonely, elderly, or sickly.

Nancy concluded our conversation with an ominous statement, "Courting

Richard is courting global conflict. We're not talking water pistols here—nuclear bombs!"

Nuclear bombs!

What had I done?

I was scared to death, but I had to ask, "Nancy, are you positive your information is…"

"Impeccable like always, Doc."

"Then what do you think I ought to do?" I asked, angry with myself for the little girl question and tone of voice, but I felt I was drowning in roaring floodwaters and a hard rain was continuing to fall.

"Simple," Nancy said. "My best advice to you is to get Richard Bailey out of your house, your life, your world… and the quicker the better!"

"Oh…" I managed, wondering why Nancy thought disposing of my new husband would be so easy.

She must have been reading my thoughts for she went on, "Have Trevor, your houseman, pack Richard's bags immediately and make sure all of his personal belongings are gone from the premises. Then when Richard comes home tonight, tell him in no uncertain terms that he must leave."

"And when he objects? Good grief, Nancy! If everything you say about Richard is true, he might become violent. Should I call the police first? What should I do?"

"No! You don't need the police or the publicity, believe me. Make sure your cell phone is handy and Trevor is standing by, as well. Then you tell Bailey you came across information about him you are definitely uncomfortable with. Doc. Just show that man the door!"

Nancy's advice seemed like the perfect solution, but my nascent loyalties to Richard were stronger than I thought. I wavered. Wondered. Waffled.

"I'm gonna wash that man right outta my hair," Nellie Forbush began to sing in my ear as confident as ever, and for a minute, I thought I could handle it.

"Okay, Nancy," I said. "I'll do it… Bye!" But my voice lacked any conviction.

Just then *Thin Air* came by messenger, tucked inside a big brown envelope. I remember the young man as handsome. The book, on the other hand, was ugly. Thin and mean and dark grey in appearance, the cover displayed four, small, triangular holders that normally secure snapshots except the photo itself had disappeared. Clever, I thought, disappeared into thin air. But the most horrifying part was in the lower right-hand corner, a cluster of almost too red blood drops, a terrible reminder of what I was dealing with.

An aura of foreboding seemed to surround the book's jacket, daring the viewer to become a reader. My mouth was suddenly dry, and I was aware of my own pulse. The cliched "moment of truth" had arrived. I hesitated. Then I thought, why not? If Richard has nothing to hide, I should read the slander. If, on the other hand, he was everything Nancy, Colonel Pick and Mr. Rizzo said he was, I needed to read this book, this indictment of Richard. After all, it was the only hard news available I realized, forgetting that was how the boys in the South Pacific described Tokyo Rose in World War II.

Still afraid to open the book, I remembered two recent revelations with stunning clarity. First, I recalled an admonition of "Colonel" Pick's to never take my eyes off my water or wine glass as long as Richard was around because Pick was of the opinion that Richard did "something funny" with drinks. Of course, Pick never specified what, exactly, Richard did.

And then there was and the realization that had followed me to my pillow last night: "I might be sleeping with a killer." I couldn't believe that there was even the slightest possibility that this was true. Those bizarre predicaments only happened to other people, those who were featured in T. V. and movies. Not to me!

I pushed these terrible thoughts aside and opened the little book, trying to gather information objectively. Right away, the first paragraph chilled me to the bone, and I kept rereading it. Without being aware of what I was doing, I memorized the words like a school girl fighting to master a catechism:

It was about half past ten in the morning on Thursday, February 17, 1977, when Helen Brach, the sixty-five-year-old widow of one of the three founders of the Chicago-based E. J. Brach and Sons candy company, Frank Brach, and heiress to a fortune in property and securities estimated at the time to be worth $21 million, placed what was probably the last phone call of her life from her room at the Kahler Hotel in Rochester, Minnesota…

The words puzzled me as they would anybody, but I had an extremely busy work schedule that day. There was no time to read on. I put the book back in the envelope and slipped it inside my briefcase. I arranged to leave the office early so that I could glance at the book before Richard got home.

I was so stressed by everything that was happening to me that by the time five o'clock rolled around, it felt more like midnight.

Around ten o'clock that night, I told Richard I had correspondence to take care of, to go to bed without me, and that I'd wake him for a kiss when I joined him later. He seemed to have no problem with my made-up-on-the-spot-lie.

Then, all alone in the family room, I forced myself to once again open the damming book, fearful of each turn of the page, but driven to know the facts of every mystery surrounding Richard Bailey. My desire to understand this complex man has not abandoned me to the present.

I managed a brush-through read that failed to answer many of my questions and presented facts that seemed to be seriously at odds with what not only Colonel Pick had led me to believe, but which also did not sit squarely with my impressions of what Mr. Rizzo told Nancy Lewis, or, for that matter, what Nancy had told me.

Yet, I could not erase the downright crushing impact of Nancy's fax. Its contents painted Richard so Stygian black that besides robbing me of my sleep, the information left me confused about my new husband, what had been said and what my personal feelings were.

Thin Air was a factual account of the life of candy heiress Helen Jorhees Brach. Only a few sentences referred to my husband Richard Bailey. He was an excellent dancer and took Mrs. Brach dancing a few times and also sold her three racehorses. Helen Brach loved to dance with Richard's impeccable manners, upbeat personality, and charm; it was understandable that she enjoyed his company.

Chapter 7

My final thought before leaving for the office Wednesday morning was that I was still unconvinced for Richard's guilt, but was very, very concerned about my predicament. After all, whatever gamble I was willing to take, I would have to take for my children, as well.

As the day wore wearily on, I became even more concerned about everyone's safety because the growing list of anomalies and factual discrepancies about Richard would not allow me any peace. Eventually, my maternal instinct prevailed, and I had Trevor take the one daughter still living at home over to stay at my friend Marian's.

Once that had been accomplished, I set about getting ready for my confrontation with my husband. Although I could have handled the situation in a number of ways, I chose an ambush as the optimal form for our separation. Possibly the shock of a blind-sided attack might shake the truth out of Richard.

Making sure that the houseman Trever and Robert, my bookkeeper of many years, would be present in my home should I need the physical presence of a man or two, I waited for Richard to arrive. Like Henry the Fifth planning the Battle of Agincourt, I decided to station the two men in reserve and out sight, yet readily available should reinforcements be needed. To this end, they would be ideally positioned in the kitchen from there both men would have a perfect vantage point to see and hear everything taking place between Richard and me in the nearby family room.

There were a number of reasons the kitchen was the ideal location: Only a four-foot-high wet bar and short wall separated the family room from the food preparation area, so the visibility was optimum; the kitchen was on a higher level than the family room below; and there were large mirrors on a wall in the family room as well as in the hallway and living room beyond. Most importantly, my reinforcements were only a couple of bounds away from the sofa where Richard and I would be seated.

In order to be certain I could be rid of Richard as easily as Nancy had promised, I took her advice and committed one other small subterfuge. At my orders, Trevor had placed all of Richard's belongings in the cloak closet at one end of the family room. So, the stage was now set for my denouncement of the mystery surrounding my magical lover and I was also prepared for my husband's subsequent and swift departure.

Richard was due home after 5:00 PM. Like English highwaymen, Trevor, Robert, and I were in the kitchen, ready and waiting for his arrival, but when I went to let Richard in, he was carrying a beautifully wrapped gift. I was so unbalanced by the turn of events that I could not decide how to handle the situation. What to do? What to do? Ah, the best laid plans of mice and men, I thought as I waived Robert and Trevor back into the shadows of the dimly lit kitchen and walked Richard into the family room.

We sat down together on the soft and silky sofa and a beaming Richard handed me the present. The pink and silver floral designs on the expensive wrapping paper and the lacy pink bow were so very elegant I almost hated to open the package. But Richard coaxed me, and I finally unwrapped it, very carefully, saving the paper. To my amazement, I found a small plain box, and inside, an exquisite gold wedding band. The card that accompanied it was the same design as the wrapping paper and said simply, "To My Wife."

Oh, please, don't be sweet to me now, Richard, I thought. Not now. I resolved to stay strong. Things I could change in the future.

I accepted the ring, fighting back clouds of internal objections, then steeled myself for what was to come. With a tremulous voice, I said, "I'm sorry, Richard, but I received a fax from a private investigator and your background check didn't paint a very complimentary picture of you. The truth of the matter is I feel I have been deceived. I have to return this wedding band to you."

Richard seemed startled and very hurt. It was as if I had slapped him across the face hard enough to draw blood. Was he acting? Impossible to tell.

But he began.

"Richard," I broke in, "I want you to leave my house until I can figure out what to do next." I had, but I was afraid of what he might do next… yell so loudly he would alarm the neighbors, throw furniture around, punch Trevor or Robert or me, but none of those things happened.

The perfect gentleman, wrapped in a soft aura of understanding, said slowly and in a very low voice, "Nothing has changed… I just want you. I want to be with you, want to spend the rest of my life caring for you. I am so much in love with you. But I will do whatever you ask of me."

Then we just sat there on the sofa for a moment, staring at each other. I could see tears filling his eyes and I wanted to tell him that he should have been more straightforward from the first night at The Waterfront, but I was so tense sitting there face to face with the man I loved that I couldn't get the words out. Besides, if I tried to say anything else, I was afraid I'd break down and let him stay.

But Richard, of course, was unaware of these fears. He held up his hand for a moment as if to stop any more negative words, and then, with his voice breaking, said, "If you have heard that I have been with many women, well, yes, that is true, but you should remember I didn't marry any of them.

I married you.

Even the sketchy history I had in my possession bore out the truth of those words. Marriage was never a part of any of Richard's schemes. We sat for a moment longer with Richard shaking his head, then I called Trevor and asked that he put Mr. Bailey's belongings in his car.

Upon hearing this, Richard gave me a sad smile, touched his fingers to his lips, kissed them, then gently pressed them against my mouth. He then walked into the foyer and gave me a kind of jaunty Fred Astaire wave. The wave was an act to hide his true feelings. I knew in my heart his tears had been real.

Trevor moved quickly, gathering Richard's bags and I stood in the foyer and watched the two of them walk out the front door and down the walkway to the street. For some reason, Richard, who was trailing behind Trevor, left the door open.

I was still standing in the foyer when I suddenly heard Richard and Trevor screaming at the tops of their voices, but I couldn't see what was happening because of the high walled fence in front of my home. The first thing that came to mind was a fist fight. I ran out to the street.

Three teenagers had just slashed Richard's convertible top in an effort to steal a pair of snakeskin boots in the back seat, and Richard and Trevor had apparently caught the boys in the act. The men were running as fast as they could after the young kids, but the teenagers outran them. There was nothing more anyone could do so I walked over to the fence gate and stood, waiting.

When Richard returned, I could see he was panting and looked terribly sad. I turned to go inside and just then, Richard's Mercedes' engine rumbled to life and smoothly purred away. My loving husband was gone forever, and I was absolutely devastated by what I had just done. At that moment, I could not begin to imagine how I would live through the coming weeks, much less the rest of my life.

I thanked Trevor and Robert for their help and told them I needed to be alone. After they left, I sat down on the sofa Richard and I had been sitting on and reflected on the events that bad passed. My marriage was over… and Richard had never been less than a perfect gentleman.

Then, even though I was deeply hurt, I began to think. I was faced with an unknown, and the unmasking of unknowns in the scientific community always began with an assessment of available facts. Although I had read through *Thin Air* very fast, I had arrived at a conclusion and it was a strange one.

So, what?

The book asked more questions than it answered. True, Richard's name was in it, but…

So, what?

At first blush, *Thin Air* was completely objective and there was nothing inside which proved that Richard Bailey murdered Helen Brach… or had it? Was it wishful thinking on my part? Had the devil blinded my eyes or had God softened my heart?

What did *Thin Air* prove?

The answer came in a nanosecond.

Nothing.

The proof that Richard was the murderer of Helen Brach was simply not to be found in *Thin Air*.

In fact, when pointing out a possible murderer, the author leaned in another direction: Jack Matlick, the heiress' houseman and an ex-con. I was now more confused than ever. What were Nancy, Rizzo, and the Colonel talking about?

Was my husband really a murderer?

I didn't think so.

If murder really was Richard's game, then why hadn't he struck out at me when I threw him out of the house? Wasn't that what murderers did—they became violent when things didn't go their way?

I seemed to be pulled in so many directions. I wanted with all my heart to be married to Richard, but I didn't want to be involved in a dangerous situation. There were other allegations and seeming facts I also had to deal with at the same time that just didn't add up.

Chapter 8

As I was leaving for the office the next morning, Nancy Lewis called. She congratulated me for getting Richard to leave, then recommended I get an immediate annulment. The annulment, she counseled me, should be easy as the marriage was unconsummated. Even though I still cared for Richard, I had to agree with her course of action. The reason was obvious. I had been pulled back and forth so many times I had partially lost my own will to act and make important decisions. Nancy suggested that I try to get a full disclosure from Richard.

As soon as I hung up, the phone rang again. I expected Nancy wanting to tell me something she had forgotten, but the deep bubbly voice said, "Hey, hey, my beautiful doll…whatever's not working, let's get together and fix it!"

My knees felt weak. My first thought was, "He still loves me!"

Then I did a double take.

He… what is he up to?

This time I was determined I would say what was on my mind. "Richard," I said, "I am so confused about your past I don't even think the head of the C. I. A. could shed any light on it."

"Ask me anything."

"Anything? Well, for starters, did you have anything at all to do with the disappearance and presumed death of Helen Brach?"

"Absolutely, positively not," Richard said slowly. His voice was serious, precise, more importantly, it had the ring of truth. A small voice inside me said, "Believe him... he's not lying." I didn't know what to do with that insight, so I continued my interrogation.

"Then why didn't you tell me you were once a suspect in the Brach case?"

"Because if you had known, you would have walked! I wanted you to know the real me first, then I was going to tell you. I can say this... I was never, ever charged with anything."

I took a long deep breath and let it out as slowly as I could, forming my thoughts as I did so. "Helen Brach is just the tip of the iceberg, Richard. Your other deceptions are equally hard to deal with. I also have to consider the way your past affects my family, my business, and my health."

I paused for a moment, then went on, "If only you had proposed properly without all the pressures, tricks and games, I probably would have married you sooner or later, and you would have had ample opportunity for full disclosure of your past... from the Helen Brach matter to your financial fiascos."

I hesitated, trying to keep my emotions in check and Richard said, "Go on. Finish what you need to say."

My voice was getting shrill, but I couldn't help it. "It's not a crime to be questioned by the police about a friend's disappearance, not a crime to be sued. Neither is it a crime to file for bankruptcy, but we who love without reservation must also trust with reservation, and you should have been more honest and forthcoming about your past, Richard!"

"May I say something?"

"No!"

The thoughts were just flying out of my mouth and I didn't want to stop. "Instead," I went on, "you let me find out all these terrible things about you in a decidedly less wholesome way, by an investigator's report and a conversation with that awful man Pick. Why?"

"Because I —"

I cut him off, "And that's not all! Because you didn't have collateral for a credit card, I ended up stuck with the Vegas hotel bill! You know, Richard, I never would have found out you were lying had I not been forced to look through your belongings trying to find your next of kin!"

"I was going to tell you but…"

"But how can I believe you, Richard? You lie by omission… by keeping silent. Oh… and I almost forgot… what about the women you cheated?"

"Most of those cases were settled out of court twenty years ago! You have no idea how badly I now feel about the way I used to conduct my business. Had I had a better education, I would never have lived my life so dishonestly. Surely you can tell I'm a different person now."

"Are you a different person, Richard? I have no way of knowing. All I ask is that you don't phone me for a while. I need time to think!" I slammed the phone down hard without saying goodbye, something I rarely do.

I immediately felt relieved. I had said what I was truly thinking, feeling, living. My hands were shaking and knowing I had almost become hysterical for a moment; I was angry for the display.

All I could think was that there was no way on earth Richard, and I could ever resolve the chasm between us. It was enormous, as big as the Grand Canyon. But I had no more time to devote to my personal problems. I was late in getting to the office.

Later in the day, Nancy Lewis rang me up again in my private office and said she had learned that Richard had made an appointment to see his lawyer that very afternoon. What now? I thought. Nancy told me not to worry, that she had someone in that particular lawyer's office who would tell her what transpired.

I didn't know what to think about this new wrinkle. Would an ethical investigator have plants in attorneys' offices? Did attorneys leak such information? How could Nancy know everything? What kind of an attorney would allow his attorney-client trusts to be breached by one of his staff? The dark intrigues that permeated law offices was a world I had heard of but was certainly unfamiliar with firsthand. I withheld any comment. "Okay, call me" was all I said.

The minute I hung up the phone, it rang again and once again, I thought it was Nancy calling back.

"Everyone in Chicago's talking about you and Richard!" the excited voice on the other end exclaimed.

"Marian! What are you talking about?"

"WCFL... Clark Weber! He did a program on people who got married on the spur of the moment... said he had spoken to some man at Marshall Fields who was buying a wedding ring for a lady he had only known a few days before marrying her in Vegas."

Marian giggled, "I just knew it was your Richard... held never go to 'Needless Markups.'"

Richard... the beautiful ring... and Marian was right. Neiman Marcus would not be Richard's store of choice.

Part of me wanted to tell Marian about all the heartache I was going through with Richard, but I didn't have the luxury. I had patients waiting. I made my excuses, told Marian I would call her later, then I was out the door, running to the life ring of my life... my medical practice.

I had just finished seeing my last patient when Nancy Lewis called again. She informed me that Richard's lawyer had advised him to disappear for two or three years because by Illinois law, he would not be able to attach any of my assets that I had up to the day of the wedding, but that he could attach half of my subsequent earnings until there was a formal divorce.

There it was.

Richard was apparently the gold digger Lewis, Pick, and Rizzo made him out to be!

Whether or not the information was ethically come by, it was something I had to deal with. Half my earnings! I took a very deep breath. Those earnings would be significant. I would not believe that there are men and lawyers on this earth who would put a scheme like this together to rob a single mother of her income.

I still had more questions than answers, but as a mother, I had to very quickly make some extremely important decisions to protect my family from my new husband.

I couldn't lash out at Richard anymore, I had sent him away, and according to Nancy, just in time. There was no place for my anger, so I lashed out at myself.

I have always been ay too trusting and often naive regarding the intentions and scruples of others.

Even though I was angry, I eventually began to pray in a more rational way and like always, my meditation produced a certain calm. If I could not get divine answers, a brief tranquility, I told myself, was the next best gift.

Painful as it was, I had to read *Thin Air* again.

Alone that night, I found the dreary little book, carried it to my bedroom, locked the door, and curled up in bed. I murmured for insight and understanding as I once again turned to the first page. I closed my eyes for a moment, then began to read the familiar words.

Ringgg!

When the phone jangled at my elbow, I actually jumped. I picked up the receiver and much to my surprise, heard, "Hey, hey, my beautiful doll. Can we talk?"

"Not right now, Richard. I told you… I have to think! Will you be staying in town?" Without realizing what I was doing, I closed the book and traced my fingers around the blood drops on the cover.

"I'm your husband. I'll stay as close to your side as you'll let me."

"Is that what your attorney advised?"

"I haven't seen an attorney…"

"Not today?"

"Not any day. I spent all day at my brother's."

"Somebody has certainly been filling your ears with lies about me… maybe time is the only cure," Richard said evenly.

He was right. I was now convinced I was getting bad information from a number of sources. "Richard, I desperately want to talk, but not now. Can I call you at your place in a couple of days?"

"I won't go out of the house."

I hung up, fixed a scalding cup of apple-cranberry tea, crawled back in bed, and practically ripped *Thin Air* open. I was going to read and study that book, word by word, line by line, paragraph by paragraph, and ambiguity by inconsistency.

Richard Bailey

In the coming days, I would repeat that reading countless times, along with endless prayers for protection, first for me, then as I began to sense Richard's innocence, for my husband, Richard Bailey.

Chapter 9

My previous readings of *Thin Air* had left me with a number of vague conclusions. From the outset I knew (or thought I did) that Richard was probably a sharp horse trader. I felt I could live with that, and when I analyzed my reasons, they seemed sound enough. In the first place, my intuition told me that most people in the horse-trading business were swindlers of sorts, always playing up the strengths of their horses and avoiding any discussion of the weaknesses. Somewhat like the thousands of commercials one sees in a lifetime for weight loss clinics, diet fads, wonder health foods, and engine oils that will transform your rattling Chevrolet into a roaring Jaguar.

Chicago, in particular, seemed to be a hotbed of swindlers and swashbucklers like the Pullmans who came up with the idea of franchised sleeping cars and who also created the ultimate company stores that robbed their workers blind. Chicago also had the meat packing families who bragged of pure hot dogs then sometimes slipped in the animals' "other parts" long before the trend became fashionable. The swindlers were all there in the railyards and stockyards, bilking the public while dishonoring and abusing their employees.

Chicago was a swindlers' mecca… from the Chicago Board Options Exchange scandals to the pork belly frauds of the futures markets. There was a long Chicago history/tradition of con men like The Yellow Kid who always wore yellow kid gloves during his elaborate confidence games. And of course, the movie, The Sting, with Robert Redford and Paul Newman, was centered around a horse swindle and after great consideration, set in the city of Chicago. Chicago had the Black Socks, Al Capone and the Teamsters' frauds, corrupt policemen by the hundreds and a general police intolerance of outsiders that manifested itself in the riots of the 1968 Democratic Convention. This same police corruption allowed the fraudulent sale of "voting rights" for the names on gravestones in various area cemeteries.

I was not a person who would support frauds, but they were part of life like smallpox or car dealers who wouldn't live up to their warranties.

I was aware of defense attorneys who traded their criminal clients with the prosecution, letting a guilty but rich man go free in exchange for incarcerating a poorer albeit innocent man. I had heard of doctors by the score who removed perfectly healthy, human body organs for the sole purpose of putting their children through college or purchasing a new sailboat with which to play on the waters of Lake Michigan.

I was not naive to the evils of the world, but I knew that every con game depended upon the greed of the victim in order to succeed. Therefore, I was tolerant of those endless scams in which the rich and greedy were trapped in the web of their own avarice when it came to horses. And I also knew another fact: No one on this earth could, with absolute certainty, tell you which horse was better or worse than another on a given day, never mind the week after next. This was best evidenced by the fact that on the day Seattle Slew, the Triple Crown Winner and arguably one of the best horses ever to race, was purchased for a mere $17,500 by a sawmill owner and his wife looking for a tax loophole. Other horses that would never win a race (or even run a race) have been purchased for over $100,000 and no one ever screamed "fraud."

With my mind now pried open, I set about reading and evaluating the book in my hands.

Thin Air was written by Pat Colander and published by Contemporary Books, Inc. of Chicago. Although I suspected the publisher was some sort of Vanity Press, I decided to discard that bit of information as too prejudicial for my purposes and proceeded as if the work had been disseminated by a mainline New York publishing firm. In short, unless I had hard information to the contrary, I was prepared to believe everything the book said for the purpose of that reading, and then make my decisions as to which portions to double check on later.

The first chapter basically retraced the last few hours before Helen Brach disappeared in February of 1977. As is expected in the genre of True Crime Stories, the focus was on the more sinister aspects of her exit from the public eye. There was also a seeming attempt to paint Helen Brach as a solitary soul, having a few friends and being somewhat meanspirited in terms of her ability to give gifts, etc. to deserving individuals. I found Richard mentioned twice in that chapter, in one instance as a playboy (which he was), and in another where it stated that Richard had sold Brach a horse that had just won a rice in Florida. So, much for at least part of the allegations by Pick that Richard sold only worthless nags.

Helen Brach had had a spotty, unremarkable career on her way to becoming the heiress to the candy maker's fortune. In her hometown of Hopedale, Ohio, she had worked as a ticket agent for a trolley system, a pottery finisher, billing clerk and a ticket seller at a local ballroom. After moving to Miami Beach, she took a job as that check girl in an exclusive country club, and it was there she met the scion of the Brach millions, Frank Brach.

The chapter was long and like others of the genre, used mountains of nonrelated historical information about the protagonist and her past (including a lengthy genealogy) as a filler.

Her connection with Richard was not very clear in the book. He had sold her some horses and went to Argentina to purchase another. Some of the horses were terrible, some winners. One thing was clear: She enjoyed his company and from the outset of the book, I had the impression that there was nothing sexual in their relationship. Helen Brach liked to dance, and for a woman who enjoyed ballroom style dancing, Richard Bailey would have been a gift from heaven.

It's a gift from heaven, I reminded myself.

Richard Bailey

On the day Helen Brach disappeared, there was a fairly solid trail up to a point. She was staying at the Kahler Hotel in Rochester, Minnesota. On the morning of February 17, 1977, she got up, called her home in Chicago, and spoke at length with Jack Xotlick, her houseman. She then walked over to the Mayo Clinic, was checked out by her doctor and paid her bill. Knowing she had been given a clean bill of health, she stopped at a gift shop and purchased some towels, a soap dish and powder box, and after telling the clerk her "houseman" was waiting for her, instructed the woman to mail all the purchases to her new home in Florida.

Apparently, I concluded at this point, Helen Brach was planning on moving away from Chicago, something the book hinted was going to upset a lot of people. She paid her bills with checks (and here the author included the check numbers, which lent credence to the work), and flew home to Chicago. After this point in time, no one on earth claims to have seen her except her houseman, Jack Matlick.

In reading on, I discovered Jack Matlick had claimed he had watched Brach sign a number of checks, all made out to him. The checks were later found to be forged. After Brach disappeared, Matlick also burned her diaries and automatic writings, yet he was never arrested.

It appeared, even back then, that the officers involved from the State Police had another suspect in mind, Richard, and at one point, they took him in for a deposition by manipulating the civil inquiries going on. At this time, Richard did something that was very incriminating in my eyes, something that will probably haunt him to the end of his days, and made it look like he had much to hide. At the advice of his lawyer, Jo-Ann Wolfson, Richard pled the Fifth Amendment to every question he was asked.

It was, in my opinion, this action that had put the entire focus of the investigation on Richard from then on, despite the fact that he had proven he was in Florida at the time Brach disappeared.

Despite the ubiquitous vagueness in the work, the book did a fair job of listing all the people who might have had an interest in seeing Helen Brach dead (even though her body was never found, and Jack Matlick was all but accused of buying a meat grinder on her credit card to do away with the body).

The suspect list was long.

Jack Matlick, her houseman who would lose his cushy job, his farm, and a lot of perks if Brach had moved to Florida, Matlick also invoked the Fifth Amendment, and the police showed no further interest.

Her brother, Charles Voorhees, who helped Jack Matlick burn her diaries and other records and who stood to inherit a large sum of money.

Everett Moore, Brach's accountant, was a vague suspect, despite his uncovering of a number of checks that Jack Matlick had forged on Helen Brach's account.

Belton Mouras, an Animal Protective Institute executive, was believed to have a motive because investigators thought he might have had something to gain by Helen Brach's death.

Howard Fulton, a county dogcatcher, did not escape the author's net as well, and by the time I reached this level of suspicions, I had pretty much concluded that *Thin Air* was based on facts, many, many facts. But as a credit to the author, the facts were all there; the problem was to determine which ones meant anything.

As I was carefully checking the book for the suspects, one fact leapt out at me on the bottom of page 63. There had been a $100,000 reward for information on Brach's disappearance yet that amount of money did not bring anyone forward. The disappearance "with foul play" allegations of the Illinois State Police had been referred to the U.S. Attorney's Office and the Federal Bureau of Investigation. Since then, the F.B.I. had an interest in the case, and Richard was a prime suspect. Someone had, in fact, been trying to focus the investigation on Richard by spray painting messages on the roadside saying, "Richard Bailey knows where Mrs. Brach's body is. Stop him! Please!" and another equally sinister warning, "Bailey killed Brach." Normally one would think the F.B.I. would have leapt on the case at this point.

Not so.

The reward kept going up, reaching $200,000 by 1978, the year after Brach's disappearance, and still there were no takers!

Richard Bailey

Frank Jayne then showed up as a suspect. Frank Jayne was the nephew of Silas Jayne, the most feared of all the notorious Jayne clan. The two Jaynes had more than a few reasons to set Richard up for a fall with the murder.

Silas Jayne, who did six years in prison for the murder of his own brother, was a long-standing enemy of Richard's. Many called him "The Godfather of the Chicago Horse Mafia," and I assumed they meant the horse swindling set that Richard belonged to in the North Chicago stables area.

According to the book, by 1981 the reward for information about the missing heiress had grown to $250,000 and still no real leads had developed.

A friend of Silas Jayne's showed up with a story that he had been offered $10,000 to relocate Brach's body. His name was Morris "Slab" Ferguson, but his stories were not credible. Nevertheless, he became a suspect, as well.

I put the book down after reading a chapter entitled, "Jack Matlick and the Perfect Crime," on page 117. Matlick was everybody's choice as the murderer. Then why the focus on Richard?

Colonel Pick was a man with an ax to grind.

Nancy Lewis was so rushed by my need for information that she gave me a report full of holes and shaded by her own feelings of protectiveness toward me.

I knew Richard Bailey did not kill Helen Brach.

Perhaps the person who knew who killed Helen Brach was the man with the spray can who had run around painting signs saying that Richard did it. I did not know who was behind that campaign, but one day, I knew everybody will find out who and why.

When that happened, I would find out who Richard's real enemy was in this bizarre mystery. I just did not believe that the culprit had surfaced as yet.

I put the book aside for all time.

Chapter 10

Five days after the marriage, I awakened one morning and took inventory of my life. Most of the discord in my life at that time had focused down to the dichotomous nature between my magic relationship with Richard and the relatively sterile life in which I had merely existed before the advent of our union.

On the romantic side, I was still madly in love with Richard and desperately wanted to work things out. On the practical side, I remained a very high profile, professional person who was financially dependent upon the quality of my public image.

It was becoming increasingly obvious (even to me) that I could not have it both ways. It was time to make a decision. The problem was that each of the options available was terribly repugnant to either my practical or my romantic nature.

Choice One: Part ways with Richard and deal with my broken heart.

Choice Two: Stay with Richard, watch my practice fade and my family dissolve.

Family first, my Reformed Dutch upbringing demanded, and my conscience agreed.

I called my lawyer, Stanley Kaplin and told him that I wanted an annulment. Stanley assured me he would phone me back just as soon as he drew up the necessary papers and schedule an appointment.

While waiting for his call, Richard rang me up, asking what my intentions were. "You tricked me, Richard," I said. "I thought I would be living with you in Sleeping Beauty's castle and now I find myself a prisoner of your past." My fingers tensed, tightened around the receiver, but I went on, "I could not be more miserable than I am right this minute! I want to get an annulment!"

There was a protracted silence and I steeled myself for burst of outrage, but then, like a warm fog boiling up from cold darkness, Richard said softly, "Please reconsider. We can reach an understanding because we love each other. My feelings are unchanged… I still truly love you. We have something that most people seldom find, a love that will endure. You'll see."

"No, Richard," I said, my voice more firm than one would suspect considering my ambiguities and the palpitations of my heart. "I can't make lifelong decisions based solely upon my feelings for you. The world is not as simple as black and white, good or evil, yin or yang, and we are caught in the vortex of one of the gray areas. Please understand that I have other issues besides just you and me to think of… there are other lives to consider… and yes… protect."

I took a very long and deep breath, then said, "What I would like to do is to date you for two or three months after the annulment. We could have a normal courtship, an opportunity to reconcile the many dissonant differences of our life models."

I paused, thinking that Richard would want to say something at this point but only heard silence on the other end, so I went on, "I'm entitled to some time to adjust without any pressure, so are you. Surely we have seen enough of each other to trust that our love, assuming it is as real as we perceive it to be, can only grow."

"And then…"

"Then if we still feel we care for each other, we'll have a proper, decent marriage which is in keeping with my at professional standing and values."

In the end, Richard agreed to the conditions. He had to. I placed no caveats on him… don't do this or you're out of my life, but I gave him no other options than to accept the conditions. "This time," I said, "our relationship will be built on trust and understanding, but we must break clean and then grow back together."

"You make us sound like broken bones."

"No… broken hearts… but the principle is the same."

"We'll be stronger after the break and a healthy regeneration."

"Go ahead and draw up the papers," Richard said finally, "and I will sign them." He chuckled softly. "I have never ignored a doctor's prescription in my life and won't start now. Besides, I only want to make you happy."

Later that day, Stanley called, saying he had drafted the annulment papers and wanted me to drop by and go over them. I could not bring myself to read them but told him to finalize the drafts as I had a clear understanding the dissolution had to happen.

I was deeply depressed but nevertheless, Richard and I went to dinner that same evening. I was loving and caring that night which really wasn't hard because I was truly in love, but I could not deal with the black hole of Richard's past in any rational way, and I was unable to change his history.

The next morning, Richard stopped by the house, and we drove to the Currency Exchange with Stanley is legal papers for signature guarantee. I could see the strain etched on Richard's face and felt my own pinched into a mirror image. How different from our smiling happy faces in Vegas.

The end of my painful dream came with surgical indifference: snip, clip, sponge, and suture. With a shaking hand, I signed the annulment papers without looking at either the coldly worded document or my crestfallen ex-husband. Richard dutifully signed right after me. To this day, I do not remember what either of us said when we parted. The sadness has folded over my memory like a black velvet glove.

On Friday, April 22, 1994, Richard and I met once again, this time in judge's chambers. What I had thought would be a fairly intricate process was a done deal in a matter of minutes. Our marriage was annulled. Technically over.

The judge was very specific and succinct with his instructions, "You each have thirty days to appeal the decision."

Immediately after the judge's pronouncement, I didn't know what to do. My attorney was busily fiddling with some of his papers, and Richard was just standing there, smiling sadly. I wanted to grab him and kiss him, tell the judge that it was all a mistake, but before I could put thought to action, Richard turned and walked softly out of the room, his gait measured, his back proud and tall. I knew I was looking at a genuine man who took his adversity with grace and courage. I slipped myself the intellectual pill of remembering my shock at the first disclosures of his untruthfulness, but the bitter medicine did nothing to soothe the tremors of hurt rumbling through my heart.

Sensing my pain, Stanley said, "You've done the right thing." He patted my shoulder for a moment then touched my cheek with one finger. "You're a strong woman, Annette. You've told me that yourself many, many times. The only problem with announcing to hell and sundry that 'I'm a tough guy' is that every now and then some gunfighter or gut twister is going to come ambling down the street and make you prove it." Stanley smiled, made a fist, and tapped me on the chin. "It's your time now, slugger. Go on out of here just like Richard did and let me see how tough you really are."

"Yes… right… Annette Hoffman, M. D, M. A. , and a mean S. O. B. ," I said softly. The words and the tears came out at the same time, then I, too, left, fled, actually, bearing the same anguished feelings I'd experienced once in South Africa when I saw a stillborn baby delivered. What would have happened, I had wondered at the time, if that precious life had been allowed to go on, to flourish or to fail on its own? Why did God stop the beating heart without giving it a chance to prove itself?

Why was I being deprived of a chance to see my marriage blossom?

After the stressful meeting with the judge, I took a taxi and returned to my office. There I went to work with a vengeance, hoping to bury my pain in activity. For the few hours I was in the office, my plan worked. I slowly began to relax, unwind.

Then five o'clock rolled around. There were no more patients. The door closed, was locked. My staff went their separate ways. Alone again, a terrible depression quickly fell over me. All I had to look forward to was another lonely night in my empty castle.

But I was in for a big surprise.

When I returned to my home that evening, Richard had moved in, bringing all his clothes! I had never heard of anything so outrageous in all my life!

Moving in after an annulment?

We might as well be trailer trash shacking up for a few days every now and then. No, I told myself, you're still technically married. "Married with an escape hatch" was the way Marian described it.

Nevertheless, my first reaction was repressed anger at Richard's audacity. It was a such a shock to see him there. I had also finished reading *Thin Air* again that very morning and had hundreds of unanswered questions, scary questions, filling my head, but even then, I was certain Richard was no murderer. Playboy, yes, but he simply did not have the mindset of a killer.

In the end, I gave in and let him stay.

Maybe we were meant to happen after all, I thought. My mind was now focused on how we might mesh as a social couple… did Richard and I have the give and take to make our already shaky relationship work for an extended period of time?

Much to my surprise, the new arrangement worked out well for both of us. During the next few weeks, Richard was absolutely wonderful, very caring, and unusually domestic.

Whenever he saw a problem of any sort around the house, he fixed it. He never had to be told. He even cleaned up my kitchen! It was all too good to be true.

And once again, it was only the beginning.

Each day that passed, I saw my home becoming more and more organized with Richard correcting the thousand and one problems an unscrupulous builder had left me earlier (after inflating the price of his work by $200, 000 above the contract price). Richard finished the landscaping job, planting flowers tastefully and yet in profusion. He cleaned the swimming pool, not just scrubbing around the edges; he had it drained and then scrubbed. He tightened door knobs, fixed locks, and cleaned the house each day with an attention to detail that would make any professional service envious. And he never once let me feel less than the most important person in his universe. He brought the paper to my bedroom (every morning!) along with breakfast in bed, which we shared, and yes, I discovered that despite our original abstinence, Richard was an extraordinary lover, showering me with the epitome of my sexual experiences.

Marian summed it up one day when she said that Richard was the only man she ever met who knew how to properly care for everything, even a rubber plant! I remember blushing at the time, reflecting on how wondrously he was taking care of me!

I couldn't help what happened next.

I fell even more in love with him.

His caring ways extended not only to me, but also to my teenage daughter. He was only too happy to drive her and her friends to the movies, but unlike me, he refused to let them come home in a taxi. It was far too dangerous, he would say, young girls alone in the city are innocent targets, and he would drive into the loop to pick them up. He was the ultimate protector.

Even if he dropped off one of my daughter's little friends at her home, Richard would always wait until she had safely walked to the door, and he made sure there was a responsible adult inside to accept the child. In those days, my daughter couldn't help but like him. He treated her like the very special person she was.

I begrudgingly began to count off the days on the calendar, never wanting the month hiatus of the annulment process to come to an end. When it did, I really didn't know what to do next, what decision would be best for me and my daughters. Was my judgment being clouded because I'd been alone for so many years? I wasn't sure. I did have to admit that it was nice to go to bed with someone I loved, be held in his aims all night, and then to wake up with that same someone the next morning.

But it was more than that. I had actually spent an entire month laughing! What a joyful change for someone as serious and emotionally overextended as I had been!

Aside from sleeping with someone I loved and being happy around the clock, there was an added unexpected bonus.

Richard talked in his sleep.

And what he said while sleeping was a miraculous revelation. Night after night, Richard brought up Helen Brach and how he was worried that people thought he had something to do with her death. Over and over, he said he wasn't guilty and wanted to hire some lawyer from Ohio with a fabulous reputation to clear his name from the *Thin Air* allegations. During those times, Richard would also say he loved me, and that he didn't want me to have any doubts about him.

When I told a couple of non-professional friends about Richard's ramblings, they scoffed, saying I was being manipulated by a slick con man, but I had more than sufficient medical training to know if a person was faking sleep. I had operated on thousands of patients under anesthesia, and they often talked when the anesthetist brought them to the cusp of full unconsciousness.

How could I tell Richard's behavior wasn't an act? Because when he talked in his sleep, it was the way a person spoke when he was asleep, slurred speech, broken speech, but what he said was understandable.

Also, Richard's breathing was very even. If a person were putting on an act and trying to say this or that and regulate his breathing at the same time, it would not be possible. Why? Because when a person is sleeping, his breath comes in and out regularly as opposed to being awake, when an individual phrases his words so he can breathe. When someone talks in his sleep, this phrasing does not occur which results, of course, in broken speech. Whether inhaling or exhaling, a person simply says what his subconscious mind is dealing with.

It would be extremely difficult if not impossible to fake. A person would have to understand the complexities involved, memorize his text and practice for months in order to carry it off. At that time, I hadn't even known Richard a month.

Besides, Richard's voice was seldom over a whisper and if I had not been an extremely light sleeper, something he could not have known, I would never have heard him speaking in the first place.

It was late one night when I became aware of an interesting fact. When Richard spoke in his sleep, he was in some sort of a nonmedically-induced trance. I believed he was being entirely truthful then, and his subconscious was speaking because a trip through the subconscious is the ultimate track to the truth.

I was so stunned by this revelation that I wrote a spontaneous paper on the matter, not very creatively entitled: *Truth: The Shortcut to Justice*.

What has always bothered me about the American legal process is that you can't give a suspect an injection that will take away his or her inhibitions, scopolamine, for instance, so a person would tell the truth no matter what. A combination of sodium pentothal and valium would work as well, but there are many drugs the government could use. One can only imagine the millions of dollars America could save if they caught a criminal suspect, administered the drugs with permission and let the person simply tell the truth. The subject would have to be willing, of course, because the system is required to protect the individual's civil rights.

Injection with a "truth serum" is something I believe any innocent person would want to do in order to clear himself as rapidly as possible, if for no other reason than to avoid the lengthy pretrial incarcerations that have become so common in America of late.

THE SHORTCUT TO JUSTICE IS THE TRUTH.

When I told Richard I had written the paper, he asked that I read it to him and agreed entirely with its contents. He even asked if there was a drug someone could give him to prove he was not involved with the Brach disappearance. He told me this on more than one occasion when we were walking along Lake Michigan. He even offered to let me conduct the examination so I would feel comfortable with the outcome.

Richard also said he wanted to hire an expensive lawyer to clear his name. He said after he proved he wasn't guilty, he hoped we could write a book together to pay back the expenses because he didn't want to involve me in any kind of financial difficulty. He knew I was a working woman and always respected my position and the needs of my family.

Golden Tongue

The thirty days of the appeal period were up. I steeled myself and told Richard (once again!) that he had to leave. "I will continue to see you," I promised, "but I need space and time to make up my mind about our relationship." Richard was a modem day genie. My wish was his command. He simply went to our bedroom, packed up his clothes and left. He never argued with my decision or tried to upset me in any way. As always, I was his first and only consideration.

Having been in an "on again, off again marriage" for six weeks, I thought I had toughened somewhat. Not true. I was completely devastated and felt like a mouse in a B. F. Skinner Approach/Avoidance conflict study. The closer I got to Richard, the more anxious I became, and the further I got away from him, the more anxious I became. When it came to Richard, there did not appear to be ANY middle ground where I was comfortable.

My image of the conflict was so clear that sometimes at night I could close my eyes and actually see the experiment take place. The mouse was kept alone in a dark box and fed through an opening at one side. one day, the end of the box was opened by remote control and suddenly the mouse was staring at a huge block of cheese far down a long passageway. Without hesitation, ears and whiskers twitching, the little fellow galloped off down the corridor and bit into the cheese. At that precise moment, he was delivered a very strong electrical shock, causing him to jump back and run to the security of his little black room.

That night, the mouse was given no food, and the door was opened again the following morning. This time the cheese was even larger, more aromatic, and the mouse trotted down to the cheese, sniffed about for a moment, then touched his nose to the cheese. The electric shock was stronger this time and the mouse ran in terror back to his little room. That night he was not fed.

The next morning, the mouse, now bordering on starvation, was up when the door opened. He started toward the cheese, remembered the shock, stopped, headed back to the box, remembered he was starving, turned back to the cheese, was terrified by the possibility of another shock, and turned back to his safety zone.

At this point, the mouse, afraid to approach the prize and yet driven to, was also unable to avoid the prize because of his hunger. Now, he had nowhere to go that was safe as his home at the end of the box would become the cell in which he would starve to death.

There was only one logical outcome, a nervous breakdown, and the mouse suffered that alternative. He continued to spin wildly from cheese to what had once been his safe haven until he forgot about both and died, chasing his tail instead of his dreams.

Richard was my cheese.

My dream would become my life.

My past empty life was my little black box.

The electrical shocks were the violent disapproval of my family and friends.

Who pulled the switch? I still didn't know, but if it was the Devil doing it, I knew I had a chance. If it was God, Fate or Destiny doing it, nothing could help me, not even my Guardian Angel (who had been markedly absent for some time).

What to do when faced with the ultimate Approach/Avoidance conflict?

Pray, you ninny, I told myself.

And pray I did… by the bucketsful.

Chapter 11

For the next few months, Richard and I spoke every day on the phone and saw each other constantly, usually for dinner followed by a night of dancing. These were happy times, caring times, perfect times with never an unkind word for each other. There was only love and laughter and Fun with the ever-present capital IF, just like the very first night I met Richard at The Waterfront. Oh, I knew the old axiom: "He who loves least controls the relationship," but our love seemed to be an ongoing dead heat.

No matter how hard I tried, I could not dispatch the feelings I felt for this man or the many concerns I had about him. I told myself that if I survived the experience, perhaps I would end up a much stronger person.

A fortune teller at a charity bazaar had once told me that loving a swashbuckler was definitely not a pastime for the timid I had giggled at the phony advice and said, "What? You mean I'm going to fall in love with a pirate?"

"There's all kinds of pirates, dearie," she had replied and clicked her long purple nails against the crystal ball. Her words had come to haunt me.

I also remembered the advice of a famous sushi chef in Chicago who told me one night that falling in love with an adventurous man and eating sushi were two proclivities not compatible with a faint heart.

And then, of course, there was the old warning from Colonel Pick to keep a close watch on whatever I drank when Richard was around. Oh, yes… I had found out that Colonel Pick had more lawsuits against him than Marshall Fields had men's suits in their store.

So, it had come to that.

Advice from cooks, crooks, and sorcerers flooded my mind.

I even had a dream that I asked Julia Child to concoct a recipe for my perfect mate and Richard showed up in a one-dish cookbook, but Freud showed up too in the same dream, yelling, "Father/Fraud!" and then Jung appeared, yodeling wildly about youth on the wing. Freud may have been on the money, but I had no hint I was going through any sort of midlife crisis.

As Richard and I saw each other more and more, every now and then, he was painfully honest with me, and in the process, he would tell me little things I didn't like. Minor flaws, I decided, but still comments that weren't completely moral or honest, like the time he overstated the bloodlines of a horse to make a deal. I'm forgiving to a fault and as time passed, I tended to overlook these moral transgressions just as I tolerated the fact that one of my female acquaintances (and one of Richard's worst detractors) was married to a man (high society, highly visible, big executive) who was forced to retire from his company for embezzlement.

Embezzlement!

Richard's pecuniary transgressions paled in comparison.

Besides, a little voice in my head kept pointing out, "Richard was raised in poverty and is the twelfth of twelve children. Probably his mother didn't give him her all when it came to imparting values and teaching him the difference between right and wrong." In my mind, Richard's focus on instant gratification was all completely logical based on his childhood years of struggling, but I failed to make the connection between his poor start in life and one fact noted in *Thin Air* that Richard's targets were all women.

One Thursday in mid-July, Richard dropped by the house and said quite unexpectedly, "Let's you and I run away, spend the weekend together in the country!"

I thought for a moment and said, "Why not?" It had been ages since I spent any time out of doors and I envisioned a stay at one of the health spas up north in Wisconsin, possibly one of the artsy-fartsy, country "retreat" hotels by Lake Geneva or the Wisconsin Dells. Tourist traps where everyone went.

I should have known better with Richard.

The following Saturday when we were loading our luggage into my Mercedes, I saw these ominous looking, black carrying cases, long, thin and made of a hard material. My God, he's going to teach me how to play pool, I thought. We got trouble right here in River City, and that begins with "T" which rhymes with "P" and I'm talking about pool! The lines from Music Man were chased out of my mind by the thought that the cases might also be used for carrying and/or secreting hunting rifles.

Wrong again.

The sinister looking tubes contained a mystery but one that I was not to solve until we reached our destination.

Kohler, Wisconsin.

Across from the Kohler Factory.

I should have known that with all the water images I had come to associate with Richard and me that Kohler had to be the company which made the faucets that spouted water for the basins of the world.

Of course, with that realization, I figured out what the ominous tubes in the trunk contained.

Fishing poles!

But I kept my guess to myself and said nothing for the moment.

A big surprise was Richard's choice of hotels. The American Club was a large, red brick structure with an Old-World ambiance that reminded me of the better European hotels, I quickly fell in love with the oriental rugs, the Vermeer marble floors, the handcrafted woodwork and my favorite, The Greenhouse. This elegant cafe was encased in stained glass and located in the hotel's courtyard where pastries and coffee were served to its guests. It was there I learned from a waiter that Mr. Kohler had built the hotel for his immigrant workers in the early 1900s, calling it the American Club because he wanted his employees to all become citizens.

After checking into our room (complete with our own whirlpool bath!), we dressed casually and did virtually nothing for the rest of the day except make "Happy Talk." We chatted endlessly, shared secret thoughts and feelings, discussed films, dreams and ideas, our children, our futures, and just silly inane subjects like how many napkins were in the nine restaurants throughout the resort, and What would happen if Popsicles had never been dreamed up by some creative soul. Once again, I was completely relaxed during these times. The truth is I have never felt more comfortable with any human being than I have with Richard.

Without trying to do so, time and again, Richard made me forget about all the other men I had known in my lifetime. When we were together, there were only the two of us, and while we weren't against the world (like in the old saying), the world did seem to be a better place because of our love.

On Sunday, we took a long, long walk in River Wildlife, a five-hundred-acre, wilderness preserve adjacent to the hotel offering many rustic trails and its own meandering river. Richard and I saw God's handiwork everywhere we looked, and I enjoyed still more meaningful conversations, conversations I can recall even today and will still be able to recall years from now. Most men talk at women to accomplish a goal or to try and turn their heads in order to seduce them. Women on the other hand want to share their thoughts, their feelings, their lives. Richard understood this completely. He was and is the most wonderful listener I have ever known. How different our talks were, I realized, from most of the inane chats I have had in my lifetime. Most of my associates were too busy counting things to speak of anything else. I remembered the old saying, "There is nothing as empty as a life full of things." How true.

During our walk in the woods, I was very impressed at how much Richard knew about nature, including the names of various trees: birch, blue spruce, white pine. He also pointed out many different birds my untrained eyes would have missed-owls, eagles, grouse, quail, pheasant, partridge. True, he wasn't a college graduate, but he was the most "street-smart" person I had ever known, and the knowledge he occasionally unveiled never ceased to amaze me.

On the drive back to Chicago, Richard stopped on the shores of Lake Michigan. It was then he finally brought out the poles. Not just ordinary poles, poles for fly fishing, and scores of hand-tied flies, mostly royal coachmen green and brown and white-striped flies.

"Let's try our luck!" Richard said excitedly, nodding at the poles.

"Why not?" I said, thinking I was probably going to hate the experience. But the minute I picked up a fishing pole, I could feel myself giving in to the moment. And who would not? The water couldn't have been more clear and cold, the air more clean and pure, the sky more bright or blue, and the company more strong and reassuring.

It occurred to me that the only man in the world who would have been able to perceive that I would thoroughly enjoy fly fishing and then having the courage of his convictions to actually get me doing it was this man I had married in great love and haste and then discarded in great love and hasty confusion. Yes, Richard was still there; quiet, strong, confident. The other men I had dated in Chicago. Not one of them had the imagination or the passion for life to take me fishing.

I learned very quickly that fly fishing was a sport in which Richard excelled. And he was the perfect teacher, patient, knowledgeable, enthusiastic. He stood off to one side at first, stripping out the line, laying the fly out farther and farther on the lake. Finally, he set up my pole and told me to mimic his actions. It was simple like that, like working against a mirror in a ballet class. Fly fishing, I quickly learned, was just another dance: one-two-three-kick, one-two-three-kick.

I came to enjoy the feel of a fishing rod secure in my hand, the way the line snakes out into the air and the waves of filaments looping and catching the sunlight before laying down ever so lightly on top of the water. I also took delight in the strange atavistic yet satisfied feeling that came over me when I caught my first fish and reeled him in. In fact, I enjoyed the out-of-doors and fishing so much I thought that perhaps in another life and time I had been a pioneer's wife. Incredible thoughts for this city dweller!

Surely I was being tested. I thought. The Devil would not have been so exquisitely agonizing as to keep forcing me to choose and choose and choose between Richard and the world. If the Devil wanted me with Richard, I would have been there at his side without impediments. No, I knew that I was being tested, and by another Power. The minions of darkness tease and tempt.

By the end of the weekend in Wisconsin, I was a fairly proficient fly caster and a much more polished philosopher. If only I could keep life as simple as the last two days together, I knew I would be alright.

I anticipated that things would be easier for me soon, but for now, my mind was just clearing.

I was absolutely certain that Richard was not a murder.

Con man?

Maybe.

But where I was concerned, where was the game?

I could see none.

And I had looked,

No, Richard's love was no con. As I told Marian, I was born in the dark, but it wasn't last night. Richard was real.

I had enjoyed myself so much in the quiet woodlands of Wisconsin that I hated to return to Chicago and the noisy echoes of its concrete jungle. But return we did, and once again, went our separate ways.

Alone in my bedroom, I replayed our outing over and over like a movie in my head. That we had a loving, compassionate relationship was a given, but morally there were still those nagging little problems (the not entirely ethical ones) that I simply couldn't overlook. My conscience told me loud and clear that there were dark things about Richard that I shouldn't like. And I could not lie to myself, act as though they didn't exist. Polonius said it best, "To thine own self be true."

It became a habit of mine to sit on my bed and look at each of these "little problems" like the individual facets of a flawed jewel, turning them over and over in my head.

What to do?

What to do?

Time was passing and I had waited long enough.

I had to make another decision and very soon regarding our relationship.

Should I end it and make my friends and family happy or should I marry this charismatic man…

Again.

My hand went out for help like a drowning swimmers to the lifeguard's ring. Meditation brought hope.

Chapter 12

After the Wisconsin trip, I spent nine soul-searching days taking stock of my situation with Richard. In the end, I was not happy with my findings. Without Richard at my side, it was becoming more and more difficult for me to stay centered, to maintain a level of calm in my life.

Exacerbating these problems, my professional responsibilities were at all times demanding and with my on-again, off-again marriage, I had to more and more become a child psychologist in order to fulfill my maternal obligations. I had come to think of my children as innocent victims in this tragedy, and this painful knowledge broke my heart.

But I could not deny what I believed to be true: Richard was not a killer. Richard was not after my money. Richard truly loved me.

Those were three big positives.

What about the negatives—aside from the obvious?

Our relationship, I had discovered, was an endless series of twists and turns that left me both breathless with excitement and emotionally drained from fear. My life was one big question mark. It was like playing Monopoly but every time I rolled the dice, I couldn't move around the board, but could only draw from the Chance pile. I never knew what was going to happen next. Just when I thought I was going down one path with Richard Bailey, I ended up on another.

Richard Bailey

The trip to Kohler had proved to be just another one of those bizarre twists and turns. was a world traveler, but never in my wildest dreams would I have chosen the backwoods of Wisconsin as a stepping stone toward my personal Bali Hai. Yet I discovered no choice in vacation spots could have brought me more inspiring spiritual and soulful moments. And once again, I owed it all to Richard! Life with him was a fairy tale, but it was all true! (most of the time) And I suffered this bifurcated reaction each and every time I went out with the man.

Absent his presence, I was once again back in the pitch-black room, waiting for Prince Charming to appear and flip on the lights. And the lights Richard turned on came in all shapes, sizes, and degrees of brightness: candle lights for intimate dinners in restaurants, strobe lights for a wild evening of disco dancing, bubble lights when I was depressed and needed to be put in a holiday mood, flashlights when I wanted something illuminated and always a soft, gentle night light of love when he tucked me in bed. The stop and go history of our relationship was a traffic light run amok, switching from red to green and back again with the confusing rush of colors of a kaleidoscope against a background warning yellow.

If God was the light of the world, Richard was the light of my life. Perhaps if the two of us were together, a married couple, all the confusion and bickering in my mind (and yes, in my family too) would finally come to an end. It was this self-awareness that made me decide right then and there that I would marry Richard Bailey.

Again.

Together, with some guidance patience perhaps there would be no more twists and turns, just a beautiful straight line of a happy couple, devoid of mysteries, double meanings, or ambiguities.

Richard had asked me to meet him for dinner at the Fountain Blue in Des Plaines that particular Tuesday evening, the 26th of July. The dinner engagement would provide me (turnabouts fair play!) with the perfect opportunity to propose. After my critical analysis, I knew in my heart that my decision to many Richard (once again!) was the right one. I would have had to have been a masochist to prefer being alone and unhappy to being blissfully content with Richard.

Yes, I would ask him to marry me that very evening and to seal the engagement, we would both drink from Richard's loving cup. It would be a tender moment, the most special time of all the special times we had been together, and I could not have been more thrilled about the possibility of my dream finally coming true. Bloody Mary had the right idea! There'd be no lonely island for this lady! Not with a husband as caring and attentive as Richard!

That evening while getting ready for our date, I actually danced around the house, humming what lyrics I could remember from the movie that was becoming my life: "Some enchanted evening, you may see a stranger, you may see a stranger across a crowded room." Yes, it had been crowded that night… "and somehow you know, you know even then, that somewhere you'll see him again and again." And again, I thought… hopefully forever. "Who can explain it, who can tell you why? Fools give you reasons, wise men never try… Right! Who could possibly explain what had happened to me? It was enough that I had found him… found him… "and once you have found him, never let him go… once you have found him, never let him go, or all through your life, you may be all alone."

Alone?

No way was I going to let that happen!

Richard and I were meant to be together!

The fates had decreed it!

And no matter what anyone else thought, our marriage was going to work!

I dabbed a new Chanel behind my ears and carefully selected what I would wear for our once-in-a-lifetime evening: a shell-pink silk suit with crystal and gold buttons, pink pearl earrings and cream-colored heels with matching hose. As I slipped into my shoes, I was thinking ahead, wild with excitement. Just for fun, maybe we could honeymoon on an island in the South Pacific. I laughed secretly at the prospect of our actually living my dream.

That night, I arrived at the Fountain Blue ten minutes late, expecting Richard to already be there. He was the most punctual man I had ever known and was usually already waiting for me whenever I was to meet him. But when I asked, the maître d informed me that Richard had not arrived.

Had not arrived... Richard?

I immediately experienced a queasy feeling. Something was amiss. But I was so excited about my imminent proposal to Richard that I momentarily wrote off the ill omen of his absence. He's worth the wait, I told myself.

Thirty minutes later, he still hadn't arrived.

By now, my heart was pounding, my palms sweaty, and I was experiencing the first warning signs of a headache. To make matters worse, the little voice inside my head was working overtime: "Richard is tired of your constant refusals to marry him!" it screamed shrilly. "You've missed your chance and you'll never get another one! This wonderful man who could have given you so much happiness has walked, no... run, out of your life, just when you were going to tell him you wanted to marry him!"

"Hush!" I said under my breath, but the voice wouldn't stop: "Silly you! Now you're going to spend the rest of your life alone!"

I sat at a booth in the bar, alone, panic stricken, sipping a glass of Chablis, thinking how much I had been looking forward to the peace I always found in Richard's loving cup. I had been so eager to start calling people later that evening, telling them the earthshaking news that Richard and I were going to be married again and forever! I had even planned ahead, selecting flower arrangements and wall decorations in mauves, blues, and warm creamy whites. I had sculpted a truly fairy tale wedding... no plastic, gaudy pink satin, and taped music this time. Miserable, my elegant suit now wrinkled, I waited another hour before placing a call to Marian.

"Richard stood me up!" I cried into the receiver, "He's dumped me... right after a magnificent weekend together in Wisconsin!"

"What? Surely there's another explanation," Marian offered. "Maybe he had a flat tire or an accident or...?"

"No, no! He would have called by now! I know Richard and he would have called, believe me. No, he probably gave up because I put him off for so long. I mean... no one can be patient forever..."

"Stay right there!" Marian said. "I'll meet you as soon as I can get dressed!"

When I hung up the phone, I felt like life had totally abandoned me. Marian showed up a short time later and we dined together, with me salting my food with tears through most of the meal.

Marian patted my hand finally and said, "Annette, I'm so sorry he's done this to you." She paused and looked me squarely in my eyes. "I have kept silent about my true feelings as to Richard Bailey, but now I see you on an emotional roller coaster with this guy. Maybe this is a chance to get off."

"But I didn't want to get off… I wanted to stay." I moaned.

Marian ignored my despair and patted my hand again, saying, "Richard Bailey is like the tides… he rolled in all bubbly and frothy then withdrew, leaving you only the cold and chill of an empty beach. I'm telling you this is the perfect opportunity to be rid of him. So, do it…"

"But I love him!" I said defiantly and with a lot more fervor than I had expected.

"Maybe… but is any man on the planet worth what you are going through? Forget the past few months. Look at you now, this minute. You can't keep on like this. Think of your children."

That arrow through the heart ended the conversation and the evening. When I left Marian, I hurried home, thinking Richard might have called, leaving some explanation or other with my houseman Trevor, but there was no call from Richard that terrible night and no answer at his brother's. Around five in the morning, I finally fell asleep, a destroyed human being.

Chapter 13

The next morning was Wednesday, the 27th of July. After getting dressed, I followed the ritual I went through every morning: put water on for tea, made toast, walked outside, and picked up my copy of the *Chicago Tribune*. I was late that morning and walked quickly back to my kitchen. Without looking at the paper, I put my breakfast next to the *Tribune* on a tray and went to my bedroom. My routine was to relax for ten minutes before going to work.

I flipped on the classical radio station and sat on the side of my bed, nibbling toast, and sipping tea from the tray. After my disastrous evening at the Fountain Blue, I was really looking forward to one small pleasure I could control: reading the comics. I always read them first, a holdover from my childhood.

There was no way I could have been prepared for what happened next. When I opened the paper, in big black letters, the headlines announced: BRACH SUITOR HELD, CHARGED IN SLAYING. My heart fell into my shoes.

Without having read another word, I knew it was Richard.

Included with the article was a small closeup photo of an elderly Helen Brach. She was wearing a white sweater and sporting a platinum blonde wig with bangs. Her eyes were blurred, strange looking. I stared at the picture for only a fraction of a second before my eyes flew down to the leadline:

Horse swindle may have role in her killing.

Horse swindle!

It took a moment to get around the feelings of revulsion I experienced in reading those (all too familiar) words, "Horse swindle," and then I studied the article carefully:

"Suave and persistent, Richard R. Bailey wooed Helen Vorhees Brach over dinner, on dance floors and across the country."

That much of the article certainly rang true, and I began to feel as though my heart would burst from its incessant hammering. I quickly read on, looking for (but dreading to find) the explicit details of how Richard had killed this well known, Chicago socialite, never forgetting for one single moment that I, too, was a well-known, Chicago socialite.

"When at first she refused his overtures, he followed her to Florida. After she fell for him, he traveled with her to New York to ring in the New Year while bandleader Guy Lombardo played.

Brach thought she was being romanced. Law-enforcement authorities say she was being conned, something the millionaire candy heiress apparently began to suspect as she accumulated a motley collection of broodmares and several racehorses through Bailey at inflated prices. But before she could go to police, Bailey arranged for her murder, law enforcement officials say. Her body has never been found."

How will I spend a day in the office after reading all those innuendoes, I asked myself before continuing.

The article was lengthy, extending to several pages. I forced myself to read on, but as hard as I looked for the damning words explaining how Richard had carried out this heinous crime, I found none. The article was obviously leaked, filled with broad statements like "Bailey has been indicted, law enforcement sources said." There was not one single detail about how Richard was supposed to have killed the poor woman; in fact, the article was a condemnation of his horse dealing days, something I was already well aware of from my own investigations. And who were these law enforcement officials, anyway?

Suddenly it hit me.

The *Tribune* article was a classic "trial by press," starting out with a huge headline which no one would ever forget and followed by a lot of information that had nothing to do with the allegation that Richard R. Bailey had murdered Helen Brach.

Where were the facts?

Richard did this and this and this and this to kill the heiress of the Brach fortune. There was nothing there.

Surprisingly, more than a few paragraphs were devoted to the crimes of other people: apparently nineteen stable owners, trainers and veterinarians had allegedly killed twenty prized horses in insurance fraud schemes. Richard was not named in any of those cases.

The farther I read into the article, the more I saw the paraphrasing and timetables set out in *Thin Air*, and I wondered how much of that was the work of research by the reporters who only read the book and how much was fed to them by the prosecution. Certainly, many phrases out of *Thin Air* appeared in the article and later on, a mention of the book itself.

My initial assessment had been correct: the article didn't prove to be nearly as incriminating or upsetting as the headline. Just part of the newspaper trade, I suspected.

When I put the paper down, I knew I was still functioning, but deep down inside, I felt totally numb, my mind paralyzed. There were going to be serious consequences for me and my family because of this new development. I had to decide then and there what position I would take.

I flipped off the radio and quickly sorted through my thoughts. Was Richard R. Bailey (the man I loved) a murderer?

No.

Was he a shady character, a swashbuckler metamorphosized from a swindler?

Yes.

What should I do? Become a Tammy Wynette clone and "Stand by my Man," or cut and run, gathering my family and my professional associations up under a cloak of anonymity? I could not have it both ways. If I went to Richard's aid, the whole community would rain on me, and the deluge of bad press would drown my business, possibly harm my relationships with my family, and certainly turn me and my romance with Richard into a media circus. I had visions of walking down Michigan Avenue besieged by paparazzi like the Beatles once were, trying to shield my younger daughter from an overzealous photographer. I couldn't bear the thought... I cherished my privacy and that of my children.

I wanted to run away from the mud-slinging mess, fly to Rome or Athens or someplace in Africa, but that was a fool's dream and reality was literally staring me in the face. I had to make another important decision, but how many of these decisions must one woman make in a matter of a few months?

Exhausted beyond belief, I bowed my head, clasped my hands and prayed. All of a sudden, in one of those stunningly clear moments when messages from the unknown come to you, I heard myself saying over and over that Richard was no killer, and that I was in love with him.

So what if I wasn't the toughest lady on the block? I asked myself. I was committed. and I would just have to learn how to be tough enough to handle all of the that would soon thunder down on me from the clouds of suspicion gathering over Richard.

That morning I never finished my breakfast. On an impulse, I walked over to the window facing the street and opened the blinds. Although there was no one outside, it was easy to imagine the sidewalk filled with reporters waiting to tear into a wounded and vulnerable target.

Me!

No, I cautioned myself, don't panic. Who would put the reporters on you? At that second a word reverberated in my brain... Pick! Pick would send them over here... And if they're not here now, they're coming! The sharks are going to pick me to pieces! I realize for the first time the irony of Pick's last name. This is no accident, I thought.

The minions of evil are marshalling their forces. The press and the public are about to criticize me for becoming involved with Richard Bailey.

The blood was in the water now, and I was soon to discover I was Richard's only lifeboat. I noticed one other thing.

It was raining.

Bucketsful.

The showers were over, and the deluge had obviously begun.

Chapter 14

The rain and pain of Wednesday continued into Thursday, July 28, 1994. The angst I was experiencing was greatly exacerbated by the fact that I had not heard from Richard, but I assumed he would phone me whenever the jailers allowed him to make a call, probably that evening. "Call me immediately if you hear from Richard!" I told Trevor and (somehow!) managed to drag my broken spirit off to the office.

The peace I normally found in my medical practice was absent that day as the media continued to bathe Richard in the worst possible light. Time and again they hit him with pejorative language. From the tenor of the headlines and the newsbreak flashes on local television, I quickly realized what the prosecution's game plan was going to be.

Public trial! Sans judge, sans jury, sans rules but most importantly, sans justice. Like Robespierre's citizen courts of the French Revolution where trials were public spectacles, Richard's trip from bastille to guillotine would be pre-ordained by the press and the press of molded public opinion.

The newspapers had hooked Richard up with over two dozen, horse trader/swindlers ranging from doctors, lawyers, and Olympic Equestrian Team members to stable lowlifes. Mixed in with the social hodgepodge of defendants were innuendoes which insinuated that Richard was involved in Helen Brach's murder. Guilt by association, a trial tactic valid from Robespierre to Rasputin to Macbeth to McCarthy.

On top of that, I could see where the love that Richard and I found and lost and found again was going to be reduced to fodder, gossip fodder, served up in a quasi-acceptable way which allowed normally staid reporters and commentators to dabble in the most lurid sorts of yellow journalism.

My fellow Chicagoans were buying newspapers like they bought gin in Prohibition. Why wouldn't they? The Richard Bailey Story was an instant sensation with something to interest everyone: murder, sex, money, drugs, betrayal, horses, fraud, and swindlers galore. Prominent equestrians and very wealthy people who traded horses professionally were hiring lawyers as quickly as they could dial their numbers. Everyone who owned a horse was suddenly at risk.

Richard's arrest, I was soon to discover, was a major media event all over the country, indeed the world. My very able surgical assistant was a native Brazilian named Nathan Mendez. His relatives were phoning him from Rio, asking for information to supplement the daily offerings in their local newspapers. I even read an article in German which had been sent to me by a friend in Switzerland. Richard's story also turned up in Pretoria. My brother, Anton lives, who still lives in South Africa, happened to read about the case in *Time* magazine and was extremely concerned about my situation. I asked if he would send me a copy of the article, but he said he was so hurt that I was involved with a man like Richard that he disposed of it. His behavior was a foreshadowing, I realized, of what I was going to endure with both colleagues and acquaintances.

The blitz that hit me when Richard was arrested has continued on through the writing of this book, making such diverse media stops as *America's Most Wanted*, *Hard Copy*, *Vanity Fair*, *G. Q.*, *Chicago*, *Time*, *Newsweek*, *People*, and all the local Chicago T. V. talk shows. Oddly enough, it was finally a woman who put it all in perspective on *Dateline*. Unfortunately, her provocative program which questioned whether or not the government had arrested the right man aired too late to give Richard any help.

Unlike other people, I bought the papers and magazines because I cared for Richard and found the reality of his situation terrifying. Like Cassandra who could only foretell the saddest future, I could see what was in store for him every time I walked up to a newsstand... and what I saw I didn't like: Richard would be tried in the press and on T. V. before he ever entered a courtroom.

I had been right.

All at once and with a single voice, the media had become the mouthpiece for Steven Miller Lt. David Hamm of the Illinois State Police. Both men were screaming for Richard's head. I knew the media had become the tool of the prosecution by comparing the truth of my own experiences with Richard to how the press had warped those same experiences to fit the prosecution's tone. So, be it, I thought. Eventually, the truth will come out and someone will have a lot of crow to eat... either the media or me.

Later that day when flipping through the headlines and searching for evidence to support my "Media-as-a-Tool-of-the-Government" theory, I stumbled upon a few very smooth examples:

"U. S. CHARGES BRACH VICTIM OF A SLICK CON" shouted the *Chicago Tribune* on July 28, 1994. Once again, when I looked for details as to how Richard had murdered Helen Brach, they were non-existent. I could only find a statement that "the charges against Bailey were the centerpiece of a series of wide ranging federal indictments that name(d) twenty-three people in the equestrian industry."

"FRAUD SCHEME LINKED TO BRACHS MURDER" answered the *Sun Times* on the same day. I frantically searched the article, looking for this "link," but just as I had suspected, the paper did not choose to demonstrate this nexus except for mentioning a connection between Richard, the Brach mystery and the killing of horses for the insurance money.

Also, on July 28, The *Daily Herald* bit into Richard with, **"THE HELEN BRACH CASE, BAILEY CHARMING TO HIS PREY."**

Prey!

Every time I had seen a woman look at Richard Bailey, I had watched a hungry person checking out a menu item... and Richard was the Blue-Plate Special! Prey, indeed!

Having been born in South Africa, and thereby growing up with a government-controlled press, I had never really bought into the American belief that there was freedom of the press here, and that the press was, therefore, completely free from the manipulations of the government. I was a cynic, I suppose, in that I believed very little of what I read in the papers or saw on television because I knew the truth: the media could easily be made to jump through hoops. How?

Simple.

If the President of the United States held a press conference and certain reporters were not invited or found themselves at the back of the room, it would be assumed in the trade that they had angered someone in the office of the Press Secretary by writing an offensive article or story. It was the same with mayors, governors and yes, even prosecuting attorneys. So, there was a direct degree of control which was exercised in the selection of favored reporters for first release on the big stories.

There was yet another even more insidious means of manipulating reporters and writers who were always in need of information.

"The leak."

Some special persons, usually key newspaper and television reporters, had "sources inside the offices" of most prosecutors. If the prosecution, therefore, warded to poison the public's mind (and thereby future jury pools), all it had to do was to leak damaging information that might not even be admissible at a trial. In so doing, the prosecution could effectively try the case in the newspapers, on television or on the radio. Although this practice was not common knowledge, leaks happened on an almost daily basis. Certainly, this tactic was used in the O. J. Simpson trial, only there it backfired on the prosecution. Still, at the time of Richard's arrest, press leaks were a working tool for the prosecutors.

Tokyo Rose.

The American press.

I decided to call this private propaganda and pejorative, prevaricate press under the single nom de guerre of Tokyo Rose.

Why?

Because much of what the press was putting out was truly propaganda (though I could not prove it); they always added just enough truth in the mix to make the stories about Richard seem believable. The indictment of Richard Bailey was a media feeding frenzy with no one pausing to find out the facts, but, of course, I could not prove my beliefs at the time. By using Tokyo Rose as a descriptive vehicle, found it somehow reassuring to make the press into a joke rather than take their outpourings seriously. So, borrowing from the Seabees, I began to work the fiction of Tokyo Rose out of my daily life.

It helped my self-esteem because I knew that of all the people now involved in the relationship that Richard and I were forced to share with the world that I was the only one who was telling the truth.

So help me God.

And He did.

But it took a while.

Oh, how I wanted to put the media out of my mind, but it was always there hovering over my head like some kind of gigantic microphone. I couldn't help but feel that way. I knew my history, knew what I had lived with as a child in South Africa.

That afternoon, I was very much surprised when two agents of the United States Government showed up at my office, insisting they speak with me. They wanted to know if Richard asked for financial assistance with respect to either his bail or his attorney's fees, I was both shocked and confused by the agents' bizarre request. Did they think I was a witness for the prosecution?

I asked if they had a problem with my visiting Richard at the Metropolitan Correctional Center where he was being held, and they said no, but that if anything unusual happened when the two of us were together, they would appreciate a phone call describing what had taken place. Why were two government agents sitting in my private office, asking me to be a snitch? I was terribly disappointed in my government that day.

Before the agents left, they mentioned they knew of Nancy Lewis' investigative report and requested a copy. I promptly ran one off and then they left.

Late that evening, a call finally came through from Richard, collect, from the M. C. C. in Chicago. I accepted the charges. This time, there was no "Hey, hey, my beautiful doll," but a simple "hello" followed by my name and I was astonished to hear myself loudly speaking into the receiver, "Why didn't you tell me you were going to be arrested? And why did you wait so long to contact me? Do you have any idea what I've been going through?"

"Please, please understand," Richard said, his normally calm voice filled with anxiety, "I had no idea I was going to be arrested… none."

"Surely…"

"No, no idea. And then the papers crucified me… I didn't think you would ever want to see me again. A suspect in a murder case! Can you understand?"

I didn't understand, didn't understand anything that had happened really since I first met Richard that afternoon at The Waterfront. But I kept my silence. Things were upsetting enough as it was. "You must have known how devastated I would be at the Fountain Blue when you didn't show up," I said, sobbing.

"Of course, my beautiful doll, and I feel terrible about that day."

Before the agents left, they mentioned they knew of Nancy Lewis' investigative report and requested a copy. I promptly ran one off and then they left.

Late that evening, a call finally came through from Richard, collect, from the M. C. C. in Chicago. I accepted the charges. This time, there was no "Hey, hey my beautiful doll," but a simple "hello" followed, by my name, and I was astonished to hear myself loudly speaking into the receiver, "Why didn't you tell me you were going to be arrested? And why did you wait so long to contact me? Do you have any idea what I've been going through?"

"Please, please understand," Richard said, his normally calm voice filled with anxiety, "I had no idea I was going to be arrested… none."

"Surely…"

"No, no idea. And then the papers crucified me… I didn't think you would ever want to see me again. A suspect in a murder case! Can you understand?"

I didn't understand, didn't understand anything that had happened really since I first met Richard that afternoon at the Waterfront. But I kept my silence. Things were upsetting enough as it was. "You must have known how devastated I would be at the Fountain Blue when you didn't show up," I said, sobbing.

"Of course, my beautiful doll, and I feel terrible about that, but I couldn't call you. They arrested me!" There was a brief silence and then he went on, "Now I need to tell you that I have done nothing wrong here... I have told you the truth, told the F. B. I. the truth, and I will tell you truly once again that I will always love you with all my heart."

"What about our future?" I blurted out. "Are we going to even have one?"

"This is all going to work out... believe me. I'm telling you I... AM... IN-NOCENT! What we're going through now is the very worst part... things can only get better from now on. I'm going to fight this... I know a first-rate lawyer and he'll be with me tomorrow for my bond hearing."

"A good lawyer... who?" Finally, a ray of hope.

"His name is Pat Tuite!" Richard said confidently, "He's a good lawyer, been around forever."

I had lived in Chicago for many years, but I had never heard of this man! If he were good, really good, I felt I would at least have heard something. Most of the people I knew hired lawyers as a living expense like household utilities. Patrick Tuite? Nothing came to mind. But Richard and I were dealing with a catastrophe and at that point, I didn't want to increase his anxiety level by whining and complaining about my immediate concerns regarding his lawyer.

Toward the end of our conversation, Richard asked me an important question, "If Tuite thinks it necessary, could I possibly stay at your home... only if my release from jail depends on it?"

Without any hesitation, I told Richard yes. We managed some small talk, and then a cold insistent tone notified us that time for the call was running out. It was very difficult to hang up and know that I couldn't call him back. Worse, that I would never be able to call him again as long as he was in the M. C. C. Also, that he would only be allowed to phone me when the jail's rules permitted, and then only fifteen minutes at a time. I was so used to being able to either talk or be with Richard whenever I wanted. What a luxury that had been and I never knew.

I felt I had walked from the pearly gates of Paradise into the fiery depths of hell. Recorded hell at that because our privacy was forfeited, as well. All calls were tape recorded by the Bureau of Prisons, and probably, I thought, whisked over to the prosecution… a chilling thought.

Ten minutes after I spoke with Richard, the phone rang again. "You don't know me," the rich baritone voice on the other end announced, "but my name is Pat Tuite, and I'm representing Richard Bailey in his defense."

"Yes, Richard just told me," I said.

"You know who I am…good! I guess Richard also told you we're in need of your help in the bond hearing tomorrow…" He hesitated for a moment, then went on, "You're okay with my telling the judge that Richard can stay in your home?"

"Yes, that's right."

Tuite paused for a minute as if he were thinking up the correct response, then said, "I can't imagine the judge denying Richard bond if you give him a place to stay."

I wanted to talk more, but Tuite said that he had business to take care of and wasn't free to talk. After I hung up, I was at once very upset and yet relieved.

Yes, Richard had been arrested but… We were going to fight back!

Pat Tuite, Esq. would help! And most important…

Richard was innocent!

On that subject, my heart and my brain wholeheartedly agreed. There was never any doubt.

That night, I repeated the word innocent, over and over like other people counted sheep as I tried to fall asleep. It didn't work for the longest time, but finally, close to dawn, I fell into a deep but fitful sleep.

Chapter 15

I was impatient and concerned!
It was late Friday afternoon. I had seen my last patient and was pacing back and forth in my private office, waiting for the phone to ring. Richard was supposed to have called right after the hearing and nearly three hours had passed since the courts closed and still no word. No word from Pat Tuite either and I began to fear the worst.

There was only one way I could find out what had happened to Richard. I called Nancy Lewis and asked her to ring up the jail, speak to someone in charge and inquire as to why Richard was not calling. She rang me back in fifteen minutes and said that Richard was throwing up frequently and had been put on a suicide watch. The news alarmed me, but I also knew there was nothing I could do about Richard's state of mind, and it was not within my power to make his warders care. I decided to keep Nancy's call to the M. C. C. a secret from Richard. Why depress him by letting him know the jail provided Nancy with sensitive information he himself would never have told me.

But why exactly was Richard so upset? His arrest or the bond hearing? Maybe both? I had no answers. I would simply have to wait for his call.

Finally, when I had almost given up, the phone rang, and it was Richard! I knew from the tone of his voice, bad news. Richard was almost always cheerful; he had this incredible sense of impending good fortune that was almost like a second skin. But that afternoon something was different. His voice was slow and measured, absent any sort of the buoyancy and staccato pace that normally characterized his phone calls.

"Bad, huh?" I said.

"Well, we didn't get a bond, that's for sure."

"But what happened? Pat Tuite thought that with my offering to provide a residence, it would be a shoo-in with the magistrate!"

"A shoo-in? Actually, it was a shoot *out*, and our guy didn't remember to bring his guns," Richard said and was silent.

"You mean Tuite wasn't prepared?" I recalled the lawyer's hesitant voice on the phone last night and shuddered.

"Well, Pat told me it was all strategic," Richard said without much conviction. Strategic… that means long range." My heart sank.

"Well, maybe Tuite's right," I said. "Tell me what happened."

"You sure you want to hear this, doll?" Richard's voice was faltering.

"Yes, please… and don't spare the details."

"Well, the magistrate was a guy named Guzman, Ronald Guzman. He never seemed to look at me, kept his head down and ran the courtroom by hand signals. The government attorney, this guy Safer, went first and began laying out the reasons why I should not get bond. I'll tell you one thing… he's a tough S. O. B. and was he ever organized!"

I did not like the sound of this already but encouraged Richard to continue. "Yes… the prosecution is supposed to be tough."

"Yeah, but they're supposed to be fair, too. Listen to what this guy said." He paused as if to organize his thoughts, then continued, "He told the magistrate that I didn't have any roots in the community, so I was a flight risk. He said I was moving from place to place and didn't have a home to stay in."

My heart began to race. I knew that I had said something similar to the government agents who had come by my office.

Richard interrupted my thoughts. "Safer said I had sold my home in Lincolnwood and was basically living on the street. You know that's not true, doll. I was getting ready to move to San Diego before I met you and was staying with my brother most of the time. Then you turned up and that was all she wrote." He chuckled, then added, "And I wouldn't have it any other way."

Richard took a deep breath I could clearly hear over the phone and said, "Then this Safer lied about you!"

"Me?"

"After Tuite said you'd let me stay in your home if I made bond, Safer jumped in and said you needed to be sworn in then because you'd made 'contrary statements' about my being with you." Richard laughed. "I remember his exact words because they were about you, baby, but what it added up to was that you'd obviously lied."

"I bet Tuite set him straight on that one," I said hopefully.

"Tuite only went on and on about how you'd said on T. V. last night that I could move in with you." I could hear a hint of repressed anger in Richard's voice, but did not interrupt to add my rage to the mix.

"Tuite said held heard I had said that on T. V. I bet the judge laughed in his face."

"Yeah," Guzman said, "you don't want me to believe everything I've heard in the media, do you?" After the judge's comeback, I had to laugh, and I could hear people cracking up all around me.

"Richard," I said, unable to contain myself, "this all sounds pretty dumb to me."

"It gets worse. Safer made it sound like I resisted arrest because I didn't come to the door right away the night I got arrested. The truth is I was in my shorts, getting ready to take a shower because it was so hot… then the cops showed up and started screaming at the tops of their voices and banging on the door. Because all I was wearing were my skivvies and because of all the noise, I froze for a moment and didn't answer the first time they pounded on the door. I certainly wasn't trying to resist arrest."

"You mean Tuite knew all this and he still let them get by with it?" I could not believe this!

"There's more. Safer then implied that I was planning an escape to Georgia."

"Where on earth did he get that idea?" Richard had told me days ago that he had a business appointment in Georgia. I saw Alice in Wonderland asking questions of the Opium Smoker.

"Well, I was joking with the cops, and I said, 'I should have gone to Georgia'… meaning I should have kept the appointment I had down there the following day. Safer just took that statement and twisted it."

I was appalled. "Did you tell Tuite what that was all about?"

"Yes." His voice was small and before he added his next words, I knew that Tuite had not protested over that misrepresentation either.

"Another strategic move, right?" I could not keep the sarcasm out of my voice.

"Well, Pat said all the moves this morning were strategic, that he wanted to let the prosecution lie and mislead the magistrate, then he could pounce on them later. But there's more… this Safer also implied I was trying to hide my wealth because when the cops asked A what kind of car I drove, I told them an old Toyota—"

I cut him off. "Why did you say that?"

"Well, the IRS was after me, and I thought they might want to confiscate the Mercedes, so I just didn't tell them about that one." He sighed, "But when Safer told the story, it sounded like I was trying to hide money and all of it was somehow related to the Brach case."

"How could your Mercedes possibly have anything to do with the Helen Brach case? She disappeared twenty years ago! Okay. What else?" I didn't want to hear it all, of course, because I had already figured out that Tuite simply went in there unprepared, his mind as tentative as our brief conversation the night before.

"Well, and believe me baby, I don't know where they got this one… Safer told the Judge that I had a lot of people who were afraid of me… and that they were going to be witnesses and would be in fear of their lives if I was released."

"Richard, that's crazy. You're sixty-five years old. You've never been arrested for a violent crime, much less convicted of one. What proof did Safer offer?"

"None that I could tell… just allegations."

"Are you telling me that Pat Tuite sat through all of this, had the information to challenge it at his disposal and did not bring it forth?"

"That's about the picture. Oh, he brought up a few things in my defense, but nothing damaging like Safer did all the time. But Pat kept saying that down the road he would get them for the misrepresentations…"

I could not help myself. I cut him off again. "Richard, we need an attorney who fights, and we need him now. I do not want to 'get' anybody… I want you out of jail and home with me. Now then… Who do you think we should retain?"

"Hey, baby, settle down. Let's give Pat a chance to straighten all this out. He's going to talk with you soon and get ready for the next hearing."

"You mean there's going to be another bond hearing?" My spirits rose. Now we could set the record straight!

"Sure! It's on Monday. Safer wanted you to be placed under oath and asked about my staying at your house. Let's not change horses in the middle of the stream, baby."

"Richard, I just heard there's a flash flood watch on this stream we're in with Tuite. A deluge is coming… we need fresh horses and fast…"

"Now stay cool. Pat has the best of credentials. He's highly recommended by my closest friend. I would trust him with my life."

Richard told me the name of the man who had given him Tuite's name, but it immediately escaped me. My mind was still back in the middle of the stream with a flood of lies coming and our wagon stuck with an old nag.

Richard cleared his throat and said, "Things will work out… you'll see. Let's give Tuite a chance and see what he can do with some warning."

"I will do as you ask, Richard, but my heart is not in the fight with this man." Richard then affirmed my fears by reeling off a half dozen more instances where Tuite let the prosecution load the record against him.

Then Richard dropped a bomb, albeit a small one, but a bomb, nevertheless. He said he needed to sell his red Mercedes as quickly as possible because Tuite was insisting on $20, 000 cash ASAP to handle the bond hearing. I was flabbergasted! I never dreamed one hearing could cost that much money, but realized at the same time, then even saviors needed to be paid. Richard gave me the phone number of his brother Bill and his wife, so I called them right away, and they volunteered to help sell the car.

They were both very supportive of Richard and when I hung up, I suddenly realized we now numbered four against the establishment instead of two (as far as I was concerned, Tuite didn't count).

But at the very least, I wasn't totally alone.

On that same morning, Friday, July 29, despite the fact that I had announced I would probably remarry Richard, the *Sun Times* proclaimed:"**TWO WIVES WEREN'T SWAYED BY BAILEY.**" The article implied that Richard had conned me, and I had found him out, then dumped him. Nothing could have been further from the truth. I wanted this man in my life for the rest of my life.

Again, where were the details? There was nothing concrete in the article because Richard had never tried to steal anything from me as long as I had known him. Neither had he tried to sell me a horse or even asked for money. In fact, the opposite was true. Except for the hotel bill in Vegas, Richard always picked up the tabs.

Also, that Friday, the *Tribune* lashed out with **"UNBRIDLED ANGER"** (Who on earth writes that pun-laden stuff?) and**"HORSE LOVERS REACT TO BRACH CASE."** Underneath those inflammatory words was a recent photo of Richard. The article described a lady feeding carrots to her horse„ wondering what had happened to Helen Brach. Once again, there were no facts, just Richard's smiling face as if to say, "Here's the murderer, world!"

The rest of the article focused on the other twenty-three people in Richard's indictment who had nothing to do with either Richard or the candy heiress, only people who had killed horses in insurance frauds. The *Tribune* quoted a stable owner as saying, "For somebody just to blindly kill an innocent horse is revolting." As I studied Richard's picture, the implication was obvious. Richard had a new label, "Horse Murderer," even though he was never involved in any of those scams.

Ah, yes… Tokyo Rose was hard at work again.

Chapter 16

On the morning of July 30, I discovered the local newspapers had stepped up their interest in me. In the *Chicago Sun-Times*, my decision to stand by Richard was announced and in doing so, the headlines made Richard seem like an orphaned child, saying, **"BRACH DEFENDANT IS OFFERED A HOME."** The paper also quoted something I told their reporter during a phone interview after the first hearing, "If he (Richard) had friends and family, they should take him in first, but I don't feel I can abandon him."

The article went on to say that, "Bailey and an unidentified co-schemer Al were charged in indictments released Wednesday with conspiring, soliciting, and causing the death of Brach…" This statement was followed by "Federal officials allege she was killed when she vowed to alert authorities to the (horse swindling) scheme."

Give me some facts, Tokyo Rose, I thought, give me some facts! Times, dates, names, places! And who, pray tell, was the mysterious co-schemer A? The press version of the case had begun to sound more and more like a plot from a Harold Robbins novel.

The phone rang quite early that morning. To my surprise, it was Pat Tuite again, wanting to see me right away. I threw on some clothes, rounded up a driver and a short time later, found myself in the attorney's office. I must admit to being shocked. His place of business was one of the messiest offices I had ever walked into, papers and legal documents strewn everywhere in uneven, skewed piles, like Grecian pillars after an earthquake. I surely hope this man manages his trials better than he manages his workplace, I thought. I remembered an often repeated saying of one of my ballet teachers, "You will perform exactly like you practice."

"God," I prayed, "please let Tuite be the exception to that rule." With that thought in mind, I began to search for signs of Tuite's competence.

But the truth was depressing. I saw immediately that there was nothing special about this man except that he was physically attractive. He was big-boned and fleshy, around fifty-eight to sixty with brown hair and eyes. For a well-known attorney, he presented an odd, disheveled appearance. His pants wore too short, his white socks clearly showing. Tuite's tonsorial ensemble went out in the thirties! I hoped his legal skills were not likewise hopelessly out of fashion.

On the plus side, he seemed fairly intelligent, had a good vocabulary and was very persuasive…but I imagined that each criminal Bowyer has their own modus operandi and hoped that his soft approach was successful in the end.

The first thing Tuite did was ask me some basic questions about Richard—where had we met, when were we married, just really ordinary things, and then, unable to wait any longer, I asked firmly, "What exactly is going to happen with Richard?"

"Well," Tuite said, leaning forward and staring into my eyes, "first we have to get him out of jail, and then we'll worry about winning his case."

"What are his chances?"

"I'm not worried about Brach," Tuite said with more confidence than I would have expected. He made a cage out of his fingers and tapped his fingertips. "It's Richard's scams on women that will probably earn him a conviction."

"A conviction! For what? How long?" My heart was racing, racing, racing.

"Well, you have to understand," Tuite said, his eyebrows raised, "the length of his sentence will depend on how many dollars changed hands. It's all determined by the new sentencing Guidelines." He nodded, seemingly pleased with his knowledge of the law, then went on, "Richard will get thirty-seven to forty-six months max, plus time off for good behavior. There's a good chance you'll have him home by Christmas."

Tuite tore off a sheet from a yellow legal pad, scribbled down some numbers, and handed it to me.

"Unh-hunh," I said mechanically, staring at the figures and thinking ahead. Two and a half years at the worst, I thought, maybe just a year at best. If faced with the maximum sentence, I could certainly wait.

Tuite cleared his throat to get my attention and smiled, his eyes drifting from my face to my breasts. I felt suddenly uneasy. I had seen that appraising look before. What was he doing? We were both professional people and I wanted him to act accordingly. I frowned and he looked back to my face.

"What I need for you to do is simple," Tuite said. "Show up in court on Monday, be sworn in and then testify that Richard can stay in your home if the Judge deems it necessary that Richard have a non-transitory residence before he bonds him out. you see, Richard will need a place of residence. He has nowhere else to stay."

I nodded my agreement, then sat there waiting for Tuite to coach me about my testimony. Having appeared as an expert witness many times before, I knew full well the importance of preparation. But unlike any other lawyer I had ever met, Tuite did not discuss what likely questions the prosecution would ask or even what I would query me about. Most lawyers, I knew, prepared a witness for direct and cross examination, and indicated certain attitudes to display when speaking to the judge or jury. Then the testimony was stronger, more forceful, more valid.

All Tuite told me was when and where to show up. I was very nonplussed by his lack of professionalism that he did not brief me rewarded but managed to calm down by telling myself that probably the questions would be so simple that anyone could answer them truthfully. Still, I was distrustful.

Suspicious? Yes, I admitted to myself, I was very suspicious, both about Tuite's handling of the case.

Finally, and with a great deal of determination (and perhaps faulty logic), I managed to dismiss my fears...at least for the moment. The process of deluding myself was simple. I was no lawyer. Why should I second-guess a man so early in the game?

At the end of our first meeting, I convinced myself Tuite was telling the truth as he saw it and had a good handle about the law and everything having to do with Richard's complex case.

Nevertheless, I kept remembering that Tuite's first remarks were about a prison sentence. Not a word about an acquittal or even a trial. Although our meeting had been brief, I was glad when it was time to go.

On the way home, I once again began to feel uneasy about Richard's choice of attorneys. All the good feelings I had mustered about Tuite flew out the window. I decided to make a few inquiries later in the day, see what I could turn up about this man who literally held Richard's life in his hands.

Back home, I ate a quick lunch, then settled down with a telephone. I had a good friend at the time who was a corporate lawyer; I called him first. We talked about the case in general terms and then I mentioned Richard's attorney. My friend was amazed. "Richard hired Pat Tuite! I wouldn't have hired him. More of his clients are in jail than out!"

I was horrified by this information but decided to place a few more calls. Perhaps another lawyer would give me some positive feedback.

I next called a female attorney I'd known for many years. We also discussed Richard's predicament, then I mentioned Tuite. "Well, I'm not in his field of work," she said guardedly. "Criminal law is a different sort of creature. Pat Tuite? I haven't heard anything really bad about him... just that he's the only attorney I know of who demands his clients pay in huge bites instead of a large retainer."

Huge bites!

I was appalled.

Measuring a man like that.

The third lawyer I called was equally depressing. "Tuite was really hot in his younger days," he said, "but he hasn't won many cases lately." He paused for a minute, and I knew he was trying to recall something, so I remained silent. "You know," he said finally, "so far as I know, Tuite has never won a single federal case… And Richard's case is federal." Of course, it is, I wanted to scream. Instead, I said nothing, was polite and rang off.

The fourth lawyer I phoned didn't want to say anything negative about a colleague at first, but I finally managed to get a strongly worded profile, "If I needed a criminal lawyer, I definitely wouldn't use Pat Tuite," he said in his calm, measured way. "The book on Pat Tuite says he's often ill prepared, but good on cross examination. The word is he relies on that crossing skill too much, makes his defenses lopsided and often fatal."

Fatal.

The word sounded in my brain like a death knell.

After I hung up, I felt I had walked into a black hole. I did have one more friend who knew a great deal about the law; he was only a paralegal, but more knowledgeable than most practicing attorneys. Dennis was always honest when it came to sharing his opinions, and I didn't expect him to be any different today. I picked up the phone and dialed his number.

"Dennis… Annette."

"Thought you might call. Well, if you want my opinion about Richard's retained counsel, I have to tell you Tuite's out of his league going up against Miller and Safer. Then, too, you have to realize that very few attorneys win in the federal court unless they've been federal prosecutors… and so far as I know, Tuite never was."

"You're certain?"

"That's what I heard. I also have to tell you that the word on the street is that Bailey's a fall guy. The Feds are really after Frank Jayne, Jr. , the Chicago version of a desperado from a Wild West show. They're hoping Richard will cut a deal, become a rat and give them Jayne."

"How can he do that? He says he doesn't know anything!"

"Knowing the Feds, they don't believe him…"

"Don't you think if Richard knew something, anything, he would give it up so we could be together? I mean… we have the perfect relationship going here and Richard's sixty-five… we don't have that many years left…"

"I can't answer for Richard, but I can say that everyone has a secret in this case. Give it some time, Annette, let's see how it plays out. But remember, the Feds don't play fair. They rewrite the rules as needed."

"Just what I wanted to hear."

"Oh, and one more thing…The cons tell me there's a Tuite Wing at the M. C. C. ;just thought you might want to know."

When I hung up, I thought I was going to be sick. My knuckles were actually white from holding the receiver so tightly.

The next time Richard called, I told him everything I had learned, hoping to change his mind about Tuite, but he was adamant. He knew Pat Tuite, he wanted Pat Tuite and that was final. No matter how hard I tried, I couldn't persuade him to go for another lawyer… even as a consultant.

I left the matter alone. Frustrated as I was. I was probably making bad judgment calls.

We had to put all our faith into this man with the sloppy office and the sloppy clothes who had never worked successfully on the federal level and who apparently was once an excellent attorney but wasn't anymore.

On top of all this, Tuite had not even prepared me to testify on Richard's behalf on Monday morning. Even though the second bond hearing was yet to take place, I could already see the headlines in Tuesday's *Tribune*: "**TUITE BLEW IT!**"

Anger and fear boiled inside me from out of nowhere, seething, burning my throat, but I pushed it away. No time to be upset, lady, I reminded myself. You have a hearing to attend, and after that, miles to go before you hear Bali Hai whisper again in her soft sultry voice, "Come to me, come to me."

If ever, I thought sadly.

On Sunday, the 31st, the *Chicago Tribune* decided to interview me before writing my thoughts for the world to see. That headline read: "**WOMAN KICKED BAILEY OUT OF HER LIFE BUT KEEPS DOOR OPEN**." After that opening salvo, the article described me in great detail so all my patients could identify me.

The story failed to mention that government agents (Treasury Department, I thought) had been harassing me, strongly suggesting that I distance myself from Richard. These unethical acts caused me to be even more suspicious of the prosecution. Why, I asked myself, would agents of the United States Government lower themselves to intimidating a woman to keep her from supporting a suspect?

Maybe the case against Richard was not as strong as the federal prosecutors were saying, I thought. Maybe they wanted to keep Richard in prison where he could not fight back effectively. These and other very unpatriotic thoughts ran through my mind. (Many of these questions have since been answered by events as the truth began to leak out from amongst the lies.)

At the time, I had no clear picture of what the truth was, and all I knew for certain was that Richard's only chance was a brilliant legal defense. Richard's supporters agreed. On a daily (and sometimes hourly) basis, I was warned, "Richard had better get a damn good attorney."

Every time I heard that remark, I pictured Tuite's office with the stacks of papers and legal documents everywhere. My next thought was always something my mother often said when I was young, "You can't work with a cluttered mind in a cluttered environment."

The mental picture of Tuite's office followed my mother's comment because a recurring nightmare I did not have to be asleep to experience. I felt the vision was an omen and nothing good would come of it. Only prayer made the image of Tuite's workplace disappear, and I thanked God that this avenue of relief was always open to me.

True, God was often silent, but I knew in my heart that He was always listening.

Chapter 17

Monday came. I dressed in a tailored suit for the hearing that was to begin at 10:00 A. M. it wasn't until I glanced at the calendar on my way out the back door that I realized it was August 1, exactly four months to the day since I met Richard at The Waterfront. Almost impossible to believe… so much had happened.

By then the government's strategy had begun to surface. The *Tribune* headline on that date read: "**BRACH CHARGE HINGES ON LAWS ON RACKETEERING.**"

Aha! No mention of a murder charge, a murder indictment or even a kidnapping!

When I reached my car, the phone was ringing. It was Dennis. He had seen the article and wanted to give me an update. The prosecutors, he said, had trotted out the old R. I. C. O. laws the government had enacted in 1970 to destroy the Italian Mafia and stop its encroachment into trade and labor unions, political movements, and legitimate businesses. The acronym R. I. C. O. stood for Racketeer Influenced and Corrupt Organizations, and on its face was the perfect tool to convict members of the Mafia who had developed "untouchable" reputations, men like the "Teflon Don" to whom no charge seemed to stick.

The strength of the R. I. C. O. Act, Dennis said, was the fact that the law could be used to string a long line of small crimes together and turn them into a bigger one. Dennis stressed that this shouldn't work for Richard as there was no "organization" with the requisite structure, and the bunch of swindlers and swashbucklers involved certainly could not be called an "organization" unto themselves.

"Then I have nothing to worry about, right?" I had asked.

Dennis was brutally honest. "Lady, if the Feds came at me the way they ambushed Richard, I'd be as nervous as a long-tailed cat in a room full of rocking chairs!"

"But you said they have no case!" I protested.

"Honey, when the Feds target you, they don't need a case! In America, a federal prosecutor has so much leeway he can indict a ham sandwich if he so wishes, and if the sandwich had an attorney, he couldn't even be present at the Grand Jury!

"Good God!"

"True. These guys could indict Mother Theresa for running a R. I. C. O. Organization designed to obviate the civil rights of males by refusing to allow them to be nuns… and they'd get a conviction, too. What's more, they would apply so much pressure that most of the nuns in the Order would plead guilty!"

"Richard will never plead guilty!" I informed Dennis, said goodbye, and hung up.

So, that was to be the government's game! Indict Richard for crimes he had already admitted to in civil court, string them together like pearls on an add-a-pearl necklace, chunk in any number of conspiracy theories and Bingo! A conviction! But in Richard's case, I told myself, there is a big difference. He wasn't involved in the Brach disappearance so there couldn't be any witnesses to something that didn't happen… and certainly, I thought, Steven Miller, who was heading up the prosecution team, would not stoop to using false witnesses. Surely the Office of the United States Attorney believed in God's commandment that "Thou shalt not bear false witness."

This thought was still on my mind when my houseman, Trevor, dropped me off at the Dirksen Federal Building. I remained somewhat nervous, but I was also excited, hoping against hope (perhaps) that the detention hearing would have a positive outcome for Richard.

When I walked into the courtroom, I was surprised to find the relatively small room crowded with people. Then I realized all eyes were on me, as if everyone had been waiting for me to show up. It was all very surreal as if Pa walked onto the set where they were filming *Law and Order* and shouted, "Roll 'em!" I took a deep breath and began to walk toward the front of the room. The whole time I stared straight ahead, avoiding eye contact, a trick I had watched Bess Myerson use in an airport once to ward off autograph seekers from invading her space.

A group of men in dark suits was standing behind the government's table. I walked over to the other side of the courtroom where Tuite was sitting, leaned over the bar, and out of the blue, he loudly exclaimed, "Where have you been all my life? Every man should have a woman like you." He gave me a knowing look and I felt my face turn a bright, bright red. There were people all around us. I didn't know who heard for sure, but I was terribly embarrassed by the unexpected familiarity.

I quickly excused myself and took a seat in the first row. This area was normally reserved for the press, but the reporters were extremely kind and let me sit there. Richard's brother, Bill, and sister-in-law, Shirley, who had become good friends while helping me sell Richard's car, sat in the row behind. They were an anchor to me at all times.

I put on my glasses and checked out the courtroom. For the first time, I was able to study the team of men who had banded together to permanently remove Richard from my life, and I was certainly unimpressed with two of them, David Hamm, an Illinois State Police Lieutenant, and Steven Miller.

Steven Miller was cut from another bolt of cloth altogether. I could easily imagine the uptight, right wing sort of environment which would produce the overachiever with the spacey almost hyperthyroid look to his face.

Just then, Richard appeared in his handcuffs and a prisoner's navy blue jump suit, and the words sacrificial lamb plopped into my head.

This was to be a bloodletting by the opposition.

I could only hope that Mr. Miller was a fair prosecutor, even if he was a hard one. Firm but fair would work for us because there was one thing I knew for sure: the man I had married in haste and planned to marry again in love, was not a killer.

When I was called to the stand, Tuite asked what I thought were very basic questions: my name, my profession, if I had traveled to Las Vegas with Richard and married him there, and if Richard had ever asked me for money. Tuite asked me very little. I would learn soon enough he would always do "very little," as well.

Co-prosecutor Ronald Safer, on the other hand, was well prepared and very tough.

He was the kind of man who was always moving, always thinking, like the restless Joe Fleishman in *Northern Exposure*.

Safer began his attack by zeroing in on my serendipitous meeting with Richard at The Waterfront. The questions that followed suggested that after Richard found out I worked in a lucrative field, drove an expensive car, and owned a Gold Coast home, he had followed a timeworn pattern of his in pursuing me: wining and dining me at first class restaurants, always picking up the tab, bragging that he was a successful businessman.

Safer was relentless in the way he presented his questions, but I must say he was good at what he did. If ever I were in trouble, he would be the first person I would want to hire.

Toward the end of his cross examination, Safer focused on the very speculative investigative report I received from Nancy Lewis after Richard's and my return to Chicago. Safer's entire line of questioning was leading to some preconceived conclusion as he continued to build and build until his objective intent exploded into realization with the words, "You did not trust him, right?"

"Right." I felt like a bug on an entomologist's pin. He brushed off my admission and went on:

Q. "And this driving school that he had operated for seventeen years, he didn't tell you that the Attorney General shut that driving school down because of fraud, did he?"

A. "I didn't know…"

Q. "Yes! He never told you that, did he?"

I found myself barely able to catch my breath before Safer was off on a different subject, each time leaving me squirming on yet another pin. This strategy worked on me because when he slipped in the comment about the fraud associated with the driving school, I let it pass by, even though I knew a little about Richard's driving school and wasn't sure at all why it had closed. Safer was very intimidating and excellent at his job.

Toward the end of my testimony, Safer asked questions about the possibility of allowing Richard to stay in my guest room for thirty days during the trial…

Q. "Now, over the course of those thirty days, you of course have no physical control over the defendant, do you?"

A. "No."

Q. "And you don't intend to give up your practice during those thirty days, do you?"

A. "No."

Q. "You are not going to babysit the defendant, are you?"

A. "No."

Q. "You could not, even if you were, you could not prevent him from leaving your home, could you?"

A. "I don't believe he will if he's not allowed to."

Q. "Well, that's not my question…"

A. "Yes."

Q. "My question is:If he wanted to, you couldn't prevent him, could you?"

A. "No."

Safer left me breathless and more than a little tired, but I had answered the questions he put to me honestly; I was an honest person. Honest to a fault, I would discover as the case wore on and on.

Tuite jumped back in when Safer was finishing up, again bringing up the fact that Richard had talked to me about his background after I read the investigative report, and that I was still considering remarrying him, depending, of course, on the outcome of the proceedings. Tuite also questioned me about whether I was willing to allow Richard to reside with me for a period of time during the trial. The answer was yes, definitely …

Then it was Safer once more, and from what I could tell, what he was saying was basically a rehash of what he had already said at Friday's hearing as to why Richard shouldn't be allowed to be bonded out. After Safer's summary, he stated that Richard's whirlwind romance with me took place only because I was a "good mark," just like all the other women Richard had wined and dined over the years.

This time the pin went through my heart.

Safer also pointed out that after Richard met me, he did not go home and tell Karen Hanson, with whom he was living part time and who knew Richard well, that he had found "this phenomenal woman." Because he did not do this, Safer said it proved that I was "just a mark waiting to happen." What Safer didn't say was that when. Richard met me; he was staying at his brother's home. Safer also threw in that Ms. Hanson refused to post bond for Richard. I knew she couldn't. She didn't have the money. Richard and I were losing, and I was terribly frustrated because the facts weren't coming out, only the impression that Safer was putting in the record.

Then it was Tuite's turn. He-brought up the fact that when the Bureau of Alcohol, Tobacco and Firearms (BATE) Agents (I had thought they were from the A Treasury Department!) had stopped by my office and asked that I be their snitch, that it was a clear violation of Richard's Sixth Amendment Rights. I was excited at first, thinking that Tuite had finally sunk his teeth into something good, but in the end, his argument was weak to the point of being appalling. The judge must have thought so too because nothing ever came of it.

It was days later before I learned the magnitude of the agents' visit to my office and how much their error on approaching me could have helped Richard. Basically, the agents had wanted to make an informant out of me, a "rat" they could control to get trial strategies from the defendant's camp. Richard had retained a lawyer and the Constitution says counsel's communications with his client are sacrosanct; there was no reason for any representatives of the

United States Government to participate in such a clear violation of the Sixth Amendment… but they had… and not only with gusto, but also with a familiarity with the process that was highly suspicious.

After a half hour or so after my testimony on the witness stand, Magistrate Guzman announced that he was going to recess until 11:00 A. M. to review his notes and the arguments of counsel.

Eleven A. M. ?

I was certainly no legal beagle but that gave the Magistrate next to no time to arrive at a decision. In my opinion, something was clearly wrong… already.

When Magistrate Guzman returned minutes later, he began to list his reasons why Richard would be denied bond: he initially attempted to avoid detection; he lied to the F. B. I. ; he lacked substantial ties to the community; he was not employed; and he was facing a life sentence. The Magistrate finished with a shocker: "Whatever Dr. Hoffman may feel for the defendant, the evidence is clear that the feelings are not mutual."

I almost choked when Guzman said those words!

An image of Richard smiling lovingly at me while standing on the banks of Lake Michigan, a fishing pole in his hand, flashed across my brain. How could Guzman possibly know what Richard's feelings were for me?

Guzman ended his decision by noting that Richard was a definite flight risk and posed a danger to the community.

Bond was denied.

I was terribly disappointed. Disappointed for Richard because I knew how difficult it was to defend a complicated case from jail. Disappointed for me because I was still in love with him and wanted to be with him. Disappointed even for Pat Tuite because he would have to work twice as hard now to get ready for the trial and I didn't think he wanted to work period.

After the hearing, Trevor picked me up in front of the Federal Building. My younger daughter was with him and the three of us drove to my office because I needed to drop off my briefcase. When we pulled into the parking lot behind my building, I was amazed to see the area was absolutely mobbed with reporters! I could almost hear their teeth snapping.

I wanted to drive off, but it was essential that I leave some paperwork for my staff. I steeled myself and got out of the car, holding my briefcase up in the air, and then the reporters began swarming around me. I yelled to Trevor to remove my daughter and shouted to the crowd, "No pictures of the child! No pictures of the child!"

I was terribly torn. I wanted to be fair with the media; after all, they were only doing their jobs, but I was also a mother who needed to protect her daughter. It was then I made the reporters a promise that I would give them a complete statement when the trial was over if they would not photograph my daughter. The press members were very considerate about my request, and the scary potential for a feeding frenzy quickly dissipated.

The reporters then asked a few basic questions, "Where did you meet Richard?"..."Why did you have the marriage annulled?"... "Do you still love him now that you know who he is?" I answered their questions as best I could, despite the fact that the answers had been given many times already, often to the same reporters.

That afternoon, tired as I was, I had to go back to the Dirksen Federal Building once again because I had been asked to meet with members of the Bureau of Alcohol, Tobacco and Firearms. Since I had been detained by the press, I was a little late, maybe fifteen minutes or so.

I ran up the steps, walked into the building and was quickly ushered into a corridor-like room, narrow, windowless and with a very long conference table. Seated around the table were six or seven men wearing what I thought of as "government agent uniforms"—dark suits, inexpensive ties, and rumpled shirts. The group looked like a mob boss meeting from an Al Pacino film. They also looked very serious. The men began to ask me the same questions I had (at this point) answered so many times before; questions like, "What exactly can you tell us about Richard Bailey?"

I looked around the room and recognized the two agents I had thought were from the Treasury Department who had come to my office a few days before. As to the other men seated around me, I was terribly confused as to who they were and which government agencies they worked for. I had just walked into this room and here were all these men who did not have the manners to stand or introduce themselves.

I was terrified, but I had come because my government had asked me to. I didn't even have a lawyer with me. Why should I? I had done nothing wrong. So, that's what they do with taxpayers' money, I thought. Frighten women.

Halfway through the meeting, Steven Miller walked into the room. He had his hands in the pockets of his wrinkled trousers and leaned against the wall, listening.

After forty-five minutes of questions, one of the men said abruptly, "That's all. Thank you for your help," and I left.

I had survived the hearing, the reporters, another meeting with various agencies of the United States Government, but when I walked out of the Federal Building, I was tired. If I was this worn out after a simple hearing, how would I manage the stress of a major trail? I firmly resolved that with Bill and Shirley for support, I would see the whole situation through to the end.

The next morning, my picture appeared in the *Chicago Tribune* with a headline stating: **"DEFENDANT IN BRACH PLOT DENIED BOND, JUDGE REJECTS OFFER BY BAILEY'S EX-WIFE."** The article discussed Magistrate Ronald Guzman's denial of bail for Richard and included some very insulting words from Co-prosecutor Safer: "He (Richard) proposed marriage in five days; not even a hopeless romantic would call that normal behavior."

Love, I wanted to shout to the press, does not run-on Adolph Hitler time tables; however badly the government agents might wish to regulate God's Great Gift, I knew they could not because they obviously did not understand the concept.

The *Daily Herald* did not do as well as the *Tribune* with their post-hearing photographs. They had taken a dark shot of me coming out of the Federal Building. I looked dazed. No wonder. The photographer had snapped my picture moments after the judge's comment that basically I wasn't able to make decisions for myself and needed the protection of the courts. When the camera clicked, I was heartbroken… and I was also scared.

Extremely so.

If Guzman had (already!) bought into the prosecution's schemes and obvious manipulations, a good lawyer would clearly not suffice against a judge who could read minds and passed judgments on those readings. Richard would need a great lawyer.

Was Pat Tuite such a brain?

I only hoped that he was, but when I shut my eyes, I still saw Tuite's messy office, only now the columns of papers were swaying as if in a catastrophic quake. I did not need to be in California to recognize that "The Big One" was obviously coming.

And still it rained bad news.

Then there was the matter of how would I visit with Richard?

Chapter 18

After the hearing, I stayed up most of the night sitting in the dark on my living room sofa, drinking chamomile tea. What I needed most was to see Richard, to sit down next to him, to touch his face (if this was allowed in jail), his hands, to listen while he told me what he knew for certain about his arrest, his future, the crimes he was accused of committing, and to pose his confidence against my wild imaginings. Meanwhile, all I had was the telephone and how could I say any of those things over a phone controlled by the prison? Worse, how could I tell Richard that I loved him with the prison staff listening, perhaps (as Dennis warned) even making obscene sexual gestures to each other as they heard our declarations of love. But I had to face the truth. Our conversations would be monitored forever... unless Richard was found innocent and released.

A personal visit would solve so many problems, and I just assumed I would see Richard in a reasonable amount of time. After all, it wasn't like held been shipped off to Leavenworth. He had never left Chicago. Unfortunately, the Metropolitan Correctional Center had other ideas when it came to the two of us getting together.

After Richard was arrested, my definition of time changed completely. It slowed down, and finally ceased to have any meaning) as my attempts to visit

Richard were bogged down by bureaucratic glitches, rules, and regulations I never even knew existed; and even if I had known about them, I wouldn't have wanted to.

Time.

There is a time to reap and a time to sow…

Days passed before Richard was even allowed to send me blank visitation forms from the M. C. C., so I could fill them out and return them. If I were approved (visiting an inmate is not a right, but a tightly monitored privilege), visitation took place every Tuesday from 12:30 to 2:30 P. M. I planned to take a late lunch on those days, pop over to the jail and spend time with Richard.

Time… time… time… creeps in this petty pace…

Ten days later, my plans to visit Richard remained only that… plans. More days passed, painful days, days expecting mail to turn up which never did. Finally, two full weeks after I had sent in my visitation forms, I received notice that I would be allowed to visit Richard.

At first, I was exhilarated!

I had won a battle, albeit a minor one!

Then another set of fears took over my life.

I was going to jail!

For the very first time!

I was absolutely terrified.

Me?

In a prison?

The time has come, Walrus said, to speak of other things… like… jail.

My imagination worked overtime, creating visions of the Tower of London and the medieval horror stories that had taken place there.

I wasn't disappointed. The Chicago Metropolitan Correctional Center was an ugly, gray skyscraper jail operated by the Federal Bureau of Prisons and, as I was soon to believe, by the darkest minions of the Prince of Darkness.

On my first visit, I was kept waiting outside the jail for an unbelievably long time, so long I thought the staff had changed their minds and canceled my visitation privileges. one of my fellow visitors in line told me the outside waiting area was like a holding pen for cattle. "The staff wants to get us upset," he went on, "so they leave us out here in the rain, in the cold like animals... they hope they'll make us so mad we'll stop coming... taxpaying citizens are a terrible inconvenience to these people." Instinctively I knew the man was telling me the truth.

Finally, my name was called, and I walked through a door into a small room, very stark and very bare except for lockers against one wall and a few chairs; I had been standing outside for what seemed like forever, but a guard told me procedure didn't allow visitors to sit down.

I suppose I had an incredulous look on my face because a little old black woman smiled at me, hanging from her upper gum like a stalagmite. "They's hateful folks here," she said, "wust I ever seed, and I got me twenty-seven relatives in jail all over... from Stateville and Joliet to Pontiac. I's seen 'em all and I's telling you, I'd rather have a daughter turnin' tricks than one working in this dump!"

Where, I thought, do they find people to work in a building whose only function is to deliver misery to the condemned and free alike? I remembered reading Oscar Wilde's comment when he was released from Reading Gaol around the turn of the century. He said when the warden needed new men, he raided the local brothels and hired everyone who was paying to watch sexual acts. The warden's reasoning was clever: He wanted men so emotionally depleted they had to watch others being pleasured to reach their own satisfaction. Such persons could be counted upon, he thought, to be watchful.

I did not stay in the small stark room over fifteen minutes before I was sent on to the next roadblock. Another room where only the handicapped were allowed to sit down. A guard behind a desk there gave me another form to fill in which I did and returned it promptly. He checked it carefully, and then, after another long wait, I was passed through a sliding steel gate, walked inside a cage, then into an elevator and was sent up to still another waiting room.

A chair at last! I took a seat and prayed. I prayed that Richard would eventually turn up. I only had an hour left to visit after all, and I could tell from the way I'd already been treated, that my time meant nothing to these people.

The jail was very poorly run, but the staff didn't seem to care in the slightest. On the contrary, complaints were met with raw insolence or silly grins.

The staff's attitude toward me and other visitors was, in a word, unconscionable. No matter who you were, no matter what your background or your nationality in the staff's eyes, you were as bad as being criminal. Forget custodians. The staff considered themselves to be judges and juries and punished the lot of us for choosing to stick by friends and family members who happened to be incarcerated. I found myself staring at the employees (who, in turn, stared nonstop at me), wondering why they felt they had the right to judge both visitors and inmates... some, like Richard, even before their trials.

Time on my hands and you in my arms.

Finally, I was taken to the area where I would meet Richard. I don't know what I was expecting, but the visiting room was like a baseball bat to the face. It was filled with tables very close together with metal chairs (welded together so they couldn't be moved) on either side.

The noise was incredible.

Sometimes I can still hear it.

It gives me nightmares.

Small children were racing about unsupervised, screaming at the tops of their lungs while adults shouted at each other to be heard. As I waited for Richard to come through the door, I heard one woman shout, "I can't hear you!" over and over to the man across the table from her. Finally, he stood up and screamed, "I love you, goddammit!"

I was so shocked I am sure my mouth was hanging open. A guard walked by just then and barked at the couple, "Hold the noise down!"

The noise.

God... the noise.

When I finally saw Richard in his navy-blue jump suit, it took away my breath. I could actually feel the color drain from my face. Even though I had seen him handcuffed in the courtroom, the reality of our situation, especially in that disgusting room, was truly shocking. It was like seeing a member of your immediate family after held been seriously injured in an automobile accident. The man I was going to propose to only a few weeks before was now an inmate, suspected of committing a murder. It was very difficult to deal with.

But my negative thoughts dissipated when Richard reached out to embrace me. After his loving hello kiss (in front of three guards!), Richard told me how much he had missed me and how my being there meant everything to him. He was all smiles and so upbeat, so positive. Everything seemed terribly surreal at that moment. Considering the seriousness of the situation, it was like we were both actors in a Fellini movie.

Time, once the tortoise had become the hare, and to my horror, I discovered that the visiting hour was almost over. True, Richard had just walked into the room, but the B. O. P. "started" the visit officially when the visitor signed in, not when the actual visiting began. Time was precious, priceless. Richard and I scurried around the room and finally found a place to sit across from each other at a table. Since we couldn't touch each other physically again beyond holding hands, we kept them on the table top (as ordered) so the guards could see.

I learned very quickly how to survive a visit without being thrown out and having visits revoked. It all had to do with "policy." As nearly as I could tell, everything two adults might do on a friendly visit was "against policy." If Richard made me laugh, I could not reach over and touch his arm. "Policy." If I needed a hug, or a shoulder on which to shed a tear, that, too, was an affront to "policy." I could not wear any dress that was higher than my knee, regardless of the fashion. Sleeveless blouses were out, regardless of the heat, and normal cleavage was not allowed either. "Policy." I could not go to a vending machine with Richard; I had to go alone, buy our food, and bring whatever I bought to the table. We could not write, take notes, or memorialize our experiences. All against "policy."

On the first visit, I walked into the toilet, but never used the facilities; the bathrooms were filthy beyond belief. Apparently, they were not controlled by Public Health policy.

The food in the vending machines was inedible, and greatly overpriced. The purpose of the price gouging was to provide funds for the Bureau of

Richard Bailey

Prisons' employee club parties. The vending machine "policy" should rot the socks of any member of any society in western civilization. The very concept of making a profit to party on from food sold to downtrodden women and impoverished children is a concept that is beneath the dignity of a civilized nation.

All these negatives aside, Richard and I were happy just to be seated across from each other at a table. He was smiling broadly and was genuinely happy to see me, like a little boy. I could always tell when someone loved me... I could see it in their eyes. And Richard honestly loved me, like he'd been saying all those weeks, months. That much was obvious.

Richard asked me the normal things:How are you feeling? How is the family? What's happening at work? I asked him what it was like inside the jail, was he having any problems, but he clammed up. Whatever life was like for Richard once he left the visiting room is still a mystery. He didn't complain that first day and he never has. All of a sudden, when I was just beginning to relax somewhat, a guard announced that visiting hours were over and I had to leave.

At the end of our first meeting, Richard was allowed to kiss me (again!) goodbye. It was an extremely long, passionate kiss. I could feel how desperately he needed me, and I felt the same way, yet we had to separate.

As difficult as it was for me to walk inside the jail, I found it even harder to walk out and leave Richard behind its walls.

In the months to come, the prison staff was time and again unnecessarily harsh when admitting me... almost as if they... or somebody else had planned each humiliation beforehand.

Many, many times after I arrived at the jail, I was forced to wait outside (in the holding pen) for an unbelievably long period of time. When I complained to the press, the harassment changed. For the worse! The guards detained Richard for so long before releasing him to go to the visiting room, that I would have to rush off and go back to the office without ever seeing him. On those days, I had no other choice but to leave. I had appointments scheduled that I had to keep.

These were difficult times, and the only thing that kept me going was my belief that Richard was not guilty of killing Helen Brach.

I honestly felt that Richard was not capable of murdering anyone. I still don't. But as worried as I was about Richard's problems, I had problems of my own to deal with. I truly feared for my practice. What would my patients think of me now that my name had been linked to a murder suspect? And my children… I adored them… how would my involvement with Richard effect our relationship… both now and long-term. I had suspicions and many, many fears, but no real answers.

As crazy as it might sound, part of me was envious of Richard though he was in jail. At least he was hidden away from the prying eyes of the public and Tokyo Rose's giant microphone which still seemed to hover over my head.

Unlike Richard, there was nowhere I could hide. I had to put on a brave face along with my makeup every single day and face my children, my patients, and indeed the world) all by myself.

Other things had changed too. I never knew what I was going to be faced with when I walked in my office door… and each day was different. In my staff, I faced both hostility and a desperate need to protect me. I still do today. And then there were my patients. Some were negative things too but most that had known me for some time were encouraging me. But I was gradually removed from all of the permanent guest lists of many Chicago socialites. This deliberate shunning by people who were at the very least acquaintances of mine, hurt me deeply. Even my most beloved charities seemed no longer interested in my help. I was being abandoned by the City of Chicago for the crime of being in love.

Very well, so be it, I thought. My covenant was with Richard, my soul known to God, my life committed to doing the right thing. I knew that the road ahead was not going to be easy, but as Caesar said, "The die is cast."

Imagine my surprise when I also received beautiful flower arrangements and cards of encouragement from other patients, all in praise of sticking by "my man." I was astonished, then grateful for such messages as, "Follow your heart" … "What a romance!" … "This must be true love!" I was so appreciative of their kind words and still am today. I certainly had not expected anyone's support except for Bill and Shirley.

While I continued to deal with my mundane problems, life, such as it was, without, Richard went on. After a while, the M. C. C. determined that I could see him every other Saturday, but the long wait once I arrived at the jail continued to wreak havoc with my schedule. Every now and then I'd get lucky; there would be a halfway decent human being at the front desk of the jail, and I wouldn't have to wait so long, but that was a rarity.

To this day I wonder whether the hostility on the part of the staff was standard operating procedure or was it carried out at the orders of the prosecution. Perhaps it was a combination. Time and tides wait for no man… or woman.

Those visits with Richard were to become lifelines to me, not only because they fulfilled an emotional need, but also because only during those times did I learn what was happening to Richard from a legal standpoint. Even so, our brief sojourns were difficult to deal with. Aside from the long process of entering there always came the time when I had to walk out the door.

Alone in my bed at night, I thought of my life, and I had to ask myself how could I possibly have gone from Bali Hai to this?

A dungeon!

And like everything else with Richard, in such a very short time!

Time heals all wounds.

Right! Please.

Chapter 19

On the drive into the office one morning, I mentally replayed some conversations I had with Tuite over the past few days. His belief appeared to be that there was only one option remaining which could be sufficiently impactive on the court to secure Richard's freedom. Tuite had repeatedly noted that if Richard were to get married, the judge would be amenable to freeing him on bond. The judge wouldn't consider Richard a flight risk then, Tuite said, plus Richard would have definite ties to the community. Tuite's exact words were that his own personal experience with marriage was so bad that he could not advise anybody to get married, but that it would be very, very helpful to Richard if he were 'married. Tuite also pointed out that it was extremely difficult to defend a case, especially a complex one, with a prisoner unavailable to assist full time in the preparation of his defense.

At that point, I had precious little faith in Tuite's skills as a lawyer, but I was willing to go for anything that would help to give Richard a better chance.

I came to a decision just as Trevor pulled up in my office parking lot. I had to marry Richard (again!)...and the quicker the better.

That afternoon, I rearranged my schedule and went into the Loop. First, I applied for a marriage license at the Marriage License Bureau in the basement of city Hall. The clerk there told me that in addition to my signature,

Richard would also have to personally sign the application. I informed the clerk that Richard couldn't sign because he was incarcerated. With an exasperated smile, the clerk then advised me to contact Richard's assigned counselor at the Metropolitan Correctional Center and make arrangements. Twice a week, she said, someone from City Hall went to the jails in the Chicago area to get the requisite signatures on the forms. I really didn't know if the public servant she referred to ever went to the H. C. C., but if he did, he never spoke with Richard.

We were left to our own devices. I asked an acquaintance to call Washington, D. C. to find out the proper method for someone incarcerated to get married. There had to be an easier way, I thought, but I was wrong. The only legal way for a marriage to take place when one is in a federal jail, my colleague was told, was with the blessing of the staff of the M. C. C. Richard and I decided to bite the bullet and do whatever those in charge at the jail demanded.

In order to get married, the M. C. C. staff informed us, Richard and I were each required to write a letter to his counselor stating our desires. This we did. Nothing happened. I called Richard's counselor over a dozen times, wanting to find out why we had heard nothing from her, but the staff always told me the lady wasn't in, and the counselor never returned any of my calls. After securing the woman's name and office address, I wrote her again. No response. After repeated calls to the jail, the M. C. C. staff finally informed me that the counselor no longer worked there! No, I was told, no one had replaced her and no, they did not know when someone else would be hired. The jail employees gave me no reason for the Bureau of Prisons' behavior. What was I dealing with? Incompetence? Malicious intent? Orders from the prosecution? It was a mystery.

I tried everything I could think of to get the ball rolling, but to no avail. My dilemma was like the old joke when the city slickster asked the farmer for directions to the nearby rail station and after several fitful starts at giving directions, the farmer stopped, scratched his head, and announced, "You're in a bad spot. You can't get there from here!"

I was up against a bureaucratic stone wall, and the anxiety in my life was increasing. I began to feel like I lived inside an enormous pressure cooker and that sooner or later the lid would blow. On the one hand, I had Tuite calling, insisting that Richard and I be married; on the other hand, I had to interact with a staff at the M. C. C. who simply refused to take care of the necessary paperwork. And always in my mind's eye was Richard's trusting but anxious face. Frustrated? An understatement! I had seriously begun to suspect the prosecution (and I still do) for phoning the jail and suggesting that members of the staff purposely delay the marriage; but for whatever reason, plans for our marriage were at a standstill and I was becoming desperate.

I was fighting the Fates and Furies, the staff at M. C. C. and yes, even fighting City Hall! Finally, I realized that virtually no one wanted to see us married so I decided to fight bureaucrat against bureaucrat, supervisors against directors. Yes, I would fight fire with Chicago fire! I called a top politician in the Chicago area. As soon as he picked up the phone, I identified myself and said, "I know you don't approve of my relationship with Richard Bailey and my involvement with him, but I need a favor," He was at least willing to listen and so I went on, "I need someone to go over to the M. C. C. and see to it that Richard is given a marriage application to sign. I have called the jail time and again trying to get the staff to do this simple, simple thing, and they have outright refused to help me... or even allow us to help ourselves."

My worry was such that the whole time I was talking to this extremely important person, I was all too aware that weeks had passed since Tuite first told me that Richard and I needed to be married in order to bond him out. Perhaps I was too late.

Pressure... pressure.

But for once luck was with me.

Not only did the politician agree to help, but he also succeeded where I had failed. He ended up fixing everything... good ole Chicago politicians!

In a matter of hours, Richard was allowed to sign the marriage application! We had it in our possession less than two days later!

It was a miracle!

And a little bit more!

I had discovered perhaps the one and only thing the Bureau of Prisons feared: politicians,

In a November 8 court appearance before a new judge, Milton Shadur (who was to be Richard's trial judge), I announced that I would marry Richard; thereby, I said, he would have a place to stay while awaiting his trial, now scheduled to begin May 9. I admitted that my change of heart was in part an attempt to aid Richard's bid for freedom. (I still had not learned that honesty is seldom appreciated in the federal courts.)

Tuite told Judge Shadur that Richard and I had signed a prenuptial agreement that protected my financial assets. This was true. I had seen my lawyer Stanley Kaplin once more and signed an agreement that said if I died, Richard would be given a certain sum of money. Richard waived a death settlement (as I knew he would), but the clause was designed to show that if I were killed, that the contract would obviate the possibility of personal gain for Richard. This section of the agreement seemed to both impress and please the judge.

Tuite then complained to the judge that the M. C. C. bureaucracy had taken "forever" to finally give us clearance to go ahead with the marriage, even forcing Richard to be examined by a psychologist to see if he was "mentally fit" to be married. "They should do that in all marriages," Tuite quipped later. "Maybe we would have better relationships."

Also, at the hearing, Richard's brother, Bill, took the stand and pledged two commercial properties he owned as collateral toward Richard's bond, and I agreed to put up the equity in my home.

I thought Judge Shadur would rule immediately, but when Tuite went before him, the judge said, "I told you we could not proceed with this unless you had certain documents ready, and you don't have them again today." My loud sigh was audible in the courtroom. Shadur said he was compelled to hold off on the final ruling until Tuite provided more detailed financial information on the property that Richard's brother and I were willing to post. Tuite's ineptitude left me heartbroken.

Shadur did, however, conclude that he would let Richard out of the M. C. C. it we were married; if he stayed in my Lincoln Park home where he would be equipped with electronic monitoring devices; if he agreed not to undergo any surgery to alter his appearance; if he did not contact government witnesses and if properties owned by myself and Richard's brother were put up as collateral.

After the hearing, I thought that things would finally go smoothly for us, but the U. S. Attorney's Office continued to object to Richard's release, saying that his behavior toward me was proof only of his incorrigibility. In a court filing, the government said that it was not surprised that Richard had found a trusting woman, adding, "What is surprising is that the defendant would expect the court to believe that he would not violate this trust." The papers had a lot of fun with that comment.

I later I admitted to a *Tribune* reporter that I had moved up my plans to marry Richard after concluding that he was innocent of the Brach murder for hire. "I talk to him every day," I said, "and he's totally different than the monster the prosecution is describing him to be. I find him to be very sensitive, sort of shy, loving and caring, almost everything I would want in a man." After the interview, I questioned whether or not I should have come on so strong, but then I decided: Why shouldn't I say these things about Richard? They were all true.

The day after the hearing, Iry Kupcinet featured my court appearance and my offer to many Richard in "Kup's Column" in the *Sun-Times*, saying that only political candidates were supposed to make news on Election Day, but that fact hadn't stopped me and referring to me as "the lovelorn." It was a tasteless joke. If only Mr. Kupcinet knew the truth behind this tragedy, I thought, if only he knew. The columnist also mentioned that Tuite had not provided the necessary paperwork for Judge Shadur to peruse at the hearing. Tuite. Kupcinet's remarks added more fuel to the fire under my anti-Tuite pressure cooker.

The paperwork relating to the bond hearings was always horrendous, but I was willing to work with Tuite around the clock if only he would submit his motions on time. Tuite also made matters worse because he would frequently want a document ASAP, but wouldn't use the material (deeds, etc.) until two weeks later. He was very inconsiderate about my time and my schedule. Everything I had feared when I first saw Tuite's messy office was coming true. His lack of professionalism and organization were rotting the fruits of my efforts. Far worse, Richard had to suffer because of Tuite's incompetence.

The next bond hearing was scheduled for November 18. Having learned my lesson with Tuite, I called him days before and asked if he had his paperwork ready. He assured me that he did.

This time I double-checked!

I called the Clerk of the Court!

During our conversation, I learned that Tuite had filed some papers with the court putting up my home and Richard's brother's property as collateral for Richard's release. It was getting close to Thanksgiving. I was apprehensive and hopeful at the same time.

I finally convinced myself that the release was actually going to happen... Richard was going to be free to work on his case! And there was even a bonus! With luck, he would be home for Thanksgiving! Once again, the disaster my life had become did not prevent me from being happy, and I began to look forward to a family time together on this special holiday. I told Trevor I planned to buy a turkey as large as the goose Scrooge bought for the Cratchits on Christmas Day, then hunted up my old recipes for candied yams and cornbread dressing and pumpkin pie laced with rum. Yes, a big-sit down dinner with the family would be a must on Thanksgiving, and with Richard home, I would be more thankful on that day than anyone in America!

But sure enough, at the hearing on November 18, Tuite didn't have all the paperwork ready as he had repeatedly, promised, and when the judge asked for the documents, Tuite simply said, "The Thanksgiving weekend is starting, and I am leaving town to be with my family."

I had never been so furious with another human being in my entire life!

Tuite was talking about being with his family for Thanksgiving as if my family didn't exist and worse, he had outright lied to me days before about being prepared!

After the hearing, I cornered Tuite in the Conference Room outside the courtroom. As I walked up to him, he had the audacity to ask for more money! "We've already paid you $120, 000, Pat," I said in a loud voice, "and I just gave you $14, 000 more last week, and to tell you the truth, I don't see why I should pay you anything. What's more, I want to know why you can't even get a man out of jail when his brother and I have posted $1. 3 million!"

Tuite was really surprised at my outburst because I'm normally so calm and even tempered. His partner, Ron Menaker (who was rarely around), was with him that day and he stepped over and said, "You know it's normal to be angry when you're expecting something and don't get it."

I looked at the man like he was crazy.

Angry?

I was far beyond anger.

He had robbed me and robbed me and robbed me.

What he had done to Richard was far, far worse.

Tuite was unfunctional, incompetent or lazy or both. There must have been great rejoicing in the prosecution's camp when they learned that Richard had hired Patrick Tuite.

If Tuite couldn't come up with the paperwork that was required and couldn't handle himself properly in court, why hadn't he just postponed the hearing or asked for continuance as opposed to making a fool of himself and charging us for court time. For the first time in my life, I could understand why men get so angry at each other they engage in physical confrontation.

I fumed for days!

In the meantime, Richard had written a letter to Judge Shadur responding to government concerns that he might flee. Nothing, he said, could be further in his mind or thoughts. Richard also said that he had never shirked his responsibilities in the past and did not intend to start at that stage of his life.

I didn't know if Richard's letter would help secure his release or not, but Judge Shadur had set still another hearing date, this time, November 28, to finalize the conditions of Richard's bond.

Richard Bailey

Once again, I became hopeful. Even though Thanksgiving with Richard had been a wipeout, his freedom was the only real issue. I bought a broad-tipped magic marker and began to count off the days on my kitchen calendar with huge black X's.

Chapter 20

Even with the disaster of the bond denial to contend with, I was still going to and fro with the staff at the Metropolitan Correctional Center to finalize the arrangements for Richard's and my marriage. I was relaxing in my private office, having just completed a complex surgical procedure, when Richard called and told me that at long last (I had almost given up!), the M. C. C. staff had set the date for our wedding: December 3. All those agonizing weeks of around the-clock phone calls and the politician's maneuvering had paid off. I could hardly believe it.

I thought ahead to the next hurdle. Where does one get married in a jail?

When Richard called that afternoon, he said he would make it his business to find out and would call me later. That evening, he said he had learned there was a little chapel in the jail where we could be married, and that the staff was insisting that I be at the M. C. C. punctually at 9:00 A. M. on the morning of the wedding. That was fine with me. I figured if I arrived at the jail early, Richard and I would have an hour or so to visit after the ceremony. After I hung up, my thought kept returning to:

The Little Chapel.

A quiet haven within the jail where Richard and I could be joined together in matrimony. Not for long, of course, but at least during this special time for us, we would be in an area far away from the hubbub of the jail visiting room, the stern guards, and the staff.

That night, going to sleep was difficult. I lay in bed for the longest time, picturing in my mind what this chapel would look like… the intricately carved alter, the red carpeted aisle, the small but quaint nave, the mahogany choir box. While I was daydreaming, I was truly at peace… even with the demeaning aspects of a prison wedding.

On my wedding day, Trevor dropped me off at the jail and as instructed, I was there promptly at 9:00 A. M. I had asked Richard what he preferred I wear, and he had suggested my black suit with the gold trim and buttons. The Dior creation was his favorite.

After I waited and waited and waited outside in the holding pen to be allowed inside the lobby, my name was finally called, then I waited some more inside. I knew all too well how the jail functioned by now with regard to visits, and I was very much aware that at 11:00 A. M. sharp, all visits were, as they said so prosaically, "Terminated!"

Finally, the chaplain called downstairs and the man behind the desk said, "Send her up!" I was then taken to the visiting Room, Richard was admitted (blue jump suit), and I thought, we're finally on our way to the chapel I had seen only in my head, but no, they took us to one of the small gloomy attorney/client visitation rooms instead. It was like a fishbowl on one side of the room, and I found myself being stared at and pointed at by people walking by as if we were some bizarre aquarium exhibit.

When the chaplain showed up, he was wearing a dirty tweed coat that stuck up in back around his neck, baggy pants, and dirty shoes. He was very unfriendly and gave the distinct impression that Richard and I were bothering him, and he would much rather be somewhere else, than where he was. I do not mean to be critical of a man of the cloth, but I did expect something more from someone who had devoted his life to God. Or I thought honestly, maybe the lack of dedication was what I sensed.

The ceremony lasted ten minutes. Richard and I exchanged rings, we were allowed to kiss, and due to the M. C. C.'s delays (intentional?), we only had ten minutes together back in the Visiting Room with all the other inmates before it was closing time: 11:00 A. M. "All visits are terminated!" the guard shouted. My punctuality (their orders!) had counted for nothing. My nuptials were "terminated," along with the visit.

I took a taxi home and although the entire experience had been unpleasant to the point of almost nausea, Richard and I were legally married like Tuite had insisted and the judge had wanted.

When I arrived home, my older daughter, who had been interviewing for a residency that week and had just returned from Evanston Hospital, was waiting for me. It was my intention to celebrate my marriage in some small way even though I would have to do it without Richard, and so when I saw my daughter, I said gaily, "Let's go to the Ritz-Carlton for lunch!"

My younger daughter was in her bedroom at the time, but when she heard me speak, she slammed her door shut.

My older daughter said, "I can't believe you did it! I can't believe you have married that man and ruined this family!"

I was crushed by her words, but she was just getting started. She went on to say that during her interview at Evanston Hospital, when the interviewer saw my name written on her application, she became very angry and said that the hospital would not be interested in anyone who came from a family of the type that her family was, and that since she was raised by a mother who was associated with someone like Richard Bailey, that the hospital would definitely not be interested in appointing her.

I was beyond sad at that point and so very, very sorry that my connection with Richard had had this kind of impact on my daughter. I knew better than anyone how much she had wanted that particular position.

"I cannot tell you how sorry I am..." I began, expecting to deliver a lengthy apology, but my daughter wasn't finished with her tirade.

"The only decent thing you can do for our family now is to go somewhere and kill yourself!" she yelled. Then she stormed out, slamming the front door as hard as she could.

That night when I tried to fall asleep, I comforted myself with Richard's last words to me in the visiting room: "All I ever wanted was you. I never married you for your money. I married you because I fell in love on our first date."

Later, as I prayed for Richard, a peace came over me and I knew that in spite of everything, I had chosen the proper course.

Shortly after the wedding, co-prosecutor Ronald Safer was quoted in the *Chicago Sun-Times* as saying that Richard and I had been married Saturday at the M. C. C. and, "They favored me with neither an invitation nor a guest list. But I think the M. C. C. frowns on large weddings."

After everything that had happened up to that point, all the delays, Tuite's incompetence, the negative publicity, my family's outrage, I found Safer's remarks to be completely unnecessary and painful.

In the days to come, Tuite began to push for more and more money. He called me several times on the phone, real sweet, sweet, sweet. Oh, the honey could flow from that man's mouth when he wanted money.

Finally, on December 6, Judge Shadur cleared Richard's release from jail, but ordered him confined to my home on electronic monitors. Trying to block the release, the government played a tape of a phone conversation between Richard and me just days after his arrest. During that call, I had joked that the chance of a movie of Richard's exploits might be helped if he fled. I was never serious, but my comments to Richard nearly exploded in my face. The judge, however, was not swayed by the prosecution's deliberate misapprehension of my words. His response was that it would be ridiculous to think that I would give up the equity in my home to let Richard flee to chase after some pie-in-the-sky Hollywood project.

The government also raised concerns that I would use my skills as a cosmetic surgeon to alter Richard's appearance while living in my house. But then in a strange twist, Judge Shadur came to my defense, saying that it wasn't his place to psychoanalyze me, and he wouldn't let the government do it either. Even Judge Shadur must have seen the shock on my face after his comment!

Tuite's following presentation to Judge Shadur was as weak as well water and frightened me in its lameness. He said there was so much paperwork, the case was so old, Richard's brother and I had put up so much property, that there was just no valid reason to keep Richard in jail. Then he sat down.

But this time, Judge Shadur said the papers pledging the real estate for the bond were in order!

He ruled in our favor!

We had won!

I looked over at Richard, but all I saw was disbelief on his face. I completely understood. We had been fighting so hard and for so very long for this moment.

It was around 3:00 P. M. The judge said, "This is my decision. I don't think he's a flight risk. His family has shown up and I don't think he'll let them down. If you want to appeal, you'll have to go before the Appellate Court. You have one hour before it closes. Otherwise, this man is gone."

The Marshal took Richard to this horrible holding cage and put an electronic monitor on his ankle. It was a bulky, disgusting-looking, tracking device, like one that an animal would be forced to wear on Wild Kingdom, but I didn't care! I was so happy! After Richard was locked up, a Probation Officer took me into another room and instructed me on the use of the home monitoring system. The officer told me that all calls would be taped, and they would come to my home the next morning to be sure that I understood their instructions and knew how to use the device properly. I left the Dirksen Federal Building with the monitor in my hands. In my hands! Richard was still downstairs with the anklet, and I was told to pick him up at the MCI at 6:00 P. M. He was coming home.

I called Trevor from the lobby and told him to pick me up. When he arrived, I said, "I want you to go to Gephardt's (our nicest meat market) and buy Richard a stead and a bottle of the finest wine because he hasn't had a decent meal in weeks… and yes! Fresh flowers… roses… white!"

Then I went to the office.

It was fifteen minutes past four o'clock.

The phone rang.

It was Suzanne Rico from Channel 7 who was always so nice to me. She seemed kind of breathless. "Did you know that Steven Miller is delivering a motion to the 7th Circuit Court of Appeals as we speak, trying to stay your husband's release until the court can review Shadur's decision, and that your husband's lawyer isn't even present?"

"Thank God you called!" was all I could get out before I hung up.

I called Tuite. He was in his office. "What in God's name are you doing in your office when the prosecution is meeting with the three appellate judges?" I shouted, nearly hysterical. I didn't say goodbye, just banged the phone down in disgust.

I tried to calm down by telling myself that the government had no time, that they could not have prepared a good case so fast, but I had a bad feeling. Sure enough, a little before 5:00 P. M. , I got the call.

Bond denied.

Last chance.

In staying the release, the Appeals Court gave the government until Friday, December 9 to file its reason that Richard should be detained. Richard had until December 13 to respond.

The Marshal took Richard's ankle monitor off and that night, he couldn't even talk about it on the phone he was so devastated. Neither could I.

The officer from the court came back the next morning and took the monitor away. I was so crushed I didn't say a word.

When Richard called that night, all I could say was, "I don't believe it… to be that close."

It was all so horrible. And then somehow, I forced myself to keep going.

My mind focused on Pat Tuite, and despite my prayers for the strength to forgive that man, I was unable to do so.

Then things got worse.

The following week, a federal appeals court overruled Judge Shadur's decision and ordered that Richard be permanently denied bond.

There was nothing else anyone could do to get him bonded out. In despair I called Shirley.

That dream was over.

So close to freedom, yet so far away.

Chapter 21

Toward the end of February, I gave up reading the newspapers altogether (even my beloved comics). Tokyo Rose was only adding stress to my already stressed-out existence. Without the media to upset me, I could hold my own, treading water, but I certainly wasn't sinking. Then one morning, just a matter of weeks before Richard's trial was to begin, virtually everything fell completely apart… once again.

I was in my office working when I received a call from Joe Polichemi, an inmate at the Metropolitan Correctional Center where Richard was still being held. "Richard asked me to call you!" he said excitedly, "You need to go to court right away! The U. S. Marshals just came and got him! He's pleading guilty!"

GUILTY?

I was stunned!

"Thanks, bye!" I managed, then slammed the phone down.

The enormity of what a guilty plea meant literally took my breath away. Pat Tuite! Darn him anyway! He knew I would have demanded at least three legal opinions had I been forewarned of this disastrous change of strategy. To top that, Tuite didn't even have the decency to give me proper notice so I could appear in court.

My main concern was Helen Brach. I knew Richard was not guilty of killing that poor woman! Tuite better not have Richard plead guilty to murder when I knew he was innocent!

Guilty!

Of what?

I called a cab and promised the driver a substantial tip to speed to the Federal Building. My mind raced along with the taxi, attempting to find an answer, any logical answer to this seemingly out of control, turn of events. If only I had known what Tuite had advised Richard to do, I kept thinking, Richard would not be pleading guilty, but Tuite never told me. Tuite never even hinted to me. Probably that was why he never told me, I suddenly realized.

Wheels screeching, the taxi arrived at the building I had come to think of as my Bali Hails only active volcano. The Federal Courthouse. I tipped the cabbie and hurried into the courtroom. once again, it was packed with people, the reporters scribbling furiously on their notepads. The hearing had already begun, and it was obvious that the press had known Richard was pleading guilty before I did. Darn it anyway!

I wanted to shout out loud to anyone who would listen, "I never would have allowed Richard to do this, do you understand?" But it was far too late to salvage Tuite's latest game plan. I pulled myself together, and, like always, quietly sat down on the row of bench seats directly behind the defense table.

I settled in just as Judge Shadur was explaining to Richard what it meant to plead guilty, and if he understood Tuite was now requesting a hearing before the bench, meaning there would be no trial, there would be no jury, and be, the judge, would make the final decision regarding the amount of time to be served.

Served?

That meant serve time!

Richard was definitely going to prison!

The beautiful illusion of Bali Hai was gone in an instant replaced by the cold reality of a grey-walled prison girded by razor wire. Now I could only hope the sentence would not be a long one.

Richard's voice was subdued when he answered the judge's next question; "Yes, your Honor, pleading guilty is what my lawyer has told me to do."

Then the judge gave Richard three pages to read. my heart skipped several beats.

Aside from Tuite, Richard's brother and his wife, I was the only person in that courtroom who knew that Richard's reading skills were severely limited, almost nonexistent. Born in poverty with drooping eyelids which caused him to be the brunt of his schoolmates' cruel jokes and which made learning to read an almost impossible task, Richard was passed from grade to grade despite the fact that his reading skills were never developed. His inability to read coupled with his classmates' endless harassments made him a dropout by the ninth grade.

It was a great test of patience for Richard to read a newspaper. He had to sound out each individual word, syllable by syllable, like a school boy just learning to read. When he finally did decipher a word, his vocabulary was so limited, he oftentimes had no idea what the word meant. To think he could breeze through a complicated legal document when I have personally seen him take up to thirty minutes to read one page of the Sunday comics was ridiculous. But I couldn't interfere, I was merely an observer in this burgeoning Roman circus.

Richard glanced at the documents Judge Shadur had handed him, then shot an imploring look at Tuite. A secret message passed silently between them, and I knew Richard was saying, "Pat, I can't do this."

At that moment, Tuite stood up and walked over to the lectern where Richard was standing. I was wondering if Tuite was going to stand there in front of that packed courtroom, point to various words on the document Richard was holding and try to explain complex legal terminology to a man who could not even read it, let alone understand the implications of phrases like, "Surrendering your constitutional right to trial."

I didn't have to wonder for long. Richard entered a plea to a panoply of charges from the indictment, all without having read any of the papers he was still holding in his hands. He pleaded guilty to sixteen of the twenty-nine counts against him, admitting to things like:

1. Conspiring with another person to defraud Carole Karstenson.
2. Working with one Jerry Farmer to defraud Marilyn Jameson.
3. Taking $55, 000 from Joyce Carruthers.
4. Inflating prices of horses.
5. Defrauding Barbara Morris of $50, 000.
6. Taking money from Jean Robinson under false pretenses.
7. Defrauding Linda Holmwood.

After these admissions, there was a pause, and I caught a glimpse of Judge Shadur as he began to question Richard in preparation to accepting his pleas. It was the "cat who just ate the canary" look that I had often seen in my native South Africa when a judge was about to sentence a black person. A chill went down my spine as Judge Shadur asked Richard specifically if he had planned to scam his victims.

"I was trying to get as much money as I could," Richard replied. "I was charging them too much money, that's for sure."

"And when you were charging them, as you put it, 'too much money,' was it your purpose to get more than you knew that the things were worth at the time?"

"Yes," Richard admitted.

At that moment, I felt that our struggles were hopeless, that nothing, nothing good would ever happen for either of us. I wanted to close my eyes, put my hands over my ears for fear that Richard would plead guilty next to any of the charges relating to Helen Brach, but there was no way I could do this. There was no choice but to look and listen as the rest of my lifetime all my hopes and dreams fantasies about Bali Hai were shattered before my eyes. A feeling of impending doom washed over my thoughts, leaving me holding my breath as I had as a fearful child when confronted by the unknown. In the end, I had no reason to worry. Richard did not plead guilty to any of the charges involving Helen Brach.

Neither did Richard admit to proposing marriage to any of his female victims to advance his frauds. A case in point was Linda Holmwood, the alcoholic the prosecution claimed Richard had proposed to in order to make his scam more plausible.

"No, I did not propose marriage," Richard said in a strong voice. "Not as far as saying that I would marry her… I might have told her that she was a classy lady or something like that, certainly."

The disbelief in the courtroom was almost palpable.

What on earth was Pat Tuite doing, allowing Richard to answer questions off-the-cuff like that? Richard was being candid, coming on straight, and Judge Shadur was leading him relentlessly down a path of destruction. I did not know the law, but I felt I knew people, and what was happening to Richard was the most heartless thing one could imagine. For a man with his background and education, the process he was going through was horrendous. Not that he did not deserve punishment for the things to which he was admitting, but that his attorney was standing by while the judge was exacting the most damning testimony possible and putting it into the permanent record of the proceedings.

Shadur also questioned Richard about threatening people while carrying out his swindles.

Richard responded in a strong sincere voice, "I never threatened anyone in my life." Then the judge asked Richard what prison term he thought he faced by pleading guilty and Richard said, "Looks like three and a half to four years."

Yes! That was Tuite's promise! The slip of paper he had written the numbers down on so long ago was still tucked away in the end table by my bed.

Judge Shadur glared down his nose at Richard. "You realize that's not money in the bank," he warned. The silence in the courtroom at that moment was deafening.

Judge Shadur set the hearing date for two and a half months in the future, May 22, to allow time for a Federal Probation officer to write a Presentence Report. It was over for the time being.

I turned around. The spectators were making ready to leave the courtroom. I saw shock and disbelief on their faces, and in so-me cases, pity, whether for me or Richard I had no idea. Then I glanced at the prosecution team. The expressions of the men at Miller's table were of smug little boys who had pulled off an enormous prank without being caught.

Richard Bailey

I looked over at Richard. Like always, he blew me a kiss, then, somewhat dazed, I walked out of the courtroom. Out of the corner of my eye, I spotted Pat Tuite making his way down the hall. My words all came out in a rush: "Pat, what the heck was that all about? Why didn't you give me advance notice? What do you hope to gain?"

Tuite gave me a knowing smile. "The main issue here is Helen Brach. If we can just get the horses out of the way, Richard's sentence should only be thirty-seven to forty-six months, max, just like I told you that first day in my office."

I was so upset by everything I had just witnessed that I didn't even respond. As I walked away, I thought maybe for once Tuite knows what he's doing, but deep down, I didn't trust the man. I couldn't, and irrational or not, I knew it was because of the way he looked at me, a sexual predator at his prey.

I was not surprised to find myself trembling when I walked out of the Federal Building. The stress I lived with was becoming unbearable. I expected the pressure cooker that had become my new home to blow any day.

Alone that night, I finally got around to reading the *Tribune* for the first time in days. In one article, Tuite stated that Richard, by pleading guilty, expected to reduce his prison term. Tuite also said that if Richard prevailed on the procedural points at sentencing, that he could face as little as twenty-seven months in jail. Then why, I had to ask myself, had the judge warned Richard that Tuite's calculations were not "money in the bank?"

Once again, questions and no answers.

Realizing how much I needed resolution which I felt Pat Tuite wouldn't give me, I called my friend Dennis.

"Dennis," I said, after bringing him up-to-date about today's events, "I heard several of the spectators discussing Richard's Bench Trial. What will it be like?"

Dennis sighed in disgust. "First off," he said, "Richard will receive no trial—bench or otherwise. Bench trial is a misnomer being bandied about by our old friend, the media. Once again, they are misleading the public."

"I don't understand!" I snapped, then apologized.

Dennis went on. "What Richard will receive is a Sentencing Hearing in which Judge Shadur will hear witnesses, examine evidence, and then sentence

Richard based upon every single alleged act of his life—whether or not he was ever charged, tried, and/or convicted of such acts."

"That's impossible!" I shouted.

"That's the Feds! Dennis said, raising his voice, "And for the Feds, nothing is impossible… except fairness, of course!"

"Don't joke with me," I pleaded.

"I'm not joking, Annette. Pat Tuite made the mistake of his career today. Richard's exposure here is up to 245 years in prison, plus life! Are you a person who prays?"

"Yes, of course," I whispered.

"Then there's no need to advise you further." The phone clicked softly in my ear.

The day after the hearing, I gave an interview in my office to a local T. V. reporter. In answering one of her questions, I told her that I hadn't known how Richard went about his business until the day before, and how hard that day had been for me. What I didn't mention was that the details of Richard's past were particularly distressing because I did not know the real truth, only the "truth" that Tuite had made Richard agree to in order to "accept responsibility" for his misdeeds of twenty years ago.

I also told her Richard had admitted to me that he had great remorse for what he had done in the past, and that if he had known better or had a better education, he wouldn't have done what he did.

I concluded the interview by saying that "My greatest regret is being in love with someone that I can't be with, but if the sentence is reasonable, then I would wait."

The whole time I was talking to the reporter, I was thinking of Tuite's figures scribbled on the sheet of yellow legal paper—thirty-seven to forty-six months.

Just a few years, I told myself.

Just a few years.

I could wait it out.

Chapter 22

"Years ago, when a reward was placed for a horse thief, the horse thief was caught, the horse thief was hung. Today if there is a reward, you probably become a government witness because that's apparently what is going on in this case." ~ Defense Attorney Ronald Menaker during Opening Statements

Finally!

It was Monday, May 22, 1995, the opening day of Richard's sentencing hearing!

I had survived the two month wait by working around the clock, by visiting Richard at the M. C. C. , and by holding hands with him over the telephone. I was exhausted. The work was demanding, the visits debilitating (due to the Bureau of Prison's constant and malicious interference), and the telephonic hand-holding merited extra effort. Love, even spiritual love, requires energy to survive.

Trevor dropped me off near the Dirksen Federal Building around 9:00 A. M. , and as I walked toward the entrance, I was deep in thought. Surely, I reasoned, this will be the end of the worst of it. Richard will spend a little time on the witness stand, the prosecution will call a few people to testify, and then the judge will sentence him to the thirty-seven to forty-six months. Tuite promised me was the limit Richard could serve. After that, my husband and I could make plans for our future. When Richard and I would actually live as man and wife in the same household all boiled down to Pat Tuite's word.

Pat Tuite, Esq.

Who was he really?

As I walked down the street to the courthouse, I could not help but worry since Tuite's roving eyes settled more on me lately. His questions as well were becoming more personal. I was embarrassed for myself, embarrassed for this attorney who was supposed to be a professional like me.

After Richard's unconscionable guilty plea, I never knew what to expect from Pat Tuite. Logical or not, I worried constantly if he was trying to conceal yet another destructive decision from me.

I chided myself for being paranoid, then paused for a moment before entering the building. What if something terrible and unexpected should happen? What if the judge gave Richard far more time than what Tuite had promised us? What if Richard never got out?

The paper on which Tuite had written the figures he said would determine Richard's sentence was still in my possession, but I wondered if Judge Shadur read the same Sentencing Guidelines Manual Tuite was always quoting.

The pop of an instamatic flash and the sudden glare of a mini-cam's harsh spotlight jerked me back into reality. They were all there waiting, the television people, the news reporters, and the wildly and mildly curious devotees of Tokyo Rose in all her various shapes and forms from *Star* and the *National Enquirer* to the staid *Tribune*. I put on my best tight-lipped smile and climbed up the steps past the boisterous group.

The courtroom was already filled when I arrived; the judge, however, had not yet made his entrance. I noticed the prosecutor, Steven Miller, was huddled with the mysterious investigator, David Hamm, who always seemed to be whispering in Miller's ear like some ill cast Iago warning Brabantio of the transgressions of his daughter, Desdemona.

I had expected something more of the courtroom that day; I didn't know what exactly, but it seemed to me that things were a bit too informal. Reporters were chatting with each other about subjects ranging from pay raises to raising children, and there was an almost carnival air about the gathering. No one looked remotely serious and that seemed somehow wrong. After all, we were entering into the most dangerous and critical phase of the process that would determine exactly how long my husband would have to serve in prison.

Tuite had told me to bring with me that day the clothes that Richard would wear to court, and I was carrying a garment bag containing a dark blue, pinstripe suit, several changes of shirts and black dress loafers which I promptly gave to the Marshals.

The bailiffs had not yet brought Richard in, but Tuite was there, talking with one of the prosecution staff, laughing and occasionally slapping the man on the back as if some great joke were being shared between them. Tuite's attitude changed dramatically when he saw me. He literally turned from the man he was talking to and stared directly at me as though he had been caught with his hands in the cookie jar.

As I took my customary seat behind the defense table, Tuite sprang into action and hurried over, slipping through the little swinging gate that separated the courtroom spectators from those persons who were allowed "before the bar," i. e. , the attorneys, agents, witnesses, courtroom staff and, of course, the defendant, Richard.

"I'm surprised to see you here," Tuite said. "As I told you before, this testimony is going to be very difficult for you to listen to. Miller is going to drag out the worst possible tales about Richard to show to the judge, and believe me, they have some very ugly stories to tell."

I looked Tuite squarely in the eye. "My place is with my husband," I replied, hoping that he would get the hint that his overattentiveness was ill-placed on the wife of this particular defendant.

"Yes, of course," Tuite said, one hand in the air to emphasize his point, "but they are going to bring in a number of the female victims and…"

"Listen, Pat," I said sharply, "I have spoken at length with Jo-Ann Wolfson. She's a highly respected attorney and has known Richard for years. Jo-Anne tells me Miller is going to bring in several women who were supposedly getting ripped off in horse deals with Richard." I paused, glanced over at my husband's empty seat, then went on, "I agree with Attorney Wolfson. These women knew they were paying for Richard's attention when they bought horses from him. What they really wanted was to spend time with an exciting man. You will never convince me that women like Helen Brach, who knew and owned horses for years, did not know if she was being overcharged."

"The prosecution will say swindled," Tuite cut in.

"You sound a bit like the prosecution yourself sometimes, Pat. Now please, hear me out. `Richard and I come from very different backgrounds; he never had my opportunities in life, but there is good in this man. I'm not comparing myself to Jesus, but He forgave and uplifted an adulteress. 'Let he who is without sin cast the first stone, ' He told the masses one day. Now I am certainly not Jesus. Neither am I a saint. Nor am I even a saintly person, but I am a woman who loves her husband, who has forgiven him. and who wants him to pay for his transgressions, so we can get on with our lives…"

Tuite was staring at me in total disbelief. I paused for a moment, out of breath, then went on, "No one knows better than I that sitting in this courtroom will not be easy, but I will no more leave Richard now than I would have back when I thought there was no chance he was not guilty. Richard and I have talked, made amends, and we understand each other. Now you get up here and do your very best for him, and I will stay right here."

"Oh, they are going to tell the truth," Tuite said, a strange smile flickering across his face. "I just wanted to spare you from it all." With that, he spun around and returned to his seat at the defense table.

Although it was past time for court to convene, absolutely nothing was happening in the courtroom which was most surprising. I then learned that the hearing was being delayed so Richard could change into the suit I had just dropped off. Tuite had given me the wrong information. The clothes Richard was to wear for court appearances should have been delivered the Friday before, certainly not the first day of the hearing. Even in this smallest of ways, Tuite was disorganized, and it hurt me to the bone.

When Richard entered the room a short time later, we flashed quick brave smiles at each other, then he took his seat at the table with Tuite. It was so strange to see Richard wearing a stylish suit and silk tie instead of the coarse blue, prison jump suit. My thoughts were: Why, he hasn't changed at all! He looks ready to come home!

As in that moment before the first gusts of the storm, the courtroom became unnaturally silent. The trigger for the change in ambiance was the court reporter who had stood up and was watching the door to Judge Shadur's chambers.

The silence continued for a moment longer and then, with a flourish of his robes, Judge Shadur entered, looking every bit like the actor Vincent Price on his way to straighten up matters in the House of Usher.

"All rise!" the bailiff croaked belatedly, drawing a fierce glare from the judge.

I was hoping that the judge would not start his proceedings in a foul mood and sprang to my feet with the rest of the gallery of onlookers. The attorneys, acting, I suppose, on the sixth sense of survival that they all seemed to possess, were already on their feet, looking attentively at the judge.

I shot a quick look at the prosecution table and noticed that David Hamm, the Illinois State Police Lieutenant, was staring directly at Richard with an enormous grin on his face. I could not ever remember seeing a man who looked as smug as Lt. Hamm.

My brief fixation with Lt. Hamm ended when the judge sat down and in a deep resonant voice, made a short speech ending with:"This is the sentencing hearing for Richard R. Bailey. I am going to accept brief opening statements first from the United States and then from Mr. Bailey's counsel."

Steven Miller stepped up to the lectern and was immediately hit by a fit of hacking coughs. When he'd regained his breath and excused himself, he began the process of taking Richard apart and examining every point of him, at the same time reconstructing him into the monster that Miller wanted the judge to see.

He first told the judge what a fine upstanding person Helen Brach was, how she enjoyed great wealth, had friends and family, loved animals, and was mesmerized by Richard Bailey, a man Miller claimed called her a, "Golden Goose," "a lousy-biff," and "a mark." Then Miller alluded to the fact that after

Mrs. Brach learned that Richard had cheated her, sold her some worthless horses, she'd threatened to report him to the District Attorney's Office. According to Miller, Brach then "dropped off the face of the earth, never to be seen again." But, he added, and at that precise moment, he turned and stared at Richard, an executioner's heartless stare that gave even me chills. "People do not suddenly vanish without reason."

Miller went on to say that one of the people who supplied horses to Richard was Joe Plemmons, and that Plemmons would testify that Richard had solicited him and a good friend to kill Helen Brach. "Plemmons is not a killer," Miller said very precisely, "he is a con man." I felt an involuntary smile creep across my face. The same could be said of Richard, I thought, the very same. For he is certainly no killer.

At the end of Miller's speech, I was left wondering and very confused. There were so many mysteries he never even touched on. Why was there no mention of the policeman I had been reading about for months in the Chicago papers, the policeman Tokyo Rose claimed was directly involved in Brach's disappearance?

And what of horseman Frank Jayne, Jr. of the notorious Jayne Family, who was now listed in the press as being Richard's co-schemer? Why was there no reference made of Jayne whatsoever?

And, of course, there was Jack Matlick, Brach's houseman of many years and supposedly the last man on earth to see her alive. Why was this ex-con, a man many considered to be the prime suspect, left out of Miller's opening statement?

And finally, the most important question of all—who had actually killed Helen Brach? And assuming she was dead, and she had to be, I felt, after so many years, then where was her body?

Without answers to these most important questions, I truly felt that the prosecution could not convict Richard. I looked up at Judge Shadur to see if he agreed with my assessment, but all I saw was a large man with beautiful gray hair and huge bushy eyebrows who looked remarkably like a cross between the God, Zeus, and a Hollywood star of the honor movie genre.

"On behalf of Mr. Bailey, as I understand it, Mr. Menaker?" With these words, the Judge snapped me out of my reverie and back into the courtroom. It was good that he had for it was now our turn.

I was hoping for a powerful opening statement from Tuite, one that would bring the spectators to their feet, but instead, his assistant, Mr. Menaker, began to speak for the defense. Menaker's first ploy was to attack Joe Plemmons and Cathy Olsen who promised to be the government's two most damning witnesses.

Joe Plemmons was a man, Menaker said, who had once worked for Richard and who was going to tell the judge that Richard had offered him money to kill Helen Brach. Menaker pointed out that Plemmons had kept his mouth shut for nearly two decades about the alleged offer, even when there was an opportunity to reel in the huge rewards that were posted at the time Brach disappeared. I thought that was an excellent arguing point and that certainly the judge would agree with me.

Menaker went on to say that Plemmons was a career criminal, that in the seventies, he had stolen four horses from some people, fled in the middle of the night and had been running ever since. With that remark, I could hear an elderly woman cackling behind me. I turned around and managed a coconspirator's smile.

The next most damaging witness would be Cathy Olsen, Menaker said, a woman who had suffered through years of mental problems as well as drugs and alcohol abuse, and who, because of those weaknesses and illnesses, now had a less than finite memory and probably would not be able to back up her statements.

Come on, Miller, I thought, if Plemmons and Olson are all you're going to hit us with, your case is as weak as a politician's promise. But I couldn't dwell on this thought, Menaker was moving ahead.

"There is a person," he was saying, "who could help us in our understanding of Brach's disappearance, and I am not saying anything revolutionary, anything new. That person is Jack Matlick."

I wanted to stand up and cheer.

It was Matlick, I knew, who had forged thousands of dollars of checks after Brach's disappearance and who had helped burn Brach's diaries which, I had always felt, contained incriminating evidence. Hatlick who had cleaned and recarpeted a room in Brach's estate after she vanished… removing blood? More than likely. And Matlick who had helped himself to Brach's safety deposit box when she disappeared and stolen no telling what—jewels, money? And Matlick who also kept a lock of Helen Brach's flaming red hair in his bedroom.

"Jack Matlick," Menaker repeated ominously, then went on, "Matlick was Brach's reputed lover and is the likely suspect in this case, not Richard Bailey."

Yes, yes, I thought to myself, but just as my hopes began to rise, Judge Shadur deflated them with one quick question by asking Menaker, "No Federal jurisdiction on Matlick, right?" So, there it was.

Everybody in the courtroom felt, knew Matlick was the murderer, but he was not going to be tried, And Richard would be the surrogate target of the prosecution.

I knew at that moment my hope to bring the truth, the whole truth and nothing but into that courtroom was a ridiculous dream.

Whatever Menaker was trying to sell, Judge Shadur wasn't buying. The expression on the judge's face was one of complete boredom and disbelief, and I began to feel for sure that Richard was going to get the full forty-eight-month sentence. Tuite's fault, I thought. he defense through Mr. Menaker had put on a sensible counter attack through a lengthy dissertation.

The hearing ended abruptly when the judge declared a five-minute break. As his Honor left the courtroom, I noticed that State Policeman Hamm was staring at me intently and shaking his head. Richard turned around, saw Hamm, and turned back to me. Richard was obviously puzzled. It occurred to me right then that there was something going on with this man Hamm that Richard did not know about. I wondered what sort of evil surprise Lt. Hamm, like all the other men gathered around Prosecutor Miller, would try to spring on us. Just one more mystery, I thought, but all thoughts of Hamm disappeared when court resumed minutes later, and Miller began to present the government's evidence against Richard. First came Marie Holmwood Jablonski who testified that Richard was the cause of her mother's drinking problems. Ridiculous. No one person can make any other person drink. Richard certainly didn't hold a gun to that woman's head and insist she drink champagne in his office as miller would have had us believe. The daughter also said that what money Richard did not take the wine merchants did until her mother finally lost everything.

Next came Lance Williamson who met Richard when Williamson worked for Frank Jayne, Jr. This witness said that Richard would often show up at the stable with women he wanted to sell horses to, then lie about the value of the horses and their pedigrees.

John Staren, a sometimes commodities broker who had been investigated several times for his activities on the commodities market, told Judge Shadur and all present that he thought Richard was a violent man because he saw Richard take money from a man at a horse show by strongarm robbery. Most of the reporters in the courtroom chuckled at the thought of the diminutive Richard Bailey as a strongarm robber.

After these witnesses, I was exhausted and ready to go home, but they were just the government's opening shots.

There was much, much more to come that day.

Chapter 23

"I've sold horses that did not exist... I've sold horses by placing fraudulent papers with the horses... I have sold one horse to two people... I have written bad checks...I have probably done everything that you can imagine..."~ Joe Edward Plemmons during Direct Examination

After a brief recess, one of the government's star witnesses, Joe Plemmons, took the stand. Like a trained predatory bird, he perched on the edge of the witness chair, tinted blonde hair parted down the middle, leering at Richard as he waited for his handler to launch the attach. Plemmons didn't have long to wait. Miller stepped to his side, and very quickly, the witness began to tell the packed courtroom some of the wildest stories one could possibly imagine. It was black comedy with Steven Miller throwing out the lines, and from the laughter I heard and the expressions I saw on people's faces, Plemmons was a successful albeit a vicious performer.

Richard, more solemn that I had ever seen him, sat very still, chin in hand, legs crossed, and never once during the next two hours did he take his eyes off Joe Plemmons.

Plemmons cheerfully admitted that after he was introduced to the Chicago horse world, that he "had never seen people with so much money," and that he found the equestrian set to be "dangerous and exciting." He had remained in the horse business all his adult life, he said, and during that time, had participated in a seemingly endless variety of horse swindles.

Without a doubt, Plemmons was the most cheerful enthusiastic witness I had ever seen. In fact, he was so eager to answer the persecutor's questions regarding his misdeeds that at one point, Miller had to reprimand him. "You'll have to let me finish the question!" Surely the judge would not be taken in by this witness's boyish charm and his overly sincere voice, I thought, but as time passed, I became frightened I had made a mistake. Like elevator music, Plemmon's high-pitched, Southern drawl seemed to smooth out the tension in the courtroom. Even as he described a life of treachery, Plemmons' voice was Muzak for the masses.

There were many references to Richard and horse swindles, but the only damning part of Plemmons' testimony with regard to Richard concerned an alleged luncheon that took place in February 1977. Plemmons claimed that he, Richard and Kenneth Hansen (Plemmon's best friend, then awaiting trial for killing three boys), were seated around a table when Richard allegedly confided that he was in trouble, that "the Candy Lady wasn't so sweet anymore," and that he thought she was "going to go to the authorities." Richard, according to Plemmons, then threw out an offer of $5, 000 to do away with Brach. Richard didn't just want Brach dead, Plemmons added, "He wanted no one to ever find her."

At that precise instant, I remembered a long walk Richard and I took in Kohler, Wisconsin. We had paused to hug under a large shade tree, but Richard had pulled away when an ant began to crawl up his arm. Instead of killing the pest like most men would do, Richard bent down and gently flicked the insect off his arm onto the grass. Would such a man try to arrange for the murder of a friend? I didn't think so.

I was snatched back to the present as Plemmons related that Hansen then said he wouldn't kill an old lady. After that remark, according to Plemmons, Hansen left to go to the restroom, and Richard then asked Plemmons if he was interested in the job. Plemmons said he replied that he "wasn't into killing people, either."

Plemmons went on to say that on the drive home after the lunch meeting, Hansen admitted that he was insulted he hadn't been included in the Brach con, and that now, for a mere $5, 000, he was expected to dig Richard out of a hole.

Despite Miller's previous warning, Plemmons was still so anxious to convict Richard that he continued to answer the prosecutor's questions even before they were asked:

Q. "And by the way, on the ride home after you dropped Mr. Bailey off…"

A. "We talked about it."

Q. "Did you and Mr. Hansen talk about it?"

A. "Yes."

After that major slipup, I looked around the courtroom and saw more than a few embarrassed smiles. It was obvious to everyone that Plemmons was reciting a script he had rehearsed with Miller many times. A few people were giggling, but I could not join in. Too much was at stake for Richard and me.

My mind was taking in and sorting the words of this admitted liar, assimilating them, trying to reach a logical conclusion. It was an impossible task. There was no logic. If what Plemmons was saying was true, and he was so concerned about Helen Brach's fate, then why hadn't he told the authorities about the solicitation twenty years ago when the woman disappeared? I would have done so! Then I realized it would have been pointless to contact the police if the conversation had never taken place!

The facts were staring Judge Shadur in the face: Plemmons had kept his mouth shut about the alleged offer for nearly two decades! A long time. Even when there was an opportunity to collect hundreds of thousands of dollars in reward money posted at the time of Brach's disappearance, Plemmons remained silent. An admittedly greedy man of no loyalty, Plemmons remained silent! There was no credibility here that I could see because of Plemmons' previous diverse positions, but I only had to wait a few moments for the pieces of the puzzle to fall into place and to allow the truth to be clearly seen.

According to Plemmons, it was in 1992 that he first learned of a Federal probe in Chicago into horse killings for insurance money. At the time, Plemmons was in custody in Sacramento, awaiting trial for selling a horse that didn't exist. When Federal agents flew to California to speak to Plemmons, his current girlfriend was out on bond for helping with the fraud.

Then came a totally incredible bit of intellectual legerdemain: During the first interview with the agents, Plemmons did not speak up about Richard's alleged solicitation to murder Helen Brach. He had hoped, he said, he could work a deal with the government about the Chicago horse frauds without turning over another card. But he learned soon enough that the agents weren't interested in what he had to say regarding mere horse swindles.

Then came a second interview, Plemmons said, this time with agents from the Bureau of Alcohol, Tobacco and Firearms (ATF). This meeting was a little different and focused on arson activity within the equestrian industry with only a passing mention of Richard selling Brach several horses. But again, the agents offered Plemmons no concrete deals. Why not? I quickly figured it out. Because what Plemmons had to say lacked the information the government needed to convict Richard!

This left Plemmons with a major problem: Unless he could work out a deal with Miller, he and his girlfriend would be facing stiff prison sentences. Plemmons desperately needed to offer information to Miller in exchange for his freedom, but at the same time, he also needed to convince the prosecutor he was worried about his safety. The reason for this latter ploy was to get into the Federal Witness Protection Program.

Plemmons testified that he finally decided to divulge the alleged conversation he had with Richard and Hansen in exchange for the help he desired. In the end, both Plemmons and Miller got everything they asked for.

First, Plemmons' girlfriend's sentence was reduced from a felony to a mere misdemeanor, something Plemmons very much wanted. Then the U. S. Attorney's office in Chicago sent a letter to Plemmons' sentencing judge recommending that he be given a departure on his sentencing guideline, which the judge ultimately did. There was also a cash payment to Plemmons, and the government paid for a hernia operation as well as for other personal needs. The grand total was in the thousands of dollars.

But that was not the end of it.

There was still another reason for Plemmons to fabricate the luncheon conversation. Something of great interest to Plemmons, and of course, very lucrative. A well-connected writer had informed him that people in Hollywood were very much interested in the Helen Brach case. Plemmons decided he could either hire a professional to write a book about his connection with the case, or someone might be interested in buying his rights if eventually a movie was made about Brach. Yes, Plemmons admitted to Judge Shadur, the first $90,000 would have to go to the victims he had defrauded in a lifetime of crime, but after that, any extra money would be his. So, Plemmons' testimony against Richard was extremely important. Only by testifying would there be the crucial nexus between Plemmons and Brach.

With this revealing testimony, Miller was finished with his witness. Tuite straightened his tie and stood up while I tried to remain calm. Tuite began his cross examination by asking Plemmons if it was true that for years, he had hurt innocent people in order to benefit himself. Smiling pleasantly, Plemmons admitted very quickly that indeed he had. With that admission, I understood Miller's strategy for the first time.

By having Plemmons readily admit to past crimes, both to the prosecution as well as to the defense, the government had successfully diffused the ticking bomb before it exploded. Oh, Tuite hammered away at Plemmons alright, but his thunder got him nowhere. Tuite scored no points. Worse. Tuite did such an ineffective job that the judge had to lecture him on arguing with the witness and even pointed out that Tuite needed to frame his questions correctly. At one point, after Judge Shadur instructed Tuite he had to pose a clear question in order to be understood, Tuite balked, saying that was a decision left up to the witness.

"No, no," Judge Shadur angrily replied, "it's for you to pose an intelligible question!" I was so mortified by the judge's remark and Tuite's lack of skills that I wanted to crawl under my seat.

That day, I left the courtroom with more questions than answers. There was only one person who could help me sift through the day's contradictions. Late that afternoon, I got word to my friend Dennis to phone me ASAP, that I needed to talk. The call came through late that same evening.

I explained to Dennis all that happened on the first day of court, and then asked how Plemmons, who was obviously lying, could have been privy to so many details with regard to Richard.

Dennis chuckled. "Simple. The feds schooled him."

"Schooled him? You mean told him what to say? But that's illegal!"

"Right." Dennis was speaking softly now, like a conspirator in some dark backroom meeting. "Of course, the Feds can't tell a witness what to say on the stand, so here's what happens. one set of agents meets with Plemmons, hears his story, and tells him it's not good enough to get any time off his sentence, whatever. Then a different set of agents meets with Plemmons and tells him what they're really looking for—someone who had a specific conversation with Richard on such and such a day and at such and such a restaurant with so and so present. For that person, the agents promise, there are no limits to the assistance the prosecution will give: cash, tax incentives, time cuts, immunity from other prosecutions for the witness or for his friends and relatives. And, if the witness can make a convincing argument that his life would be in danger if he were to cooperate… something that's always good for the jury to hear… then the Feds will throw in the gravy train of the Federal Witness Protection Program."

"The Witness Protection Program?" I echoed, completely blown away by what Dennis was saying.

"You got it… Now, I'm talking name, being set up in business, financial support, free medical, dental, optical insurance, free housing or down payments on new housing, clothes, trips, etc. , etc. , ad nauseum."

"And then?"

"Then comes the last set of agents, once again from a different federal or state agency, and the 'witness' lays out the story he was told is the only saleable one. After this, the prosecutor is called in, the testimony is sworn and presented again to a Grand Jury. By the time the witness hits the stand, he has tuned his story like an Irish Harp, and it literally sings."

I was so taken back by what Dennis had said I was unable to speak.

"Annette, are you okay?" Dennis asked finally.

"I…I…I suppose I am… But what about Richard?"

"What?"

"Make no mistake, Annette. Lucifer is on the court, it's his ball in play, he owns the referees, and the game has already been won. Except for a miracle, Richard is going to prison for life."

"But he's innocent!" I wailed.

"That's irrelevant," Dennis said quickly, "and unimportant. What counts is what the witnesses say, and they don't have to be fully believable; they just have to pile up a mountain of words that is higher than Richard's. In a hearing without a jury, what Tuite insisted Richard be subjected to, the truth of the matter is measured by the relative height of the opposing testimonies."

"That's crazy!" I said, my voice rising.

"That's what you should have told your congressman when he voted for the Federal Guidelines," Dennis said evenly. "You and one hundred million others forgot to stand up and be counted, but you don't need the lectures on citizenship right now... sorry."

"Don't apologize; you're right." I paused, smiled, then decided to feed Dennis' already considerable ego "again," I added lamely.

Dennis snorted. "God, now you're conning me! Look, get some rest, say your prayers, and lay out your court clothes for tomorrow's session. It will be another bad one I suspect, and you'll need some reinforcement and support. Is someone going with you tomorrow?"

"Yes, very definitely yes..."

"Then good night, Dennis."

"Good night, Dennis."

On the second day of Plemmons' testimony there Was one breakthrough that I thought of interest. Plemmons said that he could recall neither the name of the restaurant the three men had visited when the alleged solicitation took place nor anything about it. All he could remember about the eatery was that there were tables, chairs, plates, silverware, and waiters.

Plemmons had to be lying!

The widely accepted truth is that when someone experiences a traumatic event, like the assassination of President Kennedy, one tends to remember the details of their surroundings with crystal clarity. For Plemmons to remember nothing about the restaurant where he claimed a solicitation for murder took place (name, location, furnishings, etc.) was really revealing;revealing because Plemmons obviously concocted the chilling dialogues with Richard out of whole cloth. He could not remember the restaurant because it did not exist, it never had. Plemmons was earning promised benefits from the federal government and augmenting his hopes of a future movie or book deal by lying to a Federal Judge.

It was that simple and that complex.

All Judge Shadur had at the end of Plemmons' testimony was his "word," words from a mouth that had first told Federal Agents that he was privy to something to do with horse fraud in Chicago, then adding arson, and finally tacking on Richard and the alleged solicitation. Why? To get out of jail, to get his girlfriend out of jail, to collect a substantial amount of money and to receive other benefits. Even a three-year-old judge could look at Plemmons' track record and understand what had happened where this witness was concerned.

Bali Hai was neither mist nor substance on my horizon.

I even began to doubt it had ever graced my imagination. I was very depressed with all that I had witnessed and all that I had learned.

As I struggled to fall asleep that night, words sang out loud and clear: "THOU SHALT NOT BEAR FALSE WITNESS."

Chapter 24

The lady(s) cloth protest too much, me thinks.

After Plemmons finished testifying, Miller was suddenly wearing an exceptionally broad, Cheshire cat grin, then he brought in the first of the elderly women he had groomed as stand-ins for the missing Helen Brach. Tuite, of course, remained seated, staring down at the table in front of him. I could not help but think that Miller was giving everyone the impression he was a perfect gentleman while Tuite came off as someone who had no respect for women.

As the hearing progressed, Miller employed the females from Richard's past quite effectively to show how Richard had "used" women. The first of these little old ladies threw me off balance. It seemed incongruous to me that the elderly woman with short white hair sitting before me could ever have attracted Richard. Then I remembered that the two had met twenty-five years earlier when both she and Richard were in that thirty-forty-something-ish area. The infamous "Midlife Crisis Zone" in which last flings occur. It was understandable. As we face the onset of middle age with its frightening specter of long nights alone, many of us are afflicted.

The difference was that because of this vulnerability, these women had been defrauded. Yes, there, had been frauds, I agreed, but for the most part, the ladies had settled their grievances with Richard by civil suits. Somehow the government had been able to bring the same suits up in court once again. I would have thought this was double jeopardy, but it seemed any subversion of the law was possible under the R. I. C. O. statute.

My friend Dennis, who had surprised me by showing up in court, was sitting behind me, and touched my shoulder. I turned around and whispered, "Are these twenty-year-old frauds serious enough crimes to merit a life sentence?"

"They shouldn't be," Dennis said and chuckled softly. "Look, if a man in his fifties takes up with a bimbo in her twenties, and she gets him to buy her a car and a condo in exchange for her company, then she up and dumps him, what does society do?"

"Laughs and looks the other way?"

"Right! In Richard's case, society didn't look the other way because the gender and the age difference were reversed. Richard was the young 'have-not' while the older women were the 'haves,' and make no mistake, they wanted to have Richard, both as escort and lover. But when Richard got the car and the condo, so to speak, and dumped the women, everyone became angry. It's a double standard. Society is used to the young woman/older man relationship, and the fact that the young woman's company is, in one way or the other, 'purchased.'"

"The difference…"

"The difference in Richard's case was that he was the younger consort and a man, and he took his escort fee out in horse transactions. It was a good working arrangement. Since the women didn't want to pay a gigolo's fee, they helped Richard make money on his deals instead. Their monetary 'gifts,' they reasoned, made him love them all the more."

"But that's not too terribly smart."

"Smart has nothing to do with it! Let's go back to the bimbo and the fifty-year-old man. The man gives her money and expensive gifts to buy her love; the young girl, in turn, 'sells' her company to the older man. Neither is guilty of prostitution, but the net result is the same: time, love, and sex are purchased."

I cringed but nodded in agreement and Dennis went on, tapping his finger lightly against the back of my seat. "Remember this important fact: The same wealth and power many men use to manipulate young women, they also use to protect the older ones. The protection of the 'mother' image is a shared male conscience in America, and you better believe Shadur is going to protect those older women now, today, in his courtroom, because they are most assuredly, 'mother' images."

My heart skipped a beat. "Then Richard's in a worse position than I suspected?" It was hard to keep my voice at a whisper level.

"Unless Tuite et al. can make the point with the judge that I just made with you, that in the past, these women were basically 'renting' Richard Bailey… yes."

"God…"

"He could help," Dennis said, smiling.

Chapter 25

Tuite: "(Arthur Katz) It's your testimony that this police officer said to your father: 'I don't want to hear anything about discussing the race horses. I believe it's the houseman (Jack Matlick) that did it. ' That's what you are telling this Court?"

Katz: "He kept pushing the story about what he knew about the houseman."

Tuite: "So, is it your testimony, sir, that that police officer just didn't even want to talk to your father about this alleged information that he had?"

Katz: "That's correct."

In a counterpoint to the prosecution's carefully orchestrated ballet of these very shaky witnesses, still another witness took the stand who began to pick away at Richard's past.

Arthur Katz.

This somber-faced, flashily dressed son of William Katz, a Chicago engraver of cemetery markers, testified that his father had erected an elaborate family crypt for Helen Brach in Ohio, even including gravestones for her dogs, Candy and Sugar. Speaking softly in a clipped Midwestern accent, Katz also claimed that Brach had visited his father in their place of business a short time before she disappeared, and he had overheard their entire conversation while standing in a shared office.

Katz alleged that on that particular day, Brach complained vehemently to his father about Richard, saying he had conned her out of some money she paid for horses. The elder Mr. Katz, who Arthur Katz admitted was a close friend of Brach's, offered to accompany her to the State's Attorney's Office to report Richard when she was released from the Mayo Clinic, and Brach, Katz claimed, agreed.

So, much had been made out of what would have happened if Brach had actually gone to the authorities and reported Richard, and how there would have been a big investigation which would ultimately have sealed his doom, that I could not help but smile.

It was all baloney!

Factually what would have happened if Helen Brach had spoken with the State's Attorney's office was exactly what had transpired in every other case that involved Richard and a wealthy woman who thought she had been conned: Brach would have complained, the prosecutors would have called it a civil matter, and there would have been a civil suit and a cash settlement.

Richard knew that, and William Corwin, Richard's former stables manager, had said as much in his testimony earlier that day. Corwin claimed that Richard told him early in 1977 that Brach might be moving her horses from his facility because she felt she had been swindled. Richard, Corwin said, felt at the time that Brach might sue him.

Sue him.

Nothing more.

As I sat in the courtroom listening to Katz talk on and on about how Helen Brach had planned to accompany his father to meet with state officials and report Richard, I wondered if anyone believed Brach's wealth and position would have caused the State's Attorney's Office to begin an investigation. If so, this was flawed reasoning. Practically every woman Richard had ever dated was extremely wealthy, some even wealthier than Helen Brach! None of them could move the State to prosecute Richard criminally,

During the course of his testimony, Katz kept changing the amount of time that had elapsed between the date he alleged Brach spoke of reporting

Richard and the time she ultimately disappeared. Katz set dates that were thirty to fifty days before her disappearance. There was a "to do" in the courtroom over those inconsistencies, but I didn't think it made one bit of difference. The problem with Katz's statement about Brach's alleged promise to his father was obvious. The time frame was illogical. What person would be angry enough to put someone in prison, but would wait five minutes, let alone the fifty days Katz swore to on the stand, before making a move? Katz's lesser estimate of thirty days was no better; it would have put Helen Brach and Richard together in New York, ringing in the New Year with Brach picking up all the tabs.

No matter how Katz wiggled, the timing did not add up.

This inconsistency brought up still another unanswered question. Why would Brach treat Richard to this fabulous time in New York, spend thousands and thousands of dollars on him, if she were planning to put her "dream date" in jail? Surely the judge was not going to believe such pathetic offerings.

I had several other observations regarding Katz's testimony. In the first place, a lot of it was hearsay, and in the second place, it was hearsay from a deceased person, Katz's father. Finally, it was hearsay testimony from a deceased person that was not presented to the authorities at the time the alleged conversations took place and therefore, none of it would have been admissible at a regular trial!

If only Richard had been given what the Constitution guaranteed every American citizen: a jury trial!

As I listened to Katz's testimony winding down, I suddenly realized there was yet another unanswered question staring us in the face and Tuite was just sitting on it. Why was William Katz, the only person who ever admitted to living with Helen Brach, who visited her regularly both in Florida and Ohio, who vacationed on her houseboat, why was this individual, who had, in his son's own words, "a very good, close friendship" (with Brach), never questioned as one of the possible suspects in her disappearance? Another mystery? Or another coverup? Maybe the truth was not being sought, or when the true picture was found, it did not fit in the big frame the prosecution had constructed.

I also had to ask myself why Arthur Katz had kept this alleged conversation between Brach and his father a secret for almost twenty years. True, the younger Katz had written a letter to the administrator of Brach's estate way back in 1979 when he was seeking reward money, but he never mentioned Richard. If I were trying to collect a reward and knew who the suspect was, I would put his name at the top of the page! Who would not? A person who did not have the name, that's who.

It was also true that an investigator stopped by to talk with William Katz after Brach disappeared, but apparently the officer, believing Matlick was the murderer, disregarded Katz's information, never followed up, and both father and son simply let the matter drop.

If Arthur Katz truly was the law-abiding citizen he claimed he was, it would have been his civic duty to go to the authorities and report what he knew. I would! Who would not? The person who didn't have a fact or a clue, that's who! Not one word of Katz's testimony made any sense.

Arthur Katz was the last person to testify that day, and never in my life had I seen a witness so anxious to leave the courtroom. Why was he in such a rush, I had to wonder, thinking of all the mysteries piling up before me.

As I walked out of the Federal Building, I recalled Katz's testimony and found it to be flimsy, but the judge later gave it great credibility, like it was prearranged. People might hate me for saying this, but it's what I believed. I asked myself over and over why Katz didn't go to the police in February or March or April 1977 when Brach simply vanished from the face of the earth? If not the police, why didn't he seek out someone in authority and insist on being heard?

These were questions that would plague me until I could prove he was simply another false witness.

Chapter 26

Tuite (Ms. Olsen): "Would it be correct to state that because of the pressures that you have had in your life and the abuse that you've given your body because of these drugs, that you don't remember a lot of things?"

Olsen: "To certain degrees, yes."

Tuite: "You have made things up, have you not, if you thought it would be to your advantage?"

Olsen: "Yes."

Disturbing admissions on cross examination were to be the entire substance of the next person to testify, Cathy Olsen.

Olsen was yet another government paid informant, a witness for hire. Daughter of the notorious Chicago horseman, Frank Jayne, Jr., she was once a stunning woman. I knew faces and I knew bones and I could tell. Now she had the timeworn face of a vintage bag lady, and when she walked over to the witness stand, her gait was the slow and unsteady shuffle of a mentally disturbed person.

Once Olsen was seated, I looked into her tired, expressionless eyes and could not rule out that she was suffering from withdrawal symptoms or had sustained brain damage from prolonged alcohol or drug abuse. The image of an egg sizzling in a flying pan popped into my mind, but perhaps she had taken a mood-altering drug before she showed up. There was no way to tell.

Testifying under AUSA. Miller's grant of immunity, Olsen began to relate a pitiful tale of hard drinking, hard men, and hard drug abuse. I had seen women like her before in my volunteer work with the poor. She had traded her love for liquor, her teeth for narcotic prescriptions and ultimately, the balance of her self-respect for a free ride in Steven Miller's highly personalized witness program.

For the hearing, she was wearing a floral-print blouse and blue denim skirt purchased with money the government had given her. Someone had obviously styled her hair in an attempt to soften her appearance; long blonde curls framed her face, but the image was still that of an empty-eyed woman staring out at you from an American Gothic painting. Even though I knew she was bent on destroying our lives, I had to feel sorry for her.

But I felt even sorrier for Cathy Olsen when I learned that Miller had given her money, tax payers' dollars, before she testified, money she probably used to keep her drug addiction going. As a matter of fact, I soon learned that Olsen had been on the government's payroll (and free drug wagon) since 1990 when she hooked up with David Hamm and two ATF Agents! Why the government fed Olsen's habit instead of sending her to a drug rehabilitation center remains a pathetically sad mystery.

No wonder, I thought, that America is losing Reagan's War on Drugs!

Our own government is one of pushers!

Speaking in a slurred, husky voice, Olsen testified that she gave Brach her very first riding lesson back in the seventies and later warned the wealthy widow that her father, Frank Jayne, had sold her some worthless horses. Brach, Olsen said, confronted Jayne about the swindle, and the horseman retaliated by giving Olsen a severe thrashing for not keeping her "blanking mouth shut."

With this statement, Olsen's eyes darted around the courtroom as if she were looking for her father. I thought perhaps if he were there, she was afraid held drag her off the witness stand for yet another beating. Richard had told me stories of Frank Jayne yanking Cathy off a horse she hadn't ridden properly, then throwing her onto the ground and whipping her. Olsen was traumatized by fear, and I knew she would always be looking over her shoulder for her abusive father.

Olsen went on to say that also in the late seventies, she had been working in her father's outer office when Helen Brach walked inside Jayne's inner sanctum and complained once more about the worthless horses. With her father, Olsen said, were two men: a policeman and Richard. With the mention of Richard's name, my heart began to pound.

Further, Olsen said, she occasionally worked inside a medicine closet in her father's outer office where she prepared illegal drugs for horses. The syringes and pills, she told us, were used to hide lameness or temperament problems from potential customers. Olsen claimed that sometime before Brach's disappearance, that she was working inside the closet and overheard Jayne, Richard, and the same policeman discussing the candy heiress. The gist of the conversation was that Brach "knew too much" and needed "to be shut up." Olsen revealed that Jack Matlick, Brach's chauffer, was also present during this second meeting, information she had never spoken of before.

As the minutes ticked by, I found myself straining to hear this important testimony, but due to Olsen's dentures and whatever other reasons, it was becoming increasingly more difficult to understand what she was saying. To make matters worse, she began to leave words out of her sentences, especially "I." It was as if Cathy Olsen had no ego.

Shortly after Brach disappeared, Olsen further testified, she was again working in the small closet and overheard still another conversation. This time the policeman told her dad and Richard that Brach was (now) "shut up." With this remark, the courtroom became very quiet as if all the spectators had suddenly stopped breathing.

I, too, was taken back by Olsen's comments but her testimony didn't add up. What were the odds that on three separate occasions Olsen "would just happen" to be working in her father's busy office and "would just happen" to overhear the same three men talking in three consecutive meetings, meetings in which she claimed she heard them (1) speak with an angry Helen Brach; (2) say Brach knew too much and had to be shut up; and (3) announce that she was shut up. Taking into consideration the fact that Olsen had a very busy work schedule at the stable, giving lessons, medicating horses and relaying phone messages, the chances against her overhearing the three alleged conversations in the manner and time frames she described had to be astronomical. She was simply not credible.

Administering illegal drugs to horses also created another credibility problem for me. What reliable person would willfully and knowingly inject a foreign substance into defenseless animals just to make them saleable or useable? Such a person couldn't have a conscience or any integrity, but Olsen's testimony was having a devastating effect on Richard and myself. Even today many people despise Richard because they think he killed horses. In truth, not a single witness during the hearing said Richard ever hurt a horse. Cathy Olsen was a liar. Bought and paid.

There was endless proof of Olsen's mendacities. During the time frame when she claimed she overheard the chilling remarks in her father's office, she admitted she was addicted to marijuana and alcohol. In fact, Olsen testified that when Brach disappeared, her regular routine was to smoke marijuana, drink beer and tequila all at the same time! Such a combination would have a permanent effect on a person's memory, and Olsen's memory, insofar as Richard was concerned, was critical. Her testimony, like Plemmons' earlier, was supposed to back up Miller's claims that there had been a plot to do away with Helen Brach.

There was a long, long list of admissions on Olsen's part that also negated her credibility:

1. Olsen admitted that she had allowed kids to sell drugs out of her apartment, that she was instrumental in selling these drugs, receiving a commission on their sales, and that she was getting drugs from these children to use herself.
2. Olsen admitted that she had herself committed to a mental hospital to avoid going to jail.
3. Olsen admitted that for over five years she took money from the Bureau of Alcohol, Tobacco and Firearms (ATF) in exchange for information, money she spent on drugs.

4. Olsen admitted she wrote bad checks, all while under the supervision of ATF Agents who were giving her money and to whom she also lied.
5. Olsen admitted she tried to kill herself twice, in the seventies with aspirin and with sleeping pills in 1990, which she later admitted was actually cocaine.
6. Olsen admitted she "made up stories" to get into a mental facility, then to get out.

And was Cathy Olsen making up stories when she testified before Judge Shadur? The facts spoke for themselves. Up until September 11, 1990, when the police added Richard to her testimony, she had never stated in three previous police interrogations that either Richard or Matlick was present at the meetings in her father's office in which Brach was discussed. Her sworn testimony before Judge Shadur added both men to the confab. Her schooling was blatantly obvious, but when the prosecution was finished, Olsen's lies were on the record.

Then it was our turn. When Tuite first elicited the name of the man who had written the statement Olsen read at the Grand Jury in 1990, my heart nearly stopped.

David Hamm.

Lt. David Hamm of the Illinois State Police. It was then that I reassessed my previous thoughts that Olsen was looking about for her father as she testified. Perhaps I had been wrong... perhaps she was really looking for Lt. Hamm to get his approval of her "improved" testimony.

During her Grand Jury appearance, Olsen, reading from the statement prepared by Hamm, said she had walked into her father's office and overheard one conversation.

One.

Today she swore she was hidden in a medicine closet on two occasions and was working in the outer office on a third occasion to overhear a total of three conversations!

Obviously, Lt. Hamm was making adjustments to Olsen's "sworn" testimony, changing the facts to fit the needs of the prosecution.

Also, when reading the statement Hamm had written, Olsen swore to the Grand Jury that when she walked into her father's office, he was saying, "You ought to do something about her (Brach). She ought to be dead."

Today Olsen swore she had never heard her father make those statements!

But seconds later, Olsen admitted to Judge Shadur that she couldn't remember whether her father had made those comments or not. Whew! It was impossible to keep track of all the contradictions! I was beginning to think of Olsen's testimony as "Variations on a Theme." But a peek over at Steven Miller revealed that his face wasn't even red. All I saw was a confident confidence man, his paisley tie laid carelessly across his chest.

Tuite interrupted my thoughts about Miller by asking Olsen to tell the judge the types of stories she claimed she had "made up" to be admitted to a mental hospital only one short month ago. The witness replied she told the staff she was hallucinating and hearing people's voices. This set of lies (on top of everything else), was particularly disturbing! Was Olsen truly hallucinating or was that just a coverup attempt styled by one of her government pushers? Certainly, Miller would not want his star witness committed a matter of days before a high-profile case! It would destroy her credibility!

With these thoughts, a myriad of questions raced through my brain: Was Olsen hallucinating when she thought she saw Richard in her father's office? Or was she just lying?

Was Olsen "hearing things" when she testified, she heard the three men discuss the fate of Helen Brach? Or was that, too, just another lie?

I might as well have tossed a coin to find out the answers because there was simply no formula to discover the truth where Olsen was concerned.

The sad thing was that this admitted liar was destroying my husband. The scene was all too horrible, yet the judge was letting it go on… and on… and on.

Tuite kept going back to Olsen's previous statements.

She claimed she had little memory of a 1989 interview with the Glenview Police Department and an Illinois State Police officer in which she made no mention of Richard being present when the alleged conversations about Brach took place. This man, one Carl Anderson, interviewed Olsen extensively before she met David Hamm and his ATF buddies, and in the Anderson statement, she never brought up Richard Bailey.

The only untainted testimony Olsen ever gave and now she said she couldn't remember.

Her revelations were amazing! She couldn't remember what she said six years ago, but she could remember with stunning clarity what she heard twenty years ago!

With Safer handling the recross, he asked Olsen if anyone from the federal government had appeared before a judge and resolved any of her current cases.

When Olsen replied that they hadn't, I received a sharp jab on my shoulder from my friend Dennis.

"What a cute bit of footwork!" Dennis whispered.

"What do you mean?"

"Olsen's been schooled. Before you can get into the Witness Protection Program, all charges against you have to be dropped! Olsen had to know the facts but was probably told to not mention this in court."

I closed my eyes and tried not to hear whatever testimony Olsen was continuing to give. I already knew what I thought of the witness and what she had testified to and had reached my own conclusions.

I believed with all my heart that for the purpose of Richard's hearing, that Olsen had been helped to make up the additional conversations she now said she heard almost twenty years ago. She had already admitted to Judge Shadur that in all of her statements and testimony prior to May 24, 1995 that she had only mentioned hearing one conversation when she walked into her father's office to give him a phone message.

I also believed that because Olsen had cases pending against her she had been forced to expand on what she told the agents five years previous by including Richard in each brand-new lie.

I thought Olsen was also given additional dialogues to repeat for each meeting, very simple dialogues, dialogues she could remember to say in court even under pressure: that she heard the men say they needed to shut Brach up, and that they had shut her up.

The purpose of Olsen's sworn but perjured testimony was astonishingly clear even without Dennis' input. Due to a legal technicality, her father, Frank Jayne, had never been indicted along with the other defendants. As far as Brach was concerned, Jayne was "untouchable." What Olsen achieved by mentioning her father's presence at the meetings was to "nail" him theoretically; by adding Richard to the group, she used the same hammer to pry out the nails.

Why?

Because no matter what had happened in the past, Jayne was still her father.

The killer sadist.

With this rationale in place, Olsen had gladly given Miller the substitute held purchased: Richard.

Her lies were obvious.

If Richard had truly been in on the meeting/meetings from the beginning, Olsen would have spoken of his presence in 1989, before the statement David Hamm wrote for her for the first Grand Jury proceedings.

The fact that Olsen had not mentioned Richard previous to her meeting with Hamm proved that Richard had not been present.

I also believed that Olsen had to say whatever the prosecution wanted her to say in order to get something else she desperately wanted, needed, she felt, in order to survive: a new start in life away from her father who had so terribly abused her.

I could see how the government could easily manipulate this mentally ill and mistreated woman, especially by saying that they would set her up in a new life, giving her drug money when they should have given her help for her addictions. Olsen admitted she didn't even know how the government would accomplish what they had promised. She was just a lost soul.

All in all, it was a very trying day. Aside from Olsen's testimony, Shadur had again criticized Tuite numerous times, even correcting his methodology in questioning a witness, saying (to Tuite), "That's not proper cross examination." And on another occasion, "You know, it (your behavior) is just not excusable."

The only time the tension was broken was when Tuite asked Olsen if she had called her "Sugar Daddies" from the ATF once when she needed help in getting bonded out of jail. Shadur, admonishing Tuite, said he wouldn't hold Richard responsible for his lawyer's needless remark. "The 'Candy Lady' is gone," Judge Shadur said dramatically, "now the 'Sugar Daddies' are here. What kind of business is this?" Laughter rippled throughout the courtroom like the chuckles in a horror movie when the heroine is walking down a dark alley and a cat jumps out…comic relief for some, but nevertheless, a device used to mislead the obvious because something terrible is still going to happen.

Although I had little faith in Tuite as a lawyer, I still had faith in the saying, "The truth will set you free." When Richard blew me a kiss as I left the courtroom, I did not hear the "Cassandra" song of gloom and doom of so many other court sessions.

That night as I prepared to go to bed, I realized that Cathy Olsen, the false witness, had been unmasked in front of all and sundry. Surely Judge Shadur would take her testimony into account when the time came to reach a verdict. With this thought in mind, I slept sounder than I had in months.

Chapter 27

"**I** heard what I heard, what I heard." ~ Pamela Milner during direct examination

On May 30, I was introduced to someone new from Steven Miller's bag of tricks. Pamela Milner. The prosecution's newest "star" was a surprise witness who ended up surprising everyone, even Judge Shadur. The anorexic young teacher wore no makeup and flaunted the brightest whitest stockings I had ever seen. She sat down in the witness chair and immediately began to rock back and forth, picking at the hem of her short green skirt and pulling at her hair. Anyone could see she was frightened out of her wits, and I thought everyone in the courtroom probably felt sorry for her. I glanced at Steven Miller. He was smiling, obviously pleased by the pathetic picture Milner presented. I myself was dumbfounded by her appearance in the courtroom. Who exactly was Pamela Milner? Was she mentioned in *Thin Air*, and I had somehow missed her name? And why was she so studiously presenting herself as the consummate victim? Did Miller hope to elicit from this unlikely looking witness the question all Chicago was asking: What truly happened to Helen Brach? I leaned forward, eagerly awaiting this witness's testimony.

Speaking in a voice little more than a whisper, Milner began by describing how she met Richard. While driving past his stable one day, she said she saw a gorgeous Thoroughbred named Mongo, then later made inquiries about the horse. Shortly thereafter, she claimed, Richard tried to con her into buying Mongo, persuading her to give him a $500-00 deposit. The sale was never finalized, she said, because the horse was far too costly.

All of a sudden, Milner began to hide her eyes with her hands and hang her head. Was she ashamed or frightened of what she was going to say next? I figured it had to be one or the other.

The witness crossed and uncrossed her legs, took a deep breath, and said that she dated Richard on and off for a year in the late eighties, and that one night he took her to a "dump" where something highly unusual happened. After a strange man offered to buy them drinks, Milner said Richard became very belligerent. I had no idea where she was headed with her testimony but could tell by the way her face and hands were twitching that she was even more anxious than when she sat down.

Apparently, Miller had the same awareness. He began to protect his star witness, coaxing her, coddling her. "Would you describe for Judge Shadur what he (Richard) did and what he said? And if you'd feel more comfortable, you can just look at Judge Shadur and tell him what happened."

Milner, her eyes now on the floor and in a voice barely audible, claimed that after the stranger's offer, Richard told her that he didn't have to take any insulting behavior from anybody, that he could take care of everybody, and that he alone had taken care of the Candy Lady.

WHAT? Was she saying Richard had taken care of the Candy Lady like in… in… doing away with her?

I was shocked by Milner's words, I felt as though an atom bomb had exploded inside my brain, and the shock waves were bouncing off the spectators in the courtroom, then all the people in Chicago, the world, and extending out into the COSMOS. In the still moment that followed, I pulled -myself together, waiting to hear what she would say next.

I didn't have long to wait. Miller asked the school teacher if Richard had then showed her any part of his body, and Milner replied that he showed her his hands, asking her to look at them, to feel them. She did what he asked,

Milner claimed, and found his hands to be "real rough and callously." She further testified that Richard said, "They've (his hands) done it all," hinting that Richard had strangled Brach with his strong hands.

Milner further claimed that after Richard said this, that she became "hysterically frightened," and felt her own life was in danger. She went on to say that she never wanted to hear what Richard had told her, but that she heard what she heard.

Just then my friend Dennis whispered in my ear, "I'll bet you a cookie that 'poor little Miss Milner' never heard that confession from Richard. And I'll bet you another cookie that 'She heard what she heard' from David Hamm."

"Him again?"

"Right… Milner's testimony is absurd," Dennis assured me. one of Richard's pet sayings was, 'I've never had a callous since I was a kid.'"

"I remember that," I whispered. My heart was beating wildly.

"Besides," Dennis added, "who in their right mind would make such a gratuitous confession?"

I shook my head, not knowing what to think at that point.

For some reason, stick-like legs reminded me of a praying mantis, but I pulled my thoughts together and stared down at my own clenched fists. This young woman was no government paid informant, no headline hunter from the celebrity horse business, but a highly respected member of the community, a role model. Unlike Plemmons who was just a jailbird trying to get out of prison, the school teacher had no reason to lie that I could think of. Therefore, she had to be telling the truth! Was Dennis wrong?

My brain was crowded with contradictions and conflicting images. Milner surely would have called the police after she left Richard that tell-tale night, I thought. They would undoubtedly have records of her phone call and statement. There had to be some reasonable explanation as to why this evidence had not surfaced before now. Possibly Miller was just being clever in not bringing the information forward at this time. It was also possible that the police had simply misplaced the file. Things like that did happen after all, but as I was learning, those losses were not always "accidental."

I stared dumbly at the demure school teacher. Her testimony had undermined Richard's defense before he even got started. She was clouding my future, and I was angry she had brought this new and devastating information into the hearing, but if Richard had truly caused Brach's disappearance, then Milner was certainly right in coming forward. At that moment in time, all I wanted to do was throw in the towel. This frail woman, who appeared to be on the verge of fainting, was hammering me with the proof I had dreaded discovering for so, so long...

Richard was guilty after all.

My mental anxiety and rambling had caused me to miss a few seconds of her testimony. When I again picked up on what she was saying, Milner was describing a plan she had devised to protect herself from Richard's wrath. While in the privacy of her home, she claimed she took some paper out of her purse and wrote down everything that had taken place that evening in the bar. Later, she claimed, she put the document in a safety deposit box where it had waited all the intervening years until she felt compelled to contact Steven Miller.

But apparently this was no ordinary piece of paper she recorded the information on.

No.

Milner testified it was a partially torn pay stub from her employer where the date 2/3/89 appeared at the top. On this small piece of paper, she wrote the following:

If I die, then it's for love.

Richard Bailey scared me at the restaurant after that strange man left... he told me about the Candy Lady and that he took care of the Candy Lady too...

There was an embarrassing moment for the prosecution when Miller first translated the remaining few lines as, "This is the key," and was corrected by Judge Shadur who said he thought the sentence read, "Read this key." Miller immediately corrected himself. How strange, I thought. Miller didn't even know what his own star witness had written on the pay stub. We then learned that "key" was short for Kevin, Milner's brother, who was, of all things, an Assistant United States Attorney.

Milner further claimed she also wrote:

He (Richard) mentioned, "Joe can go to hell."

I assumed the reference was to Joe Plemmons who had testified earlier.

Milner, whose testimony had been terribly confusing up to that point, then began to repeat certain words, "Yeah. I… I… yeah. I just… I had… yeah. I just had to… enough is enough, is enough. Is enough."

Finally, Miller said he had no further questions for the witness, court recessed, and I was left pretty much speechless by everything I had heard. A glance over at Tuite told me he was as surprised as I was. Then Miller asked for a side-bar with. Judge Shadur and together with Tuite and Milner, they all left together for a meeting in judge's chambers.

When Richard stood up to leave, there was a special, reassuring lilt to his smile. "She lied," he mouthed, blew me a kiss, and walked away.

She lied?

Not this time, Richard, I thought.

Not this time.

It's over.

I talked with Richard on the telephone the night after Pamela Milner testified. I was unkind. Who could blame me for my behavior? Richard had misled me in the past, and he had not warned me about how damaging Milner's testimony was going to be.

The phone conversation went roughly like this: "Hi, hi, my beautiful doll!"

I bit my tongue, took a deep breath, and said, "Richard, you apparently forgot to tell me a couple of minor details." I couldn't help being sarcastic; I was very angry and more than a little hurt.

"Hey, she lied! What can I say?"

"Say it isn't true for starters," I replied coldly.

"It isn't! I never, never, ever took that woman or any woman to a joint like she described! You know me! I would never take a lady to a dive… And the meeting with the tough guy and the confession about Helen Brach, why those things just never happened!"

"Richard, I want to believe you, but let's take a look at the record because you know that's what Judge Shadur's going to do. First, there's Plemmons saying you tried to hire him to kill Brach; then there's Olsen backing him up, and now this! And you say they are all lying? I mean, where does it end? Do I have to go to my grave believing that the prosecution, representatives of the United States Government, is priming these witnesses and making them lie?"

I paused, out of breath for a moment, then added, "Steven Miller is a slickster and a dangerous, dangerous man, but I cannot believe he is putting perjured witnesses on the stand. People he has coached into perjury at that… this is America… he can't be doing that…"

"Well, somebody is," Richard said softly.

"Who?"

"Maybe David Hamm… I don't know… I truly do not know. But those government witnesses are all making this stuff up. Listen, I confessed to everything I did. I admitted to the overcharging. You know I settled most of the civil suits regarding all of that nearly twenty years ago. But I did not ask Plemmons to kill Helen Brach! I did not ask anybody to kill Helen Brach… and I certainly didn't drag Pamela Milner off to a Sleazeville bar to confess to a crime I never committed!"

"Well…"

"Come on… You know the story about the time Joe Plemmons took his brother, Tommy, out to beat up the vet, Dr. Hugi. Hugi only weighs 150 lbs. and stands 5'6", but the little doctor whipped them both with a training twitch! A training twitch! Tommy ended up in the hospital. The Plemmons were the joke of the horse industry, still are today. Are those the kind of people anybody would hire to kill… anything? Joe Plemmons couldn't even scare a little veterinarian, let alone physically handle him. I swear to you… I did not have anything to do with Helen Brach's disappearance period. End of story."

"But who did do it then?" I was frustrated beyond belief. I think it was Jack Matlick or…" He paused, as if sifting through his thoughts. "Maybe no one did it."

"What?"

"Maybe Helen never really planned to go to Florida like she told everybody, but secretly flew to Brazil to meet that plastic surgeon she was always talking about, and then…"

"Then?"

"Then something happened. Maybe she died under the anesthesia… who knows? As far as I can tell, all the cops ever did was call and ask that doctor's receptionist if Helen showed up. No one from law enforcement ever went there and checked out the facts. Who knows?"

"Richard, I want the truth…"

"Look, the truth is I am just a convenient target, and it's a natural fact that somebody's out to get me. If it isn't Miller, then they are darn sure using him!"

Richard's voice, his selection of words, his stressed tones all indicated to me that he was, in fact, telling the truth. My heart softened. "Okay, honey," I said, "let's see if that lawyer of yours can poke some holes into this latest deluge of lies."

"Pray for that," he said softly.

Later, when I was drifting off to sleep, Milner's face when she was testifying about the callouses on Richard's hands kept reappearing, then, without realizing I was doing so, I began to picture Richard's hands. I remembered the gentle way his hands held me as we danced a waltz, remembered the loving grasp of his hands on the cups of wine we shared in restaurants, remembered how smooth his palms felt when he slipped the wedding band over my finger, and how soft his fingers felt when he lifted my chin for a goodnight kiss.

I sat straight up in bed.

Richard's hands weren't rough.

And they certainly weren't calloused.

They were soft and smooth.

Why wouldn't they be?

This was a man who did not engage in manual labor.

Why… Judge Shadur could have peeked down from the bench and seen for himself! Then I wondered about some other things Milner had testified about.

Milner had sworn on the stand that Richard took her to a dump, but I knew for a fact that that type of restaurant just wasn't in his repertoire. Oh, perhaps he took Milner to a less upscale restaurant than say, the Pump Room, since she wasn't one of his wealthier clients, but to a sleazy bar? Richard wouldn't do that!

And the police hadn't lost Milner's file as I thought earlier, or Miller would most certainly have brought it up in court! No. Milner never called the police to report Richard's confession. But why not? Most law-abiding citizens would at least have picked up the phone! Something was wrong here, terribly wrong.

Could it be possible that what Milner really wanted was to be in the limelight like that clown, Kato Kaelin in the O. J. Simpson case. The thought was horrifying, but it wouldn't go away. I could see that it was entirely possible.

Chapter 28

"I would treat these women like no one else had treated them before." ~ Richard Bailey during direct examination

In a bizarre quirk, Richard was to be put on the stand while Judge Shadur gave the defense a few days to check out Pamela Milner's testimony. As luck would have it, that was the day I overslept and when I walked into the courtroom a few minutes late, there was a buzz in the crowded room over why Richard was going to testify. Period. It was common knowledge that in all proceedings regarding Helen Brach, by advice from his previous lawyer, Jo Ann Wolfson, he had exercised his Fifth Amendment privilege to remain silent.

I thought Tuite was making a major mistake putting Richard on the stand, but Tuite was adamant. He believed that Richard needed to show he accepted full responsibility for the horse swindles and had remorse for his victims. Richard's testimony was essential, Tuite said, in order to keep his sentence in the thirty-one to forty-six-month range.

My friend Dennis agreed with Tuite but only to a point. Yes, he said, if Richard took the stand and showed great remorse for his past actions, it could be beneficial at sentencing, but Dennis was quick to mention a definite downside. In all probability, Safer would brutally attack Richard on cross examination, a confrontation Dennis compared to America invading Grenada with United Nations support.

Dennis' downside really concerned me. For weeks I had watched Safer in action. The tall thin man with steel-rimmed glasses was an intense and relentless prosecutor, a verbal hurricane of verbs and questions marks. Any confrontation between Richard and Safer would be *nollo contendre*, as far as I was concerned no contest, because Richard was barely literate, a middle school dropout.

As I walked over to my seat behind the defense table, I saw the spectators were bunched together at the front of the room. Like people at a cock fight, everyone was trying to get as close to the action as possible. It seemed all of Chicago had turned out to see Richard on the stand, a man, who, thanks to Tokyo Rose, was now known all over the world as the "Galloping Gigolo," "Easy Rider," "Mr. Golden lips," and "Mr. Golden Tongue."

When the Marshals led Richard in, a tense hush came over the gathering. I didn't know if the crowd expected Richard to look like a beaten man, but if so, they had to be disappointed. He walked straight, head up, and looked upbeat and confident (like always).

Richard gave me a quick smile, then began his testimony with what I felt was a lie. He stated he had completed the ninth grade and later passed the GED. To me, this was an impossible statement because I knew for a fact that Richard could not read the daily newspaper. How could he pass the GED? That Tuite had led Richard into this blatant "falsehood" disturbed me. I feared it was an ominous harbinger of what was to come. To quell my momentary upset, I told myself that surely Tuite would not coach Richard into further false testimony; such unethical behavior was the government's game and I expected more from his own attorney.

Richard then went on to describe how he became involved in the horse business some twenty years ago. After meeting Frank Jayne, Richard said they worked out an arrangement whereby he would buy a horse from Jayne, then resell it at a higher price, giving Jayne 50 percent of anything above the original price. Richard called this splitting up of the profits, "chopping up the watermelon," and the phrase seemed to make Judge Shadur wince.

Golden Tongue

The women came into play, Richard said, when he began to meet them at the stable and realized they were potential customers. According to Richard, he wined and dined them, always at the finest restaurants like the Ritz Carlton and the Pump Room, and the ladies would gradually, in his words, "Get a little confidence in him." Yes, he admitted, at times he exaggerated the worth of the horses or claimed the horses were younger than they were, and yes, he showered the ladies with compliments, calling them "real classy ladies." Richard also remembered that he often gave the women Chanel No. 5 or white roses, and sent greeting cards addressed, "To my classy, beautiful lady." Only occasionally, he said, did he become romantically or intimately involved.

When he embellished his answers by saying he treated the women like no one else ever had, I knew it was true. Since meeting Richard that first night at The Waterfront, I had always thought he should write a book entitled, How to Treat a Woman. I had no doubt it would be a best seller. Never in my life was I wooed with more style and class than by Richard Bailey and he was an unforgettable lover. I could easily understand why some women believed he was sexier than Mel Gibson.

When Tuite asked Richard if he attempted to sell horses to these women and borrowed money from them, Richard acknowledged that he had, but said he always intended to pay them back, even though there were times he did not. He also said he sometimes told women he needed money to buy a horse because he had already put a deposit down and would lose the horse if he didn't come up with the money.

"Was that ever a true story?" Tuite queried.

"No," Richard replied honestly.

I saw what Tuite was doing. Exactly what the prosecution did earlier with Plemmons. Defusing all the bombs before his opponent had the opportunity, i. e. , having Richard confess to whatever frauds he had already committed. Why not, I thought sadly. Thanks to Tuite, Richard had already pleaded guilty.

Suddenly, almost as an aside, Tuite asked Richard to show the judge his hands and asked, "Do you have...have you ever had calloused hands from physical labor?"

"When I was a kid," Richard replied.

Tuite smiled, glanced at the judge, and asked, "How about in 1989? Did you ever have calloused hands from physical labor?"

Richard replied, "No."

Thank God. At least Tuite had the sense to get that testimony into the record. Now Pamela Milner's story had a sizeable hole in it because she had weighed in so heavily on the side of Richard's hands being rough, calloused, strong… capable of murder.

Tuite paused dramatically, then continued with his direct, and Richard admitted that another way he met women was by running T. V. commercials early in the morning, and that he had met Linda Holmwood from one such ad. He had flattered her, Richard said, but when asked if he had a sexual relationship with the lady or proposed as she had claimed earlier on the stand, Richard replied, "Never."

But when Frank Jayne introduced Richard to Carole Karstenson, Richard said there was definitely a romantic involvement aside from selling her horses. In fact, Richard admitted, referring to sexual intercourse, "I just couldn't stop her." There were chuckles all around me and I felt my back stiffen, not from the fact that Richard was laying claim to being a Don Juan, but from the idiocy of proclaiming before Judge Shadur that this poor woman was obviously oversexed. Even if it were true, Richard's admission had nothing to do with Brach's disappearance, and I couldn't believe Tuite had instructed him to tell the truth on the stand and was now asking the kind of questions that were a virtual self-inflicted character assassination. The effect was so impactive I had the eerie feeling that Richard was now a witness for the prosecution.

But the most damning element to Richard was that he appeared to have no remorse. I was worried that Judge Shadur would make the leap from thinking that Richard didn't care about the feelings of women he had defrauded to not having any feelings about the disappearance of Helen Brach.

Dennis leaned over and whispered, "Richard is killing himself. He looks too calm."

I knew why Richard was acting that way and blamed Tuite. Any serious discussion with Richard would have revealed he was using a survival technique on the stand he developed as a child when fighting for his life. Because of the many beatings he endured due to his deformed eye lids, he learned soon enough to put his fists in his pockets and to utter something disarming to hold off his opponents. When classmates attacked him with brute strength, Richard fought back with wit and words. He had no choice in the matter. Small for his age and physically weak, winning a fistfight was a ridiculous hope. Richard's solution was to become a "sweet talker." Only by engaging in clever conversation could he avoid being whipped on a daily basis.

But being clever with words wasn't enough to prevail in a physical confrontation.

Richard also had to hide his emotions.

Showing fear made him appear weak no matter what interesting tidbit he managed to come up with, so Richard created a mask to wear, one that was always smiling and relaxed.

On the witness stand, the players were different, but the situation was the same: Richard was still fighting for his life… and thus, the mask.

It was my belief that a psychiatrist's examination would have backed up my evaluation. Why Tuite hadn't called a professional in to examine Richard when he was first arrested was a travesty of ethics. I feared Tuite had not done so because he never expected to win Richard's case. Why do anything "extra" that might help prove his client was innocent if Tuite thought the case was lost before it began? Tuite's failure to get the psychiatrist's examination in conjunction with putting Richard on the stand was unconscionable.

It seemed like forever before Tuite finally got around to what everyone in the courtroom had been waiting so long to hear, Richard speak of his relationship with Helen Brach. According to Richard, he met the candy heiress by serendipity. Back in the early seventies, he had introduced himself to a lady at a car wash, a Mrs. Hirschman, and after she turned him down for a date, saying she was married, she suggested he might like to meet her friend, Helen. Mrs.

Hirschman and Richard then made arrangements to meet at a restaurant called The Studio. She promised she would bring Helen and introduce them.

Richard testified that after he met Helen Brach, they soon became very good friends. They enjoyed dining out and dancing, he said, but they didn't have a sexual relationship because she had a "tipped uterus." I knew that statement wasn't medically correct, but I did remember the paragraph in *Thin Air* where the author mentioned Matlick, Brach's houseman, was aware of a sexual problem of Brach's, that her vaginal opening was too small for sex. And while I didn't necessarily believe anything Matlick said, I also remembered a passage from the same book where Brach had confided to a girlfriend that her first marriage might have worked out if she had been "sexier," an in confidence to another friend, that she had an arrangement with Frank Brach: "Sex, but not too often." Because those references seemed to validate what Richard testified to, basically an excuse for Brach to engage in sex, I believed what he said, that his friendship with Brach was strictly that… sex did not enter into the picture.

Richard cleared his throat, asked for some water, and then the topic of Helen Brach's horses came up. Richard said there did come a time when Helen mentioned she'd like to buy a few race horses and he had contacted his brother P. J. , a former jockey, to help out. His brother searched around, found three suitable horses, and the sale was consummated. The profit, Richard admitted, was around $45, 000 and he and his brother split it down the middle. According to Richard, these were the only horses he sold to Brach during the entire time he knew her.

Richard did mention that in the fall of 1976, that he took Brach to the Oak Brook Stables to look at a "jumper" at the request of Jerry Farmer, but that Helen left abruptly when someone riding a horse tapped it with a crop. Helen hated that kind of thing, Richard added.

Dennis leaned over to me and said, "Pat Tuite should have spoken with Dr. Ross Hugi. He has records showing that Helen Brach was going to a horse sale with Richard at Oak Brook Stables late in February of '77. Why would she go with Richard to a sale to buy horses if she planned on putting him in jail? It's not logical! That question would really blow a hole in Katz's story too because he testified that Brach was going straight to the State's Attorney when she returned from Mayo, a date well before the Oak Brook sale!"

"Tuite must have that information already," I whispered back. "Dr. Hugi is a government witness, and they were supposed to turn over all the exculpatory evidence before the hearing started."

Dennis chuckled. "Dream on, Doc, dream on. For all the government cares, Brady vs. Maryland, the case which requires the discovery you described, might just as well be a divorce action. Brady is another rule of law the prosecution just tread upon. Before this hearing is over, you're going to find that the prosecution's hidden much more than they've delivered."

"But that's not fair!" I complained.

Dennis' smirk said, "You have a lot to learn, lady." I consoled myself with one thought: During the body of his testimony about Brach, Richard often spoke of her in the present tense, as if she were still alive. "Let me tell you something. Helen would never go to a horse show. And when she says she doesn't want to go to a horse show, there's no way you're going to convince her to go to one of those dusty shows." I couldn't help but wonder if I was the only person who was noticing this obviously unaffected reference.

Toward the close of Tuite's direct, be asked Richard about his relationship with Brach during the final months of 1976, and Richard described how they had celebrated the New Year's festivities at the Waldorf Astoria, dining together that evening and spending the rest of the night dancing to Guy Lombardo. Although they slept in separate bedrooms, Richard said that Helen had picked up all the tabs, close to $1,000, and had given him a very expensive gift, a brown cashmere sweater. If they were sexually involved, I thought, they would certainly have stayed in the same bedroom and the government had receipts that proved this didn't happen.

After New Year's, Richard said, he helped Helen get admitted to the Mayo Clinic, then left for Florida around the 10th of February. Richard said he had no records in his possession to show when he actually arrived in that state or where he stayed, but on February 16, he checked into the Colony Hotel and was joined by a girlfriend from Chicago, Chris Kubat.

Richard went on to say that while in Florida, he and Kubat visited the Winnick Farm which had a reputation for having the finest Thoroughbreds in the country. Richard said he was waiting for Helen Brach to arrive that Saturday and then he was planning to take her to the Winnick's to view some horses.

On February 16th, Richard said, he placed a call to Brach at the Mayo Clinic, and Tuite pointed out to Judge Shadur that the phone call lasted eight minutes. Richard said it was a very friendly call and I thought it had to be. If Brach were mad at Richard for whatever reason, she'd have hung up.

When Brach was due back in Chicago from the clinic, Richard placed another call to her, he said, but Jack Matlick gave him the runaround and wouldn't put him through. He placed another call later, Richard said, and again Matlick refused to connect him. After more phone calls to Brach, and the same routine from Matlick, Richard finally decided she wasn't flying down to Florida after all. Richard then flew back to Chicago, placed still another call to Brach, and again, Matlick refused to put Brach on the phone.

At that point in time. I had practically memorized certain passages from *Thin Air* and realized that once again, Richard's testimony dovetailed with something I had read in the book. There was a long paragraph describing how the Glenview Police Chief found it highly unusual that Brach was supposedly at home during the time period Richard described and yet she had spoken to no one. Brach was a "phoneaholic," yet an examination of the calls made from her home after her alleged return from the clinic and interviews with people who also tried to phone her proved she had never as much as lifted a receiver. But Matlick did, and he had given callers a variety of excuses why Brach couldn't speak: she had just stepped out, was in the tub, was indisposed, or was just plain unable to come to the phone.

I put aside my *Thin Air* ramblings as I heard Richard say, in response to Tuite's latest query, that he finally stopped calling Brach altogether, figuring she had acquired a new boyfriend and he was out of the picture. But that had not been his original game plan, Richard quickly pointed out. In the beginning, he said, he had planned to be with Helen for many, many years because she had a long, long bank roll.

Richard denied categorically ever meeting Ken Hanson and Joe Plemmons in a restaurant in an attempt to solicit either or both of them to kill Helen Brach.

Richard denied categorically ever being present during any conversation at Northwestern Stable with Frank Jayne and others where discussions were had that Helen Brach had to be shut up because she knew too much.

Richard denied categorically ever taking Pamela Milner to a "dump" where he confessed he had taken care of Helen Brach.

Richard denied categorically ever having calloused hands in 1989, the year Pamela Milner said he had asked her to touch them.

And finally, Tuite asked Richard what he called, "the ultimate question:" "Did you have anything to do with the death or disappearance of Helen Brach?"

Richard responded, "Definitely not" in a strong clear voice.

Chapter 29

"They have no lawyers among them, for they consider them as a sort of people whose profession it is to disguise matters." ~ Sir Thomas More

I had been keeping an eye on Safer the whole time Richard was testifying and felt my earlier fears of the prosecutor would soon be justified. Safer had written more notes on a legal pad than a failing law student cramming for the bar. Not being a lawyer myself, I was uncertain as to why he went to so much trouble. Surely Tuite had succeeded in getting Richard to admit to defrauding women. From where I sat, Tuite had already done Safer's work for him.

Was I ever wrong!

After a brief recess from Richard's direct testimony, Safer began his cross examination using the same rapid-fire questions with the zingers at the end that had destroyed me at the earlier bond hearing:

Q. You lied to hundreds of customers over the years, didn't you?

A. A lot of them I lied to, yes.

Q. You lied about the fair market value of horses, didn't you?

A. Yes.

Q. You lied about the investment potential of horses, didn't you?

A. Yes.

Q. You lied about the soundness of horses, didn't you?
A. Yes.

And on and on and on and on. In fact, for the next 178 minutes, Safer did nothing but get Richard to repeat what he just said or Tuite. The entire testimony was redundant. Surely Judge Shadur would notice this, I thought… or, had Tuite made another terrible error and allowed the government another opportunity to hammer into the judge's head that long ago, Richard had been a horse swindler?

Dennis leaned over and whispered, "Safer's frying Shadur's brain with Richard's prior misconduct serving as the grease. Tuite should never have put him on. Safer's far from safe. Plus, he's a bully!"

Safer was a bully, but instead of using his fists on Richard, the prosecutor used derogatory words to hit him in the ego. Safer was also into raising his voice and yelling at Richard, shaking his finger in his face, and waving his arms.

Richard countered by wearing his zombie mask because he didn't know what else to do. He was scared. Worse. He was paralyzed, a deer caught in the headlights. He sat back in the witness chair, clasped his hands, crossed his legs, and tried to tell the truth. But instead of coming across as truthful, everything worked against him. Because he came from a poor rural family, his choice of words was coarse, his speech patterns very definitely those of a street-wise hustler. At times, Richard also looked stupid, in particular, when Safer pushed documents in front of his face. I knew Richard couldn't read them and Tuite knew Richard couldn't read them, but to cover up his illiteracy, Richard had the habit of waving them off, as though they were unimportant. Summed up, Richard's statements seemed indifferent and uncaring; and because his body language was so strange, leaning back in the chair, looking perfectly calm, he appeared to be cold and intransigent.

I had feared the worst and now I had to deal with it. Richard's days on the witness stand were adding up to a complete disaster.

And it never had to happen.

How could Tuite make so many terrible decisions?

Richard's cavalier remarks about Carole Karstenson came back to haunt him when Safer pounded Richard with the fact that he had joked about her being oversexed. I was horrified to see Judge Shadur frown, his bushy eyebrows coming together in a point, when the subject came up again. I glanced over at Dennis and his shrug was as clear as if he had said, "I told you so."

By that time, Richard had been on the stand for over two hours. I knew he was tired, but because he was wearing his mask, I was afraid people would think he was actually enjoying himself. From time to time, he took a sip of water from a plastic cup one of the Marshals had brought, and I thought even this small gesture made him look insensitive.

Safer was focusing on trying to get Richard to admit he had known all along that his business transactions with women were unlawful. Richard replied that if he had known he would have ended up in criminal court because of his actions, he would never have conducted his business the way he did. I believed him. Still do. Richard simply did not have the education and background to fabricate lies on the witness stand.

This was evident in even the simplest of exchanges:

8. (Safer): You lied about a horse's breeding, didn't you?

9. The breed they was, you mean?

Or another time...

Q. You have more at stake here than you've ever had before in your life, isn't that right? A. I don't understand what you're saying. More at stake... And on another occasion,

8. (Safer): You've lied to avoid being arrested, haven't you?

9. No, they already arrested me.

At this point, I felt so sorry for Richard because he was becoming incoherent, and in the process, looking as though he was even more recalcitrant.

I also regretted that the attorneys involved in Richard's civil suits never warned him that what he was doing was blatantly criminal. I knew Richard and I knew he would never have continued with this type of behavior with a jail sentence lurking in the background. In Richard's mind, because he truly wasn't educated, I think he confused civil with criminal, and when he settled the civil suits, he truthfully believed he had paid for his error.

At the end of the session, Safer's questions had become so repetitive that I wondered if even Judge Shadur was getting bored. Finally, when I didn't think I could bear another one of Safer's, "didn't you's," Shadur admitted he was indeed bored (or something close to it anyway):

The Court: (To Safer) "I gather you're only part way through your cross? Is that a fair statement?"

Mr. Safer: "That is fair. A large part of the way through."

The Court: "Well, I had hoped that."

After Shadur's remarks, a ripple of nervous laughter swept through the courtroom, then Richard, who had been on the witness stand for nearly three and a half hours, was allowed to step down.

The only positive point coming from Richard's testimony involved Barbara Morris who was "supposedly conned" into purchasing a stallion. I had learned from Jill McEwan, a world-renowned expert on the value of Thoroughbred horses, that the horse had, in fact, sired foals worth hundreds of thousands of dollars. I hoped Tuite would bring this information up in his re-cross because it made the entire transaction with Morris not a fraud but, in fact, a good business deal that she backed out on.

I talked the Morris incident over with Dennis later, and he told me that he would like to put up $50, 000 and get back three or four times his money even if it were calleda fraud.

I saw Dennis' point. Who wouldn't want to be "defrauded" into a position where they made four times their investment? Good, I thought. Now Tuite had some ammunition and tomorrow was another day.

I was exhausted, but I had to keep going. Richard was scheduled to testify again at 9:30 A. M. the following morning.

"Mr. Bailey," Judge Shadur opened the next day's session in a loud deep voice, "you recognize that you're still under oath?" After those words, Richard was back on the stand and Prosecutor Safer was back on the attack, pounding away at the prosecution's theory that Helen Brach knew nothing about horses and was, therefore, the perfect victim for Richard.

Occasionally, Richard tried to insert into the record the fact that Helen Brach and her husband had owned a number of race horses during their marriage. Each time Richard tried to clarify these points, Safer brushed Richard's protestations aside.

Dennis tapped me on the shoulder, leaned over and whispered, "Safer just dug himself a deep, deep hole. Helen Brach was a licensed race horse owner with the Illinois Racing Commission. When Tuite hits him with that, he'll destroy that whole portion of the government's theory."

"If he inserts it," I whispered back angrily.

The balance of the morning's testimony was basically one rehash after another about points already made. For what seemed to me the zillionth time, Safer asked Richard if he was an expert on Thoroughbreds:

Q. (Safer): "As you sit there, you don't know anything about… race horses?"

A. "Well, I know they run."

I had to chuckle. True, Richard wasn't a Ph. D., but he had disarmed Safer with his play on words.

About a half hour into Richard's testimony, Safer began to focus on Richard's whereabouts on February 11, 1977. The date was important, I knew, because that was the day the prosecution theorized, the solicitation for Helen Brach's murder took place.

But Richard had a major problem. Safer was talking twenty years ago, so long ago, that Richard could not remember where he was on that precise date. When he had informed Tuite weeks earlier that he couldn't remember his whereabouts on that particular date, Tuite had given him some terrible advice.

He told Richard to lie.

It was easy for Richard to tell the truth on the stand, that wasn't complicated. To lie was a horse of a different color… it was almost impossible. First, Richard testified that on February 10th, he was in Florida, saying he couldn't recall exactly where he stayed, but maybe it was a hotel close to Miami. No, he said, he couldn't remember the hotel's name, but that he stayed there five to six days, then checked into the Colony Hotel. The government already had receipts showing he had stayed at the Colony from February 16 to February 23.

When Safer finally asked Richard if he was positive he wasn't in Chicago from the 10th to the 16th of February, Richard replied, "I could have been. I'm not sure. It goes way back."

Safer followed up: "You didn't give then (the police) receipts from any other hotel, did you? Because you didn't stay in any other hotel…"

"Wrong," Richard replied sternly.

Richard then went on to say that to the best of his knowledge, he was in Florida, in a small motel, playing tennis, golfing, and having fun.

But Richard was doomed. The government later came up with an old billing statement for Richard's Lake Shore Drive apartment, showing that calls were placed from that address from the period of February 11 through the 15. The people who received calls were all people Richard would normally have contacted: girlfriend Chris Kubat, Richard's handyman, and Northwestern Stable. Richard could not possibly have been north of Miami as he testified to earlier.

I didn't need my friend Dennis to tell me that Richard was in deep, deep trouble, He had lied on the stand, and it was obvious. Members of the media came up to me in the hallway after court, wanting to know what had happened when Richard was testifying. I didn't know what to tell them, but everybody knew that Richard had gambled big time and lost.

When I walked out of the Federal Building, I happened to catch Tuite giving a press conference. He was trying to downplay Richard's shaky testimony about his whereabouts immediately before Brach disappeared. "So, he was wrong about something that happened twenty years ago," Tuite was saying, unconvincingly shrugging his shoulders like a used car dealer showing a customer a broken-down automobile. Tuite wasn't explaining, he was apologizing.

But nobody believed Tuite. The people standing around me were all saying that Richard had lied on the stand. It wasn't like it was a big secret, but I was the only one who knew for certain what had happened when Richard testified. He had lied about his whereabouts because on that one point, Tuite had previously instructed him to do so... and in the most unbelievably stupid way imaginable. He told Richard to lie over the Bureau of Prisons monitored telephone.

I felt in my heart that Richard's lie and the telephone billing record presented serious problems for Richard and could possibly do more damage to his defense than all the prosecution's witnesses combined. Intellectually, I knew this wasn't possible, but I had a very bad feeling about Richard's appearance that day.

After Richard finished testifying, Tuite and Miller had spoken before Judge Shadur, and Tuite had placed great emphasis on his need to get an affidavit from Kenneth Hanson. The same Kenneth Hanson who had been indicted for murdering three boys with whom held had a homosexual involvement. Fine, I thought. Now Tuite was going to hinge Richard's defense on the testimony of a child molester and murderer.

At the end of the day, I realized there were other shortcomings with Tuite's performance which also bothered me. He had promised Richard he would subpoena Jack Matlick, Brach's houseman, to testify, but he never did. When Richard had asked Tuite why he hadn't done so, Tuite nonchalantly replied, "Because we don't need him." Richard was heartbroken by Tuite's response. I was devastated but at that point, I was no longer surprised by anything Tuite did.

Tuite's redirect had also been a disappointment and unremarkable except he missed the opportunity to make points out of the Barbara Morris issue and did nothing to capitalize on Safer's allegation that Helen Brach knew nothing about race horses.

My prayers that evening were brief. Although I tried hard to be cheerful for Richard when we spoke on the phone, it was always Richard who was the more supportive one, who was congenial and charming, who worried unselfishly about my welfare. Since the first night I met him, a stranger at The Waterfront, he had never once changed his demeanor.

For the life of me, I didn't know how he managed the endless torrents of Tuite's ineptitude.

Chapter 30

"**I** would like to simply make a request of the media just as a matter of courtesy. And that is, I would hope that because Ms. Milner is not a part of this proceeding at this point, it is as though she had not come to the stand, that the members of the media would respect that and would not choose this as an occasion to pursue the matter further with respect to Ms. Milner. Treat her, if you would, as a private individual who is not in this case because the consequence in legal terms here is that it is as though she had not been called to the stand." ~ Statement by Judge Shadur after Pamela Milner was caught in boldfaced lies constituting perjury.

The entrance to the Dirksen Federal Building was well stocked with sharks on Friday, June 2, the morning that Pamela Milner was to go back on the stand, but I didn't care. Something good was going to happen, I just knew it. Days of daily meditation had given me a calm I had seldom before experienced during the entire ordeal.

Inside the courtroom, much to my horror, the euphoria of the morning quickly dissipated. Pamela Milner was already on the stand waiting for Judge Shadur, and Steven Miller was once again smiling his Cheshire cat grin. Ron Safer was beaming, too, as though he didn't have a care in the world. My mood changed in a heartbeat. I couldn't help it. The cavalier attitude of the prosecution's team made me doubt the inner peace I had found earlier, and my heart began to race.

This time the jittery Milner was decked out in something vaguely resembling a fortune teller's getup, a Slavic-looking purple dress with a noticeably short hem and gold earrings that seemed to have no other function but to dangle and flash, dangle, and flash, drawing attention away from her face. She looks mystical, I thought, and even more nervous than she did the previous Tuesday, it that were possible.

The Marshals brought Richard in and, like always, he gave me a warm smile followed by a broad wink, and I was able to calm myself down enough to at least stay in the room and see what would take place.

"All rise…"

I sprang to my feet as Judge Shadur whisked in and dropped into his seat. "Miss Milner," he said softly, "you understand that you are still under oath?" She replied that she did, and the judge told Tuite he could cross examine.

"Thank you, your Honor," Tuite said, then began shuffling his papers.

Tuite began gently, having Milner reiterate her prior testimony, apparently under the guise of refreshing her memory, but from his frequent glances at Judge Shadur, I sensed Tuite was leading her somewhere else. Perhaps… into a trap? Maybe, I thought, we are finally going to see a quarter of a million dollars' worth of attorney in action!

Tuite carefully adduced from Milner that: (1) She had gone with Richard Bailey to the bar and heard his confession, probably on March 17, 1989; (2) she had written that date on her paycheck stub from the Board of Education; and (3) she had rented a safety deposit box in August of 1989 just for the purpose of safekeeping the damning evidence.

Tuite then got Milner to admit she had never told anyone about the box or its contents, not her brother, an Assistant United States Attorney for the Northern District of Indiana; not her friends; not the police; the F. B. I. , anyone… and certainly not Richard Bailey. She was speaking so softly not even Tuite could hear what she was saying, and he was standing directly in front of her.

At this time, Tuite took the check stub she had sworn she wrote Richard's confession on and allegedly put in the safety deposit box. He squinted, turned it one way, then another trying to read it. Finally, he handed the stub to Milner and said, "You wrote in heavy lines, did you not, in the right-hand corner, 'Read this, Kev, do not throw away'?"

"Yes," Milner agreed.

"And you wrote it over the serial number of the check stub, didn't you?"

"Yes."

"In the sense, it would be hard to read the serial number of that check, right?"

"It never occurred to me," Milner said, hanging her head like a child with her hand caught in the cookie jar.

Tuite then went back to the numbers under the writing.

"The numbers look like… 7758979. According to this stub, men, this was for pay period Number 20, and the amount of the check was $4, 815. 84."

Milner nodded as did Steven Miller. I noticed that David Hamm's face was dead white, and he began licking his lips. Something was up!

Tuite slowly gazed around the courtroom, then allowed his stare to center on Milner.

"Can you tell us the date on the check?" he asked.

"October 6th," Milner replied.

"October 6, 1989, is that right?"

"Correct."

Tuite glanced quickly at Judge Shadur then almost shouted, "That pay stub did not even exist in March of 1989!"

Milner mumbled something I could not make out, but Tuite pushed ahead, "Would you agree if the Board of Education didn't issue that check to you until after October 6, 1989, you couldn't have put that pay stub with that writing on it in a safe deposit box in August?"

The hiss of incredulity that whispered through the courtroom felt like a palpable wave when it washed over me. Milner stumbled for words, then spoke in fragments, "Whatever check was in my purse what I wrote." A non sequitur, and something Judge Shadur had rarely allowed the defense witnesses to get by with.

With Millner's damning admission and the confident expression on Tuite's face, I realized I was watching a scene out of Perry Mason, the defendant saved at the last moment by the lies of the prosecution being deftly exposed!

I scooted forward in my seat as Tuite struck again. "In order to become a witness, you attempted to obliterate the date of the pay stub, didn't you?"

"That's ridiculous," Milner whispered.

She was more nervous than ever, her hands fluttering wildly.

Tuite pressed on. "You also tore the date off so you couldn't tell that it was not in March, didn't you?" I glanced at Judge Shadur and was surprised he was glowering at Milner through his scraggly eyebrows.

The witness, speaking in almost inaudible spurts, then admitted she had made several "other copies" and put them in what she called, "hiding places."

"What do you mean several copies?" Shadur asked suddenly as if held just been awakened by a cannon firing a screaming projectile. He had spoken gently but appeared to be genuinely shocked.

The tense Milner, still stumbling for words, said she had indeed made handwritten copies of the original, "just in case one wasn't found," but said she would tell Judge Shadur where they were "in private."

"You can't tell me anything in private," Shadur said somewhat sternly. "You are not talking about making photocopies?" Milner was clearly exasperated, floundering.

"You know, I told Mr. Miller about the other copies…" she finally got out.

I didn't need Dennis to tell me the significance of her remark. Miller had known there were other copies of this obvious forgery before he put her on the stand! Not informing Tuite about the copies ahead of time was an unethical act on the prosecutor's part.

The reporter seated behind me leaned forward and whispered, "If that exchange had come out in front of a jury, Richard Bailey would be walking out of this courtroom! Steven Miller is going to have some explaining to do!"

Golden Tongue

As if Judge Shadur had overheard the reporter's remarks, he called the attorneys and Milner to the side-bar. After a few minutes, a Marshal walked over and I overheard him say the press was complaining that since there was no jury, they had a right to be present at the side-bar conference. Then, to everyone's complete surprise, the judge stood up and with Milner and all the attorneys in tow, walked into his chambers.

The reporter was wrong!

It wasn't a jury trial, but Richard had won and any minute we'd be walking out of the courtroom . . . together!

I looked over at my husband and he was smiling broadly, showing all his teeth. "I told you so... she lied!" he mouthed.

Once again, Richard had told me the truth. The school teacher had lied... blatantly... and she'd spent time over-the weekend with Miller-and one of-his, investigators. Probably David Hamm again! That figured when I connected Milner's testimony with his expression of concern earlier.

The break in Judge's chambers gave me some time to reflect on the government's case to date. Aside from owing Richard a long apology, I also had to give more credence to his statement that Plemmons and Olsen had been lying, as well... and that thought was quickly followed by another, that Richard was right, somebody was setting him up to be the scapegoat for everything associated with the Helen Brach disappearance. It was a big frame!

People were chattering like excited monkeys all around me as they speculated what would happen to Pamela Milner. Finally, after forty minutes or so, Judge Shadur and the attorneys walked stiffly back into the room. Milner was not with them. Once again, the noise level in the courtroom rose, then the judge cleared his throat, and I waited for the pronouncement that the case was being thrown out for the obvious perjury.

"It should have been apparent that the witness was extraordinarily tense," Shadur began, making apologies for Milner in what I thought was an obvious gesture to protect her. Shadur then seemed to stare directly at me and said,

"When the issue of timing arose and the witness's testimony about other handwritten copies. It developed that in order for Mr. Tuite to cross examine, we needed access to those copies. Ms. Milner said she had entrusted them to other people and was reluctant to involve them."

I was aghast! Milner swore on the stand that she hadn't told anyone about her handwritten note for six years! She had perjured herself more than once!

Judge Shadur paused, looked down across the people sitting in the courtroom, then went on, saying that he had granted a motion Mr. Tuite made in his chambers to strike the witness's testimony. Shadur paused briefly again, then asked the media to respect the fact that Milner was no longer a part of the proceeding and requested they treat her like a "private individual."

A private individual?

How was-that possible?

She was headline news!

And what's more she tried to crucify Richard!

I couldn't believe what I was hearing. Why was the judge bending over backwards to be kind to this witness after she broke the law, not even wanting her to be interviewed by the press? Had Shadur never heard of the First Amendment?

And what about the additional copies she spoke of? Surely if Milner had given copies to other people, she could produce them for the court! The only logical explanation for her not doing so was because they didn't exist!

I guess quite a few other people thought so too because the rest of Judge Shadur's statement was drowned out by a loud buzz that erupted from the press as well as the spectators.

I felt a sharp jab on my shoulder blade and Dennis said loudly enough for even Tuite to hear, "Well, Tuite blew it!" Dennis paused for a moment, shaking his head in disbelief, then said, "Milner's testimony has been stricken! Your expensive lawyer just threw your man to the wolves, lady. Hard to believe, but Tuite snatched defeat from the jaws of victory!"

"I don't understand…"

"Too much noise in here to talk. Meet me outside," Dennis said and left.

I had no idea what Dennis was talking about… Miller… victorious… again? The image of the prosecutor's smiling face when I first walked into the courtroom flashed through my mind. "The Assyrian came down like the wolf on the fold with his cohorts all gleaming in purple and gold."I repeated dumbly for some reason I have never understood, but the truth of the matter was that I was completely stunned.

The people in the courtroom were stunned, as well.

So, was Richard. His eyes were opened their widest and he was looking all around as if waiting for a Marshal to come and release him.

But nothing happened.

Only Miller, Judge Shadur and (sadly) Pat Tuite seemed-happy with the outcome. I shot a glance at David Hamm. He was moping his forehead with a damp handkerchief.

"Why?" I whispered.

I barely had time to catch my breath before Judge Shadur was asking Tuite if he had received Kenneth Hanson's affidavit, then his partner, Ron Menaker, read the document into the record. Hanson swore that the luncheon meeting described by Joe Plemmons never took place, and that he never so much as had even one cup of coffee with Richard in his life.

Miner quickly countered Menaker's words by calling Special Agent John Rotunno to the stand who pointed out that Hanson now resided in the Cook County Jail, awaiting trial for the 1955 murders of three Chicago boys.

The murders of three children.

Rotunno's words were like a gallon of salt water poured into a gaping wound. I was certain Judge Shadur would ignore the affidavit on those grounds alone.

As soon as I found my way out of the courtroom, the reporter I had spoken to earlier rushed over to me and asked, "Do you want to make a statement about Milner for the press?"

"Yes," I said, unable to hide the fury in my voice, "but you wouldn't want to print what I'm thinking!"

"I understand," he said gently. "That was a tough thing to watch... even for a reporter."

I was looking this way and that, trying to find Dennis, but having no success. There was total pandemonium in the halls, Outside, I spotted Tuite conferring with several reporters and heard him say that Milner had contacted his office months ago, wanting to testify as a character witness for Richard, insisting he was a wonderful man and would never hurt anyone. She had testified against Richard, Tuite reasoned, simply because she wanted the notoriety, the media following her around.

"Why didn't you bring that point up in court?" my reporter friend asked.

Tuite ignored the question and went on as if it had never been asked, "It was obvious why Milner didn't come up with the copies" he said. "There aren't any." He finished his press conference lay saying he hoped Milner would seek psychiatric help.

Maybe she will and maybe she won't, I thought, but the damage has been done. No one who heard Milner's perjured testimony (including Judge Shadur), could ever erase from their mind the terrible things she said about Richard. Her lies would live forever in print and had hit home with the judge. Her testimony would certainly have a deleterious effect on Richard's sentence come Tuesday.

Just then I saw Dennis walking down the steps of the Federal Building and quickly joined him. He gave me a knowing look and said, "Milner's unique in the annals of American justice... she perjured herself and then received the protection of the court!"

"What do you think will happen?" I asked, hoping against hope.

"Now?" Nothing. "You have to understand how badly Tuite ruined Richard's chances. First off, Tuite Should have moved for a dismissal due to blatant Prosecutorial Misconduct. He certainly had sufficient grounds. Furthermore, by insisting that Milner's testimony be stricken from the record, all that information as well as Miller's suborned perjury will never become available to the Circuit Court of Appeals. Ultimately, the Appeals Court will be deprived of the entire flavor and atmosphere of Milner's testimony."

"Do you think Tuite did that on purpose or is he simply incompetent?"

"Who knows? But you have to remember that Tuite was a prosecutor in the Gray Lord investigations years ago, and he put some corrupt federal judges neatly away in jail. Judges, like lawyers, hang together. Maybe Tuite's making peace with the government by purposely losing Richard's case because it's so high profile. Maybe in the future they'll let Tuite win a few. That's just a hypothesis, you understand. I couldn't prove it on Miller."

As Dennis was talking, all I could see was Miller's smiling face. "But if Miller had asked, Milner's testimony be stricken?"

"If Miller had said, 'Your Honor, I move to strike Ms. Milner's testimony,' every defense lawyer in America would have jumped up and objected to high heaven! Really good defense lawyers like Roy Black would have wanted that perjury left on the record so they could use it as a tool to reopen the case."

"What should Tuite have done then?" I asked. I was fighting off tears.

"Simple. He should have asked for a Grand Jury investigation into the fact that Milner lied, insisting she reveal where she got the information she lied about, and I'm referring specifically to the Joe Plemmons references. It was no accident that she wrote Plemmons' name on the check stub, saying Richard had mentioned Plemmons to her when confessing to the Brach murder. Bet you a Twinkie she heard that name for the first time in her life from David Hamm. Remember she also wrote 'Candy Lady, ' which was taken directly from Plemmons' testimony."

"Oh," I said, trying to absorb so much information quickly. "You know, at first I thought Tuite had finally done something really great."

"And so will most people following the case, but the truth is that the judge struck Milner's testimony at Tuite's request."

"Unbelievable!" I said with a sigh.

"Right... Here's a woman who outright perjured herself, everyone knows it, even the mice in the walls chompin' on their cheddar, and the judge, who's supposed to be unbiased, requests that the press not print any of her lies?"

The awareness of what had truly transpired in the courtroom that morning began to seep in. "Nothing's going to happen to Pamela Milner, is it? She's not even going to be held responsible for her actions... Miller either. There's no penalty when the government presents lies!"

"You got that right!"

"Well, Milner was a great actress," I said. "If Hollywood ever makes a movie out of this mess, she should play her own part. But think of the damage she did to Richard, the damage she did to me!"

Dennis squeezed my shoulder. "I know, I know," he said. "It's all rather incredible. Like Tuite had a hotel bill in his hand which proved Richard was in Miami, Florida, the entire month of February, 1977, and he shoved it inside a bottle and tossed it in the ocean."

Trevor was waiting for me halfway down the block, but before I left Dennis, I gave him a quick hug. As I turned to walk away, I called back over my shoulder, "Tuite stuffed our lives down that bottle, as well!"

All Dennis could do was shake his head.

Chapter 31

On Saturday morning, June 3, Tokyo Rose for once seemed to be on Richard's side. The *Sun-Times* announced, **"BRACH JUDGE TOSSES TESTIMONY, TIME DISCREPANCY SINKS BAILEY ACCUSER,"** while the *Daily Herald* agreed, **"KEY TESTIMONY AGAINST BAILEY DISINTEGRATES,"** calling Milner "the federal government's worst witness nightmare." But my favorite was the *Tribune*: **"BOMBSHELL WITNESS TURNS OUT TO BE BIG DUD."**

Those headlines kept me going well into the weekend. I kept telling myself that maybe there were a few rainbows in the sky I'd missed. I certainly hoped so. I was in desperate need of some good luck.

On Sunday afternoon, the realization that Richard's ordeal was winding down consumed my thoughts. Soon I would no longer have to juggle my daily life, rushing from one courtroom session to the next. In less than one hundred hours, no matter what decision Judge Shadur rendered, my destiny would be altered for all time.

Before dinner, I treated myself to what I hoped would be a long peaceful nap, but instead my subconscious opened its velvet doors, and in the disguise of a dream, my worst fears crawled out and bit deeply into my sleep. Whether the intrusion lasted for moments or hours, I really don't know, but the result was one of the worst nightmares of my life, a silent horror so deeply inscribed in my psyche that to this day, I fall most cautiously into sleep, fearing its insidious return.

Like many terrifying experiences, the dream began innocently enough: I was lounging away a quiet summer afternoon, floating serenely on a brightly colored, rubber raft. The raft's soft textured, yellow hide seemed to cradle me as I rocked gently beneath a cobalt blue sky spotted here and there with Disney clouds. Some of the larger ones spouted brilliant rainbows which splashed down into the ocean like kaleidoscopic waterfalls.

Without warning, the fleecy white puffs appeared to blacken, rush together, the rainbows vanished, and like a mirror struggling to keep up with a fast-moving image, the sea began to swell and roll until gigantic waves came crashing over me in slimy green cascades. The raft became a living thing, shuddering and shaking as it twisted and turned, bounded up and down, fighting to keep itself from being sucked down into the maelstrom into which we had rushed. In seconds, the violent whirlpool flipped me from the raft like a barnacle from a leviathan. I crashed into the seething green water, and to my horror, began to plummet toward the profound blackness of the deep. I was sinking to the bottom of the ocean, and it was not just any ocean, it was my South Pacific! Arms flailing like windmills, feet thrashing, I struggled to recover the raft, screaming over and over that someone had changed the rules, that my Pacific wasn't so peaceful anymore and who was going to fix it?

I awoke with a jerk, trembling, grabbed a pillow and held on tightly as if it were a life preserver. It would not take a dream therapist to explain what my subconscious was telling me: I had been sailing along through life and was suddenly tossed to the elements by Richard's advent into my world. Since that time, I had been swimming as fast as I could, but no matter how I deluded myself, I was truly sinking.

My life, my love, my peace of mind were all heading toward the same place. Rock Bottom.

Chapter 32

"We do not have to prove (guilt) beyond a reasonable doubt." ~ Ron Safer during closing arguments

I had deluded myself for so long into believing the scribbled numbers from Tuite's legal pad and had survived so many bizarre and stressful situations that when the words, "closing arguments," showed up on my kitchen calendar, I was unconcerned. I was also so physically and emotionally exhausted that the specter of the hassles at the Federal Building were no longer a threat. The reporters who waited for me at the entrance, the curious and disapproving looks from the spectators and the courtroom antics of both the defense and prosecution attorneys had lost their ability to intimidate me. I was numb and felt I could handle almost anything.

What a shock it was to discover that once again, I was wrong, this time 200 per cent. When Ron Safer stepped in front of Judge Shadur to begin his closing, I found my heart was once again in my throat and beating as fast as Krupa pounding his drum set in "Sing, Sing, Sing."

All eyes were on Safer, but he suddenly turned to Miller, a secret look was exchanged, a nod, and only then did he begin closing arguments for the prosecution, "There is no reasonable explanation for Helen Brach's disappearance other than she was silenced by Richard Bailey and his co-conspirators."

No reasonable explanation!

I had heard at least twenty plausible theories myself, and there had to have been many, many more I was unfamiliar with. Although most of the alternative scenarios were extremely complex, the one simple explanation that everyone overlooked, and I believed best described Brach's disappearance and probable death was a simple burglary.

A simple burglary Helen Brach just happened to walk into.

Of course, if one accepted that theory, then her houseman Jack Matlick became immediately suspect by virtue of his presence at Brach's home during the critical time period.

But it was no time to analyze theories. Safer was off in a different direction, insisting that after Richard became aware of Brach's disappointment in the performance of her horses, she vanished, after threatening to go to the authorities about Richard's fraud. "That proved," Safer contended, "that it was likely Mr. Bailey was involved in her disappearance."

That proved nothing!

It was merely an allegation.

Where were the facts?

Safer then summed up all the testimony we'd heard so many times before, ending with, "Thus, your Honor, what you are left with is an overwhelming circumstantial case, overwhelming circumstantial evidence that Richard Bailey conspired to kill Helen Brach and successfully (did so)."

What you are left with, I wanted to scream, is no body and no case with any proof of guilt!

Safer cleared his throat loudly and went on, "Add to that Mr. Bailey's (attitude) to the authorities during the critical stages of the investigation, this then is compelling evidence of his active participation in the conspiracy."

I assumed Safer was referring to Richard taking the Fifth in previous proceedings and knew he had only done what his attorney, Jo Ann Wolfson, had advised him to do. Once again, this action on Richard's part proved absolutely nothing.

Safer went further, "Add to that Joe Plemmons' testimony. It was persuasive, corroborative… it was credible and should be credited by this Court."

Golden Tongue

Joe Plemmons' testimony was anything but credible. It was his get-out-of-jail-free card. Regarding Cathy Olsen, Safer argued that she also heavily corroborated, had no interest in the case and, therefore, no reason to lie.

But of course, she had reason. Testifying was her winning lottery ticket to paradise because any life would have been infinitely better than the abusive one she had been born into, and the ATF was her consummate drug connection and "Sugar Daddy."

Safer was insistent that if the Court considered Plemmons' and Olsen's testimonies, that it had "proof beyond any reasonable doubt that Mr. Bailey was involved in the conspiracy," and he pointed out (since it was not a jury trial), "the government did not have to prove (guilt) beyond a reasonable doubt."

Safer's words were ominous and reminded me that if this were a jury trial, the government would have had to prove Richard's guilt without any doubt.

The prosecutor concluded by saying that Richard "has lived by false words. His crimes were heinous. He should and must be punished severely." Then very slowly and precisely, he said, "He is evil."

At those words, there was a soft but audible intake of breath throughout the courtroom. All I could think was what gives you the right, Mr. Safer, to say Richard is evil? What gives you the right to judge anybody? This is a right only God has!

As I watched Safer strut so arrogantly and righteously in front of Judge Shadur I couldn't turn off my indignation. From day one, I thought sadly, you and Mr. Miller have twisted the truth to make it appear as if Richard did this and Richard did that when you knew much of what you and your witnesses alleged simply wasn't true... Pamela Milner, for instance. When she perjured herself, you knew ahead of time that she was going to lie, and your knowledge was a crime in itself... a major crime, I thought, because representatives of the government should not only be wearing the white hats, but they should also be held to higher moral standards than ordinary public citizens! If Assistant United States Attorneys had to break the law in order to convict someone, then they should be fired and at least held responsible for their actions, no matter how strongly Judge Shadur disagreed with me.

As Safer returned to the prosecution table and his buddy Miller of the eternal grin, my eyes fell on the countless stacks of documents, papers, folders, and files on the table and in trollies. So, many men interviewing so many witnesses spending so many thousands of taxpayers' dollars, just to get Richard convicted. A quick look at the defense table and all I saw was Tuite staring absentmindedly into space, on his table, just a few file folders.

This Court was surely not a level playing field. It had not been since day one. The unfairness of the situation made me nauseous, but there was absolutely nothing that I could do to change it.

At that moment, all I wanted was to hear was for Judge Shadur to pronounce Richard's sentence. I did not for one moment believe that he would be given a life sentence as Dennis, Tokyo Rose, my associates, and members of my family were predicting.

No.

Oh, there were numerous times that I had considered the possibility, but deep in my heart, I couldn't bring myself to believe that Draconian horror story yet.

The reason was clear.

The half sheet of yellow legal paper on which Tuite had written (what now seemed like centuries ago), "Thirty-seven to forty-six months."

Three to four years.

Three to four years was not a lifetime.

Chapter 33

"**I** am not in a position to deal with (Jack Matlick)…because the focus of the total proceeding here has not been on that." ~ Judge Milton Shadur during Patrick Tuite's closing statement

During the short break that followed Safer's arguments, my eyes went from Richard to Tuite, back and forth, back and forth. Instinctively I was drawn to my husband and the only man on the planet who could save him from America's lopsided system of justice. What I saw discouraged me. Richard was wearing his zombie mask, looking relaxed, and Tuite was glancing around the room while nervously fingering some papers on the desk. In a matter of minutes, he walked before the judge.

At least we get a chance to tell our side, I kept telling myself, but after a few minutes of listening to Tuite's closing statement, I realized that his summation of the case wasn't any more convincing than Safer's. To be fair, I had to realize that Judge Shadur was cutting Tuite off at practically every other word as he tried to address the Court. Shadur was openly combative, arguing with each point Tuite tried to make, often interrupting him in midsentence. I didn't understand the judge's behavior; he had rarely spoken when Safer gave his closing.

After a few minutes, Dennis nudged me and whispered, "It doesn't take a call to the Psychic Hotline to figure out where this is going. The judge is laying down his rationale for a life sentence."

"I can't believe that!" I said. My heart was pounding once more, and I laid my hand over my chest, hoping the gesture would make it stop.

"It's true nevertheless," Dennis said, "and Shadur won't believe any of the alternative theories Tuite presents. Shadur wants this conviction as badly as Safer and Miller."

"Why?" I asked. "He's a judge!"

"He's also a man, a man with a very strong sense of morality, I'd stake my life on it, and like I told you before, he's going to protect those older women. In his eyes, their honor has been tarnished."

"But everybody stole money from those women... Frank Jayne, Jr., Silas Jayne, Toe Plemmons... even Mr. Katz overcharged Brach thousands of dollars for a family and pet memorial in Ohio!"

"Yes," Dennis said, "but Richard's the only one who told those women he loved them. And I'll bet you an Oreo that Shadur's going to put him away forever for just that."

"My God," I said under my breath. "Where's the justice then?"

"Somewhere down the yellow brick road," Dennis whispered, "when all the truth comes out."

"But will that day ever come? I've misplaced my ruby slippers..."

Someone gave us a loud "Shh!" and Dennis sat back in his seat just as Tuite said, "What we have here, Judge, is theory and no proof."

For once Tuite and I agreed on something!

Tuite elaborated, saying that the government had put blinders on as far as Richard was concerned. He then detailed out the reasons why the government's theory failed: Brach had chosen to spend New Year's Eve with Richard in December of 1976 at the Waldorf-Astoria; in January of 1977, she moved her horses into Richard's stable and left them there; she allowed him to call the Mayo Clinic on her behalf; she traveled to another state and stayed in a hotel strictly on his word; and she spoke with Richard for eight minutes on February 16th from her hotel room in Minnesota when he was still in Florida.

The real killer, Tuite implied, was Jack Matlick, Brach's handyman, but the government was unable to arrest him because he couldn't be indicted under the

R. I. C. O. Statute. Neither did they want him, I thought sadly. They only wanted Richard. Close the millions of dollars of files and place them in the archives.

But the judge neatly laid Tuite's claims about Matlick aside. "I am not in a position to deal with (Matlick) because the focus of the proceeding here has not been on that."

Maybe not. But at least Shadur knew of Matlick's existence, and Tuite filled him in on a few suspicious acts attributed to Matlick when Brach disappeared. I myself have a far more extensive list:

1. Airport on Thursday, February 17, 1977 and drove her home. (Hot Blood, 82) Aside from her love of animals, Brach's other addiction was the telephone, but from February 17 to February 21(when Matlick swore he dropped Brach back off at O'Hare), Matlick did not put any calls through to Brach nor did she make any (*Thin Air* 10); and then there was the friend who stopped by Brach's home on February 18th and was told by a stranger that Brach was still in Rochester and was not expected home until the following week (Hot Blood, 85). I believe Brach didn't use the phone because she was dead, and one of Matlick's confederates lied to the friend of Brach's because the killers had not yet cleaned up the crim scene and needed the extra time to bring in the interior decorators.

2, The fact that Matlick stayed at the Brach residence during this critical weekend was a deviation from his and Brach's routine. Normally when Brach was at home, Matlick put in an eight-hour shift then drove to Schaumburg and stayed with his family; only when Brach was away did he remain in her home. (*Thin Air*. 10)

3. The day of Brach's alleged return, Matlick claimed he watched her write a series of checks; $12, 400 went to Matlick even though Brach was known for being extremely tight with her money. These checks were later found to be forged. (*Thin Air* 11, 12, 25).

   Ernie Rizzo, a private detective working on the case, told me it was Matlick's daughter who forged the checks and that she was willing to testify against the father, but no one followed up. Miller wanted Richard.

The checks beg the question that if Matlick was the only person in the house when someone wrote the forged checks, then who arranged for the forgeries other than Matlick?

And perhaps even more important, why would Matlick have someone forge the checks unless he knew that Brach was already dead and would not be available to challenge the signature?

4. On the Sunday after Brach's alleged return, Matlick called a cleaning and decorating service to have someone come to the house as soon as possible to repaint 2 rooms and replace a rug. The service agreed to send someone out the following Tuesday. (*Thin Air*, 11)

I believe that whatever happened to Helen Brach happened in those two rooms, then Matlick and his fellow conspirators cleaned them as best they could so nothing would appear abnormal to the cleaning staff. I further believe that after a paint job and new rug, all the evidence was destroyed.

5. On Monday morning February 21, Matlick allegedly took Brach back to O'Hare Airport, where, he claimed, some amazing things happened:
   a. Helen Brach had no reservation for any flight on that day or any other when she got out of the car. (Hot Blood, 86)
   b. He dropped her off at 7:00 AM, a full three hours before the earliest scheduled flight to Florida. (Hot Blood 84, 86)
   c. In freezing Chicago weather, Helen Brach gave her fur coat to Matlick in front of the airport and walked coatless into O'Hare. (Hot Blood, 82)
   d. Brach, who normally traveled with baggage cart quantities of luggage, did not take with her a single suitcase even though she planned on an extended stay in Florida. (Hot Blood, 82)
   e. Brach, who was used to being driven everywhere, had not called her Ft. Lauderdale friends ahead of time and asked they pick her up at the airport as was their custom. (Hot Blood, 69, 86)

    f.   No airline was ever able to produce any evidence to back up Matlick's story that Brach flew to Florida. (*Thin Air*, 25)

Taking all these things into consideration, it is my firm belief that Helen Brach never left her home in Glenview alive. But there's much more to consider:

6. After Brach's brother from Ohio flew to Chicago, Matlick insisted that the two of them burn Brach's automatic writings and her diaries which they did. (Hot Blood, 80-81)
7. Any evidence contained in these materials was destroyed for all time.

When Brach first disappeared, a Glenview policeman made a thorough search of her home but could not find either Brach's will (*Thin Air* 71-73) or the suitcase she had taken to the clinic. (Hot Blood, 84)

Later, authorities found an unsigned, undated copy of Brach's will in a kitchen cabinet. Matlick claimed he had shown the will earlier to the Glenview police; they deny he did so. (*Thin Air*, 71-72) The suitcase Brach had apparently brought back from the clinic was located at the same time in a second-floor room. (*Thin Air*, 72)

The discoveries caused John Menk, guardian ad item for Helen Brach, to remark about the will, "We were looking for something better… an original… something signed by Mrs. Brach." (*Thin Air*, 73-74) Menk felt he had been sidetracked in his search for the "real" will.

With regard to the suitcase, Menk said, "I don't think the police could have overlooked it (the first time they searched the house). (*Thin Air*, 74)

8. There was a packet of unused checks found in the above suitcase, numbers 4926 to 4950. 4921 and 4922 were both dated February 17 and were made out to the Kahler Hotel and the Mayo Clinic and were signed by Mrs. Brach; checks 4924 and 4925, also dated February 17, were allegedly prepared on Brach's typewriter in Glenview, supposedly after her return. Six more checks dated February 17 were

purported to have been prepared on that date and were numbered 4976 through 4981. These latter checks were forgeries. (*Thin Air*, 73)

"If Brach did bring the suitcase in question back from Mayo Clinic, then why did she not use the next numbered packet of unused checks ... found in her suitcase?" (*Thin Air*, 73)

9. The police allowed Matlick to remain in the Brach home after her disappearance. He was free to come and go, free to destroy evidence, free to move evidence about, make it disappear and reappear. This was an unconscionable act on the part of law enforcement. (*Thin Air*, 121)

10. It was not until 1993 that a Cook County judge ordered Matlick to pay the (Brach) estate $9,000, and $75,000 as reimbursement for money or saleable items that he allegedly removed from Brach's safety deposit box and $15,000 as reimbursement for the forged checks that he claimed he saw Brach write in her home. (Hot Blood, 125)

The preceding list of facts, in my opinion, should have made the houseman, Jack Matlick, the number one suspect in the disappearance of Helen Brach. That Tuite had outright refused to subpoena Matlick as he promised Richard so long ago was, I thought, a highly suspicious act. It was as if Tuite had done everything possible to ensure that Richard lost the case.

At the end of Tuite's lengthy summation, he brought up a painful subject, Richard's acceptance of responsibility with regard to the female victims. Shadur quickly brought up Linda Holmwood and Ms. Karstenson, saying they were going to be part of the yardstick against which he was going to measure whether Richard had or hadn't earned the acceptance of responsibility.

Tuite cut in, "I don't think there is any question that with respect to the crimes involved here that Mr. Bailey has told you unequivocally he defrauded both those women."

Shadur snapped, "I will tell you up front that it was extraordinarily troublesome to bear Mr. Bailey's testimony during this hearing."

Tuite fought back, "It's not black and white; I think these women did enjoy his company and he enjoyed theirs at the time."

Then Shadur lowered the boom, "All the worse… when Bailey has knowledge… they don't have, then takes advantage of it. On that score he is in deep trouble."

My heart seemed to fall onto the floor.

"But that is what con men do!" Tuite replied lamely.

Judge Shadur spit out his words, "But the time they stop being con men is supposed to be when they get on the stand because that's the time at which it is supposed to stop, and it didn't."

Tuite admitted, "We have here an unpopular defendant based upon his… egregious conduct over many years… (but) he is sixty-seven years old and does not have that many years…"

Shadur, a senior citizen, cut Tuite off, cautioning, "Careful…"

For a very brief moment, nervous giggles filled the courtroom, but it was gallows laughter.

Finally, Tuite said, matter-of-factly, "We do not submit that the government sustained their burden with respect to the Brach matter." There were a few words about Sentencing Guidelines that I did not understand, and that was the end of Tuite's closing statement.

Richard blew me his customary kiss before leaving the courtroom, ending one of the hardest days of my life. I was not surprised that my legs felt weak when I stood up.

Outside, I spotted Trevor, made a dash for the car through a swarm of reporters and leaned back in the seat, trying to catch my breath. Only then did I gain a small degree of comfort by picturing in my mind the half sheet of legal paper on which Tuite had written, "Thirty-seven to forty-six months."

In a matter of days, practically hours now, I would know how close to the mark Tuite had come.

Chapter 34

"On Saturday, I saw a newspaper coverage of our proceeding…I found that very disturbing." ~ Judge Shadur (referencing Pamela Milner's testimony) before Steven Miller's rebuttal

By this stage of Richard's ordeal, I believed wholeheartedly that the American justice system was set up only to produce prison sentences. My reasons for arriving at this conclusion were twofold. I had read that the government convicted 98 percent of the people they indicted. If this were true, and if it were also true that any Assistant United States attorney could indict a ham sandwich, a defendant had little chance.

It was depressing but only, I supposed, if a family member or someone you knew had been arrested. Before Richard's indictment, I had never given our justice system a thought. Only now did I see how unjust it was. It seemed to me that the name of the game was only winning.

The search for truth, I realized sadly, was absent in the courtroom. The need to win was everything. It was hypocrisy at the highest level with ethics trod upon with every step the prosecutor made in front of the judge. Dennis had been telling me for weeks that the justice system was like the Viet Nam War… the only thing of importance was the body count. I hated to admit it, but Dennis was right once again. The truth was staring me in the face, and I had too much respect for it to deny its existence.

Because the legal process was cut-and-dried and pre-arranged in a long sequence, I had come to think of it as a line of dominoes. First came the arraignment, then the bail hearing, followed by a guilty plea or a trial until finally the ultimate goal, the sentencing process, dropped down like the last obedient domino, and the defendant was sent off to prison.

I just wanted to get through this final segment of the process in Judge Shadur's courtroom and then initiate a search for justice in another forum, so I was terribly disappointed at the next session when Judge Shadur slowed the fall of one of the last dominoes. He announced he was putting the delivery of Richard's personal statement before the Court off a day and a half. Although part of me had been dreading the experience, I had also looked forward to getting closer to that last domino in line.

After this pronouncement, Judge Shadur clasped his hands,, frowned and looked down into the spectators' faces. His face was an angry mask, and I couldn't imagine why. There was a long silence, then finally the judge announced that he was extremely upset over a newspaper article he read over the weekend. Specifically, he was disturbed by a story that covered a portion of testimony (Pamela Milner's) that he had ruled should be stricken front record.

I myself was jubilant!

I never understood why Judge Shadur had encouraged the reporters not to print Pamela Milner's testimony. In a democracy like the United States, its citizens deserved to know what went on in their courtrooms; otherwise, this country would be little more than a police state. Besides, Shadur's request to the media was terribly naive. Didn't he realize that perjury in a high-profile case like Richard's sold more than a few newspapers?

Judge Shadur kept repeating how troublesome he found the newspaper's rendition of the facts, especially one portion which he said, "had been sealed," but he never went into the details as to exactly what had upset him. Shadur further said he wouldn't mention anything about the source of the article because he didn't know who that person was, but that he found the article "very disturbing."

People were buzzing all around me while the judge was speaking, and I could see how confused everyone was. Dennis leaned forward and whispered he thought Shadur was angry at Miller. The prosecution had forced a perjured witness to the stand, Dennis said, and left the mess for Shadur to clean up.

I had no answers to Shadur's outburst. My window to the judge's soul was not the way he protected the perjurer Milner, but the lame way he defended himself when the press took him to task for the coverup. Shadur knew he was wrong. He had bent the rules to protect the conviction like he protected Milner. What it all came down to was just another enduring mystery added on to a very long list in the Helen Brach case.

I was amazed Judge Shadur was giving the spectators in his courtroom a long lecture about Milner, yet never once did he mention her name. That took some doing. Then the judge's frown disappeared and as if he were suddenly cognizant, he was behaving in a manner not appropriate for a jurist, he closed the door on the subject by abruptly turning to Miller and asking him to begin his rebuttal.

The prosecutor stepped quickly in front of the judge and in his tight-lipped, precise way of speaking, summed up the government's rebuttal in ten minutes flat. The only new and interesting thing he admitted to was that Jack Matlick could indeed have been involved in Brach's disappearance, but even if he were, Miller contended, that didn't mean Richard was not guilty of being a member of the conspiracy. Once again, Miller was throwing out theories without any proof. He and Safer had been skating on thin ice for so long I was astonished they hadn't fallen through.

Miller really caught my attention when he then did a complete turnaround and said that Helen Brach was Matlick's meal ticket and that he had no reason to want to see her dead.

No reason?

NO REASON?

Helen Brach was going to fire Matlick because she was moving to Florida! After that notice, Matlick had robbed Brach's safety deposit box and had someone forge checks made out to him that would have been discovered if she were alive! Miller was dead wrong. Matlick was losing his meal ticket and Brach's rent-free farm in Schaumburg! No reason indeed!

When Miller finished his rebuttal, Judge Shadur asked Tuite and Richard to stand, then spoke about the Presentence Report and Richard's speech he would deliver the next day. Judge Shadur said the process would give Richard an opportunity to make any kind of statement he thought would be useful or important for purposes of his own decision about the sentencing.

When Tuite had the opportunity to speak, he finally brought up the fact that Richard's childhood was filled with meanness by other people, teasing, beatings, and rejection because of his deformed eyelids. Tuite showed Judge Shadur snapshots of Richard from his childhood, a small frail boy standing with his head tilted back, looking at the photographer through droopy eyelids. Tuite even posed like Richard had in the snapshot, squinting and holding his head back.

Even though a surgeon partially repaired Richard's droopy eyelids, when he was twenty years old, Tuite went on, the only way he could close his eyelids even today was by looking down. As a result, Tuite said, Richard built up emotional scar tissue. That was why he seemed so relaxed on the stand and had an "I don't care attitude," showing few emotions with regard to the people he dealt with over the years.

Tuite went on to explain that because of Richard's affliction and his history of being harassed, he didn't pursue Brach when his phone calls weren't answered after a short period of time. It all had to do with rejection, he said, Richard simply couldn't handle it.

Tuite was an imbecile. He had waltzed into Judge Shadur's courtroom the day before Richard was to be sentenced and talked about a tragedy in his life that could have been a major bargaining point if it had only been brought up at the beginning of the hearing' To make matters worse, the disclosure wasn't even backed up by a psychiatrist's evaluation! Without facts, Tuite's ramblings, as far as Shadur was concerned, were probably just that, and nothing more.

As I watched Tuite make his eleventh-hour revelation, I had two awarenesses that I didn't want to have.

First, I could see from the hangdog expression on Tuite's face he had lost his confidence. Second, I believed Tuite thought he had lost the case.

Because of those perceptions, I was overcome with embarrassment once again. Tuite's incompetency had to be obvious to anyone following the Helen Brach case.

Judge Shadur closed the session on a most disturbing note, that being that his mind was already made up about Richard's sentence.

I left the courtroom that day sick at heart but tried to fool Richard by giving him one of my quick braves smiles as I waved goodbye. By that time, I had perfected those smiles and often flashed them at the press as well when I wanted them to believe I was unshaken by that day's revelations.

On the way home, I kept seeing Tuite walking back and forth in front of Judge Shadur, head down, downcast, a man without confidence. Another one of Dennis' favorite sayings came to mind: "A lawyer without confidence is like Johnson's without wax: No shine. No sparkle. No clear finish."

The image paralyzed me for a moment and then my sympathies went to Richard. Boxed into his prison cell, boxed into a guilty plea by his attorney, boxed into living with the countless lies that the government witnesses told, and soon to be boxed into a sentence that I could only pray would be no more than forty-six months.

The history or grandeur "BAILEY'S HORSE FACILITY" acquisitions, of a World rated fabulous running horse, which was claimed by the 'eye of the owner, Mr. Bailey, was known for his "horse sense," not only with the horses but, the business of horses, as well. This Rulers Ile was claimed by the corporate acquisition, for the ridiculous price of $10, 000.

Rulers Ile won its first five races after a trimming of the horse's talents, by the personal direction of Mr. Bailey. Mr. Bailey's stable's view was always, the best for the horse, is the best for the rider. Rulers Ile became very accustom to the rides that would be taken through the riding trails in Tryon, North Carolina.

Rules Ile, would enjoy the trail rides so much that be never denied a jump that I ask of him…

Chapter 35

"Much of the circumstantial evidence stems from sources that clearly raise the need to engage in judgments about the believability of witnesses whose credibility is suspect for one reason or another." ~ Judge Shadur in sentencing Richard Bailey

The day of Richard's sentencing had finally arrived. Strangely enough, it was also ID Day, and the word "liberation" was very much on my mind. Since the hearing didn't begin until one-thirty that afternoon, I spent the entire morning at work as I was trying to keep my practice going and was still scheduling patients in between court sessions.

Of course, every few minutes my mind had flipped back to Judge Shadur's courtroom. Justice would be served I thought, and in our favor. After all, the prosecution had given Judge Shadur no real proof that it was Richard who had solicited the murder of Helen Brach. How could the judge send a man to prison without any evidence? This was America and I truly believed Shadur would sentence Richard fairly. Richard had admitted to the frauds, let him serve his time and then we could get on with our lives.

Around noon, Trevor picked me up at the office and drove me home. I rushed inside and dressed very carefully in a conservative but quietly elegant, white two-piece outfit. I flashed an encouraging smile at myself in the mirror and I was ready. I called Trevor and we were off to the Dirksen Federal Building.

In the security of the car, I mentally prepared myself for the grueling process of swimming through the sharks to get to the courtroom, sitting through the sentencing (although Tuite insisted the session would be short), and then once again fighting my way back through the minions of Tokyo Rose until I was safely at home.

The government's propaganda machine had already decided that (Tuite's assurances aside) Richard could get "up to life" for his crimes. I did not know if the announcements in the papers were designed to influence the judge, frighten me, or give comfort to Richard's enemies, but I did know that it was terribly, terribly disconcerting to read in black and white that there was even a possibility that Richard might die in Prison for a crime he didn't commit.

Surely not something so barbaric and basically unfair happen.

Surely not.

Trevor's mood, while driving me to the courthouse, fit right in with my optimistic frame of mind and we began to chat casually as if nothing were wrong, and he was driving me to the white Hen Pantry instead of the Federal Building.

"How's the Big Boss?" he asked lightly. "When's he coining home?" Trevor had always called Richard, "The Big Boss," and I was "Boss #1."

"Not soon enough," I quipped, "not soon enough."

When we arrived at our destination, the press was ready and waiting for me. I knew many of them felt that even though Richard was a shady character, that he wouldn't be convicted on the Brach charge. I recalled a previous conversation with one of the reporters who said, "When the judge asks, 'Where's the body? ' the ball game's gonna be over, and Bailey's gonna walk!"

When I entered the courtroom, I could see more spectators had showed up than on any previous day making the room stuffy. The next thing I noticed was David Hamm, the Illinois State Policeman. He was talking with Steven Miller. Hamm was having the time of his life, laughing, and slapping the prosecutor on the back. Here was a man in the height of his glory and that did not bode well for Richard.

When Hamm saw me, he made eye contact. What I saw was a gloating, triumphant gleam which sent shivers down my spine. At that same time, the deputies brought Richard in and Hamm's eyes cut away like those of an evil spirit exposed to daylight.

Richard looked wonderful. He was wearing the same dark suit and tie I had dropped off on the first day of the hearing. He appeared to be calm, not at all worried about the outcome of the proceedings. I knew, in fact, he was calm because held already admitted to the frauds, and he knew he was not guilty of soliciting the murder of Helen Brach. Part of me was happy to see Richard looking so confident, but I was also worried that others in the courtroom would interpret his plucky demeanor as arrogance.

Richard and I exchanged smiles, nods, and then he blew me a kiss for luck. At that moment, the Clerk said, "All rise."

Judge Shadur entered, smiled at the prosecution table, nodded coldly at Tuite, and shot Richard one of his most scathing glares. The look was so filled with absolute loathing that I was afraid he was going to pound Richard's life to pieces with the upcoming sentence.

Somehow, I found my seat and forced my back as straight as possible. If this is going to be terrible, I thought, I will take it like a lady.

Richard's allocution was the first thing on the agenda. Allocution. Because I'd studied Latin in high school in South Africa, I had a habit of tracing words back to their Latin roots. Allocution, I remembered, came from "*adlocutio,*" the Latin noun for "address." The thought of Richard addressing the judge was more than a little scary, but I knew he could make a good impression it he told the truth.

Judge Shadur began to speak and explained (once again) that the right of allocution gave a defendant an opportunity to make any kind of a statement, on an unsworn basis, that he thought would be useful to the Court's calculation of a sentence.

Was Shadur kidding?

The minute Richard finished his speech, the judge was going to render his decision! He had carried it with him into the courtroom! Richard's allocution was, therefore, pointless and would only serve to humiliate him.

If an allocution were to have any reason whatsoever for being included in a sentencing hearing, that right should have been granted long before the sentencing itself so the judge could have been moved one way or the other by Richard's speech. There was no logic in the present chronology.

The courtroom became still and then for some reason I didn't understand, Shadur allowed Tuite to speak on Richard's behalf. In a speech I could only characterize as wishy-washy, Tuite tried to point out that he and Richard had spent more time working on the defense for the Brach matter than they had on the women who were defrauded. This happened, Tuite said, because Richard had anguished over the allegation that he was part of the Brach murder conspiracy.

Shadur missed the point and cut Tuite off, saying that the issue was not with respect to Tuite's acceptance of responsibility, but to Richard's.

This on sequitur upset Tuite he dropped the subject and picked another. "I don't think there were any intentional misrepresentations on the stand when Bailey testified that he couldn't remember dates," he said lamely.

What on earth are you talking about, Pat Tuite, I wanted to shout. Everyone knows Richard lied about his Florida trip and he did so because you, his attorney, told him to do it!

Tuite concluded by asking on Richard's behalf that Richard be given some light at the end of the tunnel, and it not be a train rushing in his direction. I looked up at the judge as Tuite was saying this and saw him frown and shake his head. Maybe Shadur's arranged for trains coming from both directions, I thought, but in my heart, I was still hopeful. Tuite's promise on the little yellow scrap of legal paper was never far from my thoughts.

When Tuite finished his speech, the judge called Richard's name and Richard began to read from a piece of notebook paper. After a brief reference to his deformed eyelids, he told the judge that he saw others pulling off scams at stables and because he felt inferior, he tried to outdo them. He had wanted the company of rich or pretty women, he said, to make him feel good about himself.

With regard to Linda Holmwood, Richard said he'd been unaware the horses took all the money she had, and he was sorry for that. Concerning Mrs.

Karstenson, he apologized for revealing their sex life, but said that was why he remembered she wasn't ill, as she had claimed.

He then looked up and stared directly at Judge Shadur. "I had nothing to do with Helen Brach's disappearance," he said convincingly. "I know my sentence could be reduced if I furnished truthful information regarding Helen's disappearance, but I don't have any." He paused a moment, then added, "I wish I did."

At the end of his speech, Richard pleaded with Judge Shadur, saying that being apart from me had been "pure torture." Further, he said, "I know you must sentence me under the guidelines, but I would like some years of peace with my wife."

He looked so sad as he returned to his seat. Richard's speech had been brief, but there was a ring of truth in his statements. He had done the best he knew how to do. I could not have asked for more.

Just then an angry, red-faced Miller, rushed in front of Shadur shouting that be didn't see any of the sincerity the Court should be looking for in Richard, that Richard had not told the truth, and had even looked for additional victims, placing dozens of advertisements in newspapers, claiming he was looking for a wife.

The truth was that Richard was being absolutely honest about looking for a wife. When a relationship didn't work out, he would sometimes sell the woman a horse instead. If anything is proof that he was looking for a wife, I am that proof! He married me! And he never ever tried to sell me a horse.

Miller went on and on, venting his anger, saying that Richard was wallowing in self-pity over his eyelids, that he had not accepted responsibility and should not be given any credit for it. The prosecutor seemed to be genuinely outraged, but I felt he was play acting for the sake of the judge. He ended his tirade by asking the Court to impose the maximum sentence under the guidelines and then in addition, requested that a million-dollar fine be imposed on Richard.

I could not believe what I was hearing! That Richard would go to prison was horrible enough; to think that once freed and jobless, he would have to come up with a million dollars right out of prison was ludicrous!

Judge Shadur nodded to Miller, then cleared his throat very loudly, and glanced briefly down at the spectators. The suspense was almost palpable. Suddenly I could hear the person behind me breathing in, breathing out.

No!

It was not the person behind me.

It was me!

I couldn't help it.

It was time for Richard's sentence.

My mind focused in the courtroom; I saw us all frozen, dutiful actors in the closing scenes of a Sophocles' tragedy. Then, like an eagle focusing on his prey, Shadur's eyes fell on the Sentencing Memorandum he had placed earlier on top of his desk. I was immensely grateful that Richard's brother, Bill, and his wife, Shirley, were sitting right behind me, as they had all through these difficult proceedings.

Shadur launched a scathing tirade of his of his own as he went into great detail about Richard's frauds, things Richard had long ago admitted to and rectified in civil suits or settlements. He brushed off Richard's entire defense by saying that Richard had even sunk to using lonely hearts ads to entice women to invest with him. Obviously, the judge's emotions were clearly in control.

Shadur then highlighted the egregious nature of Richard's conduct by noting that he chose to defraud exceptionally vulnerable women such as Linda Holmwood and Ms. Karstenson.

I strongly disagreed and had always felt that Richard should never have pleaded guilty to horse fraud. First off, a good attorney like Jo Ann Wolfson could have damaged the testimony of the female witnesses on the stand in ways no male attorney would dare. Why? Because the women weren't only paying for horses but for the pleasure of Richard's company! Secondly, as most expert witnesses on horse trades will say, people who put money into horses are not being intellectually or emotionally smart. They are buying their way into a level of the social elite. There are few winners in the world of horse racing, whether you are an owner or a better, but owners get a lot of social invitations. This concept was never adequately emphasized by the defense.

The problem was that Tuite had insisted Richard plead guilty for selfish reasons. With a guilty plea, the hearing was shorter than a jury trial would have been, which had the net effect of making Tuite the same amount of money faster and with considerably less work.

I wanted to make a spectacle of myself, stand up and address the courtroom and say that the behavior Shadur was referencing was Richard 20 years ago and what did all of that have to do with Helen Brach anyway? But of course, I said nothing and besides, my thoughts were swamped with Shadur's continued exorcising of his own male chauvinistic ghosts in Richard's hearing. He went on about how Richard had lied regarding certain things in his past, things which I knew for a fact were not lies but were well documented facts that Tuite had neglected to make clear to the court.

With a grim expression on his face, Shadur said that although Richard had admitted guilt in some of the cases, the admission alone did not absolve him of responsibility because Richard had failed to show remorse. How terribly sad! Richard's defensive mask could all have been explained with a psychiatrist's report!

The judge continued to read from his memorandum. When Richard had sworn he was in Florida, Shadur said, he had "plainly lied." His story was bogus.

Then the judge discounted all of Richard's calls to Helen Brach from Florida, saying they had never taken place, ignoring the fact that Jack Matlick was, by Shadur's own admission, a suspect in the murder.

I was astounded!

I knew Richard had phoned Brach several times and had spoken to Matlick, but the houseman wouldn't put him through.

This latest reference to Matlick was almost too much to assimilate. He should have been the prime suspect, not Richard!

"WHERE IS JACK MATLICK?" I wanted to scream. "PEOPLE THINK HE KILLED HELEN BRACH, NOT RICHARD! WHY DIDN'T MILLER QUESTION HIM? AND FRANK JAYNE, JR. AND THE RETIRED POLICEMAN… WHY WERE THEY NEVER QUESTIONED, AS WELL?"

But I bit my tongue, and the judge began to speak of Cathy Olsen's and Joe Plemmons' testimonies, admitting they were flawed and posed serious credibility problems. Shadur said that he had looked at evidence from more reliable sources to see whether it corroborated or refuted these more dubious ones.

The essence of what Shadur was saying was a question of whether the Court was going to believe Richard Bailey, Joe Plemmons or Cathy Olsen. Only Bailey was totally unbelievable, Shadur noted, and a chill went through my body. I heard the cell doors close with a sharp clang on Richard, my hopes, my dreams, and my vision of Bali Hai.

It was difficult to credit Ken Hanson's testimony for the defense, Shadur went on, because he was under indictment for the murders of three youngsters.

That was no surprise.

It was the old "Indictment Is Proof of Guilt Syndrome" that permeates the federal courts; i. e. , he's indicted, ergo, he's guilty, and his testimony is, therefore, unreliable.

The most important witness, Shadur contended, was Arthur Katz, who swore that shortly before Brach's disappearance, she had come in to see his father and had said she was disturbed because a younger man she was seeing had cheated her in the purchase of some horses, and the same man had arranged her stay at the Mayo clinic. Shadur said Katz's testimony had provided him with an accurate description of Richard, and he credited it entirely.

Then, as if playing my emotions like a badminton shuttlecock, Shadur smacked me back into the arena of hope by saying that bits of evidence provided to him portrayed Matlick in a very suspicious light. But it was impossible to tell, he went on, whether Matlick was a more likely suspect than Richard because all of the evidence pertaining to Bailey had been placed before him while nothing had been provided with regard to Matlick.

There was no mention of Pamela Milner, but I knew in my heart that she had made a profound impression on the judge, and for whatever reason, he was sympathetic to her cause. I felt her testimony, perjured though it was, had most assuredly affected the decision he would soon render.

Golden Tongue

In the end, Shadur said, "In summary, it is more probable than not that Richard Bailey did commit the offenses of conspiring to murder and soliciting the murder of Helen Brach." He then had Richard rise.

He then calmly sentenced him.

He gave Richard life in prison.

I was in total shock, neither feeling nor seeing anything. The next day, someone told me that after Shadur's announcement, my hand flew up and clutched my throat, but I had no memory of doing that. I remember turning to Bill and Shirley behind me and Shirley was crying like I was. I would read in Chicago magazine two months later that when Shadur pronounced Richard guilty, "A ripple of astonishment ran through the courtrooms T. V. reporters rushed toward the doors, and an agent for the Bureau of Alcohol, Tobacco, and Firearms high-fived an FBI Agent beside him."

Suddenly I became aware that Tuite was scurrying in front of the bench, shouting, "Excuse me, Judge," at the top of his voice. He strongly disagreed with Judge Shadur about the sentencing guidelines, insisting that the judge had used the current guideline instead of those in effect when Brach disappeared. Very quickly the prosecution team jumped in and a heated argument followed. Shadur looked absolutely furious and told Tuite he should have raised the guidelines issue earlier.

Tuite, you blew it once again, I thought sadly.

The reporters were eyeing the door out of the courtroom as if they wanted more than anything in life to burst out into the hall but were paralyzed.

Meanwhile, Richard was staring at the floor and shaking his head. To my surprise, I saw one of his eyelids was twitching under the pressure. All I could think was how much more, how much more can we take? Then I heard a very loud snort coining from the back of the room. Incredible as it seemed, someone had fallen asleep and begun to snore.

The argument between the attorneys and the judge continued for ten minutes or so until finally, Judge Shadur, looking now more than a little exasperated, postponed Richard's sentencing until June 15 Nine more hellish days in limbo! Richard, ignoring the commotion in the courtroom, blew me a kiss, and the marshals took him away.

I glanced up at the judge as he left the courtroom and thought how unfair he had been when he sentenced Richard. He had the judicial power to minimize his sentence, but instead he had maximized it, giving the prosecution everything they asked for. Considering Richard's age, Milner's perjured testimony and the information (brief though it was) Shadur was privy to about Hatlick, he could have been far more lenient.

I stared down at my wedding ring, caressed it with my fingertips. The human heart, I realized as I walked out, has no place in a federal courtroom.

On the way down the Federal Building steps, I turned and looked up and there was David Hamm, staring down at me. He looked pensive. I hoped his conscience was troubling him.

I caught Tuite and Menaker out of the corner of my eye. They were dodging reporters, scuttling down the street, but I stopped and gave the press a brief statement which was extremely difficult for me because by then I was shaking very and numb. I told the reporters I most assuredly did not believe that Richard was guilty of the Brach murder. When asked what I would do next, I said honestly that I simply didn't know, that no man I had ever known had treated me as well as Richard. I wasn't up to giving any long statements and when I spotted Trevor down the street, I made a dash for the car.

I didn't have to tell Trevor the news was bad. I managed to get out "life." He mumbled something, and I don't think we spoke again all the way home. I was only too happy to take off my elegant outfit and hang it in my closet. I never wore it again. Never will. It hangs there even now like a pitiful ghost in the back of my closet.

That evening I learned quite a few people involved with the case gave afternoon press conferences. Miller stated jubilantly that the case was closed, but Richard's brother William took the opposing viewpoint: "Richard's no more guilty than I am! Somebody's got it in for him! The truth will come out someday!"

"I'm not sure this proves anything," Helen Brach's brother, Charles Vorhees, said when interviewed. "I would like to see someone charged with the murder and tried."

That evening in my bedroom, I thought of Tuite and his strong objections to Shadur's sentencing. Maybe we have a slim chance, I thought, a very slim chance. Maybe Tuite's really up on sentencing guidelines and I wasn't aware of it.

I could picture Richard in his jail cell just then. In the background, the SeaBees were singing, "What ain't we got? We ain't got dames…"

Maybe not, Richard, I thought… but by God, your freedom is all that matters.

Chapter 36

"This whole creation is essentially subjective, and the dream is the theater where the dreamer is at once scene, actor, prompter, stage manager, author, audience, and critic." ~ Carl Jung

It was 11:00 P. M. , and I was once again in my bedroom closet, picking out clothes I would wear to court the next day. At that point in time, I really didn't care what I wore and grabbed the first conservative suit and pair of black heels I saw.

I had spoken at length with Pat Tuite the day after the sentencing. He told me rather enthusiastically that Richard stood an excellent chance to get only eleven years, and of course, he said, there was always the hope that that sentence could be reduced in an appeal. He never mentioned the half sheet of legal paper in his own handwriting regarding the short sentence he promised months ago that Richard would get. I had come to think of it as a promissory Valentine, and Tuite acted as if he had forgotten all about it.

Since Judge Shadur had already sentenced Richard to life in prison, my own life had become a brand-new nightmare from which I never awoke. At first I had closed my heart and tried not to think about the judge's decision. I cried briefly, then told myself that doing so was foolish. When the tears went away, I was numb for days in shock. Slowly a partial healing took place. I say partial because after waiting for so long a time, I still had no idea what Richard's (and my) future would be.

I had scheduled patients beginning early the next morning and put my instructions for Trevor on the kitchen bulletin board. Having done everything within my power to be prepared for one final day in court, I crawled into bed, then turned the balance of my worries over to God with a simple prayer for peace.

But when sleep came, it was with a mean spirit and dragging feet. It was at least 1:00 A. M. before I dozed off, and I fell, rather than slipped, into a fitful dream. I was barely into REM sleep when the nightmare began.

At first I thought I was in a church, but I soon realized I was in the center of a roofless Greek edifice bounded on four sides by Corinthian columns. Their slender fluted pillars capped by ornate leaf designs seemed to stretch to the sky. It took a moment for me to realize that I was a sacrifice, lying flat on my back on a raised dais, shielding my eyes from the sun.

Suddenly, a deafening roll of thunder cracked the air and made the building shake. The face of Zeus appeared high overhead and hovered over me. His gray locks were wreathed by clouds pierced with jagged spears of lightning.

I wanted to speak but my lips were frozen. Then I noticed Zeus's eyes were crinkled in mirth. The god's smile turned into a chuckle and in seconds, he was roaring with laughter. What a sight! The thunder boomed, the lightning flashed without end, and in a particularly bright moment, Zeus' eyes popped open and he formed his lips to talk. At that moment, as though a child had rolled his kaleidoscope, Zeus' face shattered into a myriad of colorful prisms, then quickly reformed into Judge Shadur's visage.

Shadur was also laughing. "Cutting up watermelons, was he?" he roared, and from somewhere nearby, I heard the rasp of a thousand demons giggling. "Well, let's just see…" Shadur paused, his bushy eyebrows came together forming a point, and he said, "Oh, I know what to do… You! You woman! You're DEAD!"

"I…"I began, but the judge vanished along with the sun and the Greek building. I was alone, consumed by terror in the musky darkness.

Unsure as to what to do next, I stood up and peered into thick, foul-smelling mists of fog. I could see nothing. After what seemed like forever, I spotted a pinpoint of light moving slowly through the haze. It was coming toward me, and soon I heard the creak of oar locks counterpointed by the splash of wooden paddles dipping into water. Creak……splash, splash… Creak… splash, splash, then the fog parted, and I could just make out a wide black river.

I was standing on the banks of the River Styx!

I was dead Just like Judge Shadur said!

The boatman at the helm of the rotting craft was wearing an Illinois State Police uniform.

"My God!" I exclaimed when he came closer. "You're David Hamm! What are you doing here?"

At first Hamm said nothing. He only stared grimly into the black seething water, then hissed, "I have a job to do! Get in!" He pointed to a seat in the back of the boat.

Hamm left me no choice. I stepped into the boat and he began to row across the fetid river. For a while I heard nothing but the rhythmic dipping and stroking of the oars, then came a barely audible sound, like silk wafting in a breeze.

The darkness was suddenly filled with the fluttering of wings. Dark nebulous creatures were flying past my face without ever touching me, but so close I could smell their putrid breath. Perhaps I was being escorted by squadrons of lost souls, I thought sadly.

The boat docked with an unexpected jar. I left David Hamm to his eternal task and began to follow a pale-yellow line glowing under my feet. I was compelled to walk onward but for some reason, my fear had disappeared. After a few steps, it seemed the most natural thing in the world to stroll off into the endless night.

I walked for miles down dark corridors, never questioning where or when to turn, obedient to the path lighted by the glowing stripe. Finally, after what seemed hours, I was stopped where the line of light disappeared into a wall. A touch and I discovered it was not a wall at all, rather a loosely hanging backdrop made of gauze. I reached out again, and the thinly woven material parted with no more resistance than a spider's web. Directly in front of me was a depressing sight, even more darkness shrouded by thicker mists. I walked straight ahead.

The next barrier was a heavy black curtain, but I pulled it aside and could see bright overhead lights and hear people talking followed by applause. I hesitated, then gathered up all my courage and walked out onto a big wooden platform. I recognized the set of *Let's Make A Deal*, only the host was Steven Miller, not Monty Hall.

Miller beckoned with his microphone. "And which door do you choose, lady... and remember, we are looking here for the BIG DEAL!"

"What is the Big Deal?" I asked, feeling very silly.

"We will trade your tranquility for Richard Bailey's life!" he said very precisely. "You, too, can become a government informant... all we want to know is how Richard Bailey charms women! What a deal!"

People were clapping wildly and cheering at the same time. "If I told you, you would not understand," I said truthfully.

At that moment, Judge Shadur, wearing a white clown suit with large black polka dots, joined Miller at center stage. "Enough of this blathering!" he shouted at me. "Pick a door! Pick a door! PICK A DOOR!" He then pointed to a group of doors in a half circle behind me. Each was painted a different color and number.

Which to choose I was terribly afraid I'd pick the wrong door and Judge Shadur's wrath would fall on Richard. "I'm terribly sorry," I said, tears filling my eyes, "but I don't know which door to choose."

"Seek and ye shall find," Miller said, jumping up and down on his unusually small feet and gesturing toward the doors with a long, fleshless finger.

"Oh, take any one, you ninny!" Judge Shadur agreed. "Don't you know this game has already been decided?"

"But that's not fair," I protested.

"You want fair, go to the fairgrounds... this is Fed and Fed ain't fair... now hurry up!"

"Oh, give me the green door, Door Number 3!" I yelled just to quiet him.

Then the lights went out.

Golden Tongue

Door Number 3 opened, and Judge Shadur stepped out still wearing his clown costume. He began to wave a gavel back and forth in front of my face. "Okay, you have one more chance," he said. "If you can prove Richard Bailey is innocent, I will let you go back to earth, and we will leave you alone… BUT… if you cannot do this in one day, you will be returned here to be forever dead and quite alone to boot!" He hit the gavel against the green door as hard as he could, spun around and fixed me with an icy glare.

"That's not fair!" I screamed, "Sisyphus got thirty days!"

"Sisyphus went to the state fair grounds. This is Fed and Fed ain't fair. Now… GO!"

He raised a white gloved hand and I found myself standing on a barren plain. There was no wind, no sun, yet the landscape was brightly lighted somehow and I felt suddenly renewed.

Something good was finally about to happen! I did not see him until he was only about thirty feet away. He was moving along, his feet not touching the ground, the lapels of his white suit flapping as though he were standing in a hurricane force wind.

Was I finally to meet my Guardian Angel?

When he stopped in front of me, the man bore a striking resemblance to Emile De Becque of *South Pacific*, but how could this be? The sexy Frenchman couldn't fly!

I stared intently into his eyes. "Who are you… really?" I asked politely.

The man offered me a condescending smile. "You think I'm your Guardian Angel… or maybe the French planter from *South Pacific*? Well, you're wrong on both counts! I'm Clue Man!"

"Clue Man?" I asked. "What is a Clue Man? What does a Clue Man do?"

"This!" he said and raised his right arm. All at once, his lapels ceased their fluttering and he settled to the ground. A gentle breeze began to blow and was soon bearing huge bubbles like those from a child's biggest bubble loop.

"What are those?" I asked, puzzled.

"Clues," he said primly.

Clues.

I needed clues.

I looked closer.

The first bubble was floating toward me. I looked inside and saw Jack Matlick tossing a diary into a furnace where it was consumed by flames. A clue… real clue!

The next globule came near, and I saw Matlick again, this time chatting amiably with an unidentified man and David Hamm. My God, I thought, they're in this together!

As the third bubble passed before me, I saw a man with a spray can painting "RICHARD BAILEY DID IT" on a stable wall. A smiling David Hamm was standing behind him, watching intently. I couldn't resist. I reached out and tried to grab David Hamm's arm, but the bubble popped with a loud bang, and I jumped back. Hamm and the man had both disappeared.

"What happened?" I asked Clue Man who had never left my side.

Clue Man shook his head. "You were too anxious," he said. "Causes you a lot of problems, doesn't it?"

"But I'm in a hurry!"

"Have faith!" he warned then flew out of sight.

"Time's up!" Judge Shadur announced as he suddenly reappeared. "I only gave you one day… remember?"

"But I'm not through yet!" I said stubbornly, crossing my arms and holding them tightly in front of my chest. "And… and… I have clues!"

"Doesn't matter," Judge Shadur said evenly. "You can't break our contract!"

"I made no contract with you…you devil!" I shouted. "You may look like Vincent Price, but you can't scare me! rm not going back until Richard is free… and you know what else? I don't think you can make me!"

Judge Shadur nodded. "You're right," he said sullenly. "I can't make you go back, but let me give you my revised judgment here."

The mysterious light left the landscape as though it had been vacuumed up into a funnel cloud. The plains began to push up and up and up and suddenly I was standing at the foot of a mountain with a large round stone resting at its base.

Judge Shadur tapped the stone lightly with his gavel. "When you roll that stone to the top of the mountain, I will set Richard free," he said. He was grinning from ear to ear.

"You can't do that to me!" I wailed. "It's a life sentence! You can't give me life just for loving a person…it's not fair!"

The judge snarled, "That word again…"

"But I don't have the strength to roll that huge stone up the mountain!" I screamed. "I'm a woman… not Hercules! That job would kill me!"

"Ah, now that's fair. You were dead anyway… no loss, no damage. You'll never prove prejudice on that one." Judge Shadur laughed hysterically and disappeared in a cloud of dust. Then the real nightmare began.

Each morning, I would roll the stone up the mountain just like Sisyphus, and each night, just like Sisyphus, the stone would roll back down as I slept. I knew who was doing it. I could see them just before dawn. A mixed group of people all wearing black robes, but some carrying law books while others shuttled files back and forth between them. They were arguing constantly over mundane issues. The days and nights went on and on, yet each morning, I always found the strength to start rolling the stone up the mountain once more. I had to do it. Richard's very life depended on it.

My alarm clock's gentle purring ended the dream. I sat up, discovered I was trembling, then sadly realized I had good reason.

Dawn was breaking on June 15.

In a matter of hours, I would be at the courthouse to find out if my husband would spend the rest of his life in prison.

Hours.

Prison.

Life! My God!

Chapter 37

"If Bailey had to serve 135 months less earned good time, he would emerge from custody shortly before his seventy-fifth birthday, a time at which it would be difficult to visualize him as remaining a material threat to susceptible American womanhood." ~ Judge Shadur before re-sentencing Richard Bailey to thirty years instead of life.

Tokyo Rose had received her marching orders from the U. S. Attorney's Office once more. The media was swarming outside the Dirksen Federal Building, a boisterous crowd more befitting a guillotining than a sentencing hearing. It was apparent the group from Central Casting circa Louis XIV expected Richard to be condemned to life in prison after all.

All week Chicago had been abuzz over the Brach case and Tuite's strenuous objection to Shadur's desire for Richard to spend the rest of his life in jail. Miller had been quoted in the *Tribune* as saying that Tuite's tactic was "a desperate legal maneuver that wouldn't be successful and that Judge Shadur would follow through on his stated intention to sentence Bailey to life imprisonment."

The *Tribune* also quoted unnamed "investigators" as saying that Richard's life sentence might be the answer to solving the Brach mystery, that people who were faced with long sentences had little to lose by telling what they knew. What they had to gain was a sentence reduction and a decent prison in which to do their time. The problem with the investigators' theory was that Richard knew absolutely nothing about Brach's disappearance. He had no information to give the government that would, in turn, cut his sentence.

Still others were curious about Helen Brach's body, wanting to know its whereabouts. More than a few Chicagoans believed the remains of a woman found in a Cook County Forest Preserve in 1979 were really those of Helen Brach.

Then there were the so-called "Brach Mystery Groupies." These people thought Jack Matlick was not only the undisputed lover of Helen Brach but her murderer, as well. This latter belief was supported by Matlick's purchase of a meat grinder from Marshal Fields and the absence of a corpse.

I carried all these thoughts into the courtroom which was packed. Fortunately, the bailiff had kept my customary place for me behind the defense table. I was most grateful. Almost at once, the marshals brought Richard in and he looked chipper, flashing me one of his Go-Get-'Em smiles. He walked over to the defense table where Tuite was standing, took a seat and crossed his legs. I realized once again that one of the things I liked best about my husband was that he never gave up, he never got angry, and he never lost his positive attitude.

I was not as confident as Richard. I was terribly anxious because of the Draconian sentence imposed and knew there was an extremely dark tunnel ahead if it stuck. On the other hand, I still held out hope the sentence could be ameliorated and Richard would not be sent away forever.

I thought the objections Tuite had read to Judge Shadur were well founded, but I was no Legal Eagle. At any rates we were at the end of the line, the very last domino, and I hoped that if the sentence held, there would be an appeal. The flip side of that coin was that if there were an appeal, the financial burden would be crushing, as by that time, I was cash poor as were Richard's brother, Bill, and sister-in-law, Shirley.

Judge Shadur arrived at last and I had a difficult time containing my emotions. I cringed as his bushy eyebrows snapped to a point just as they had in my nightmare. The judge wasted no time, told everyone to be seated and went into his spiel.

Shadur said he found Tuite's objections "without legal merit;" he raised his eyebrows, cast a wry look at Tuite, then noted Tuite had every opportunity to bring up his issues earlier but had not done so. Anyone could see Shadur was absolutely furious with Tuite. Shadur then said that the sins of a lawyer may properly be visited on the client who voluntarily chose that lawyer, meaning he knew Tuite blew it and Richard paid the price. I wanted to scream, "You better believe I didn't choose Tuite, your Honor!" But, of course, I said nothing.

The judge, it seemed, couldn't contain himself when it came to our defense counsel, saying his most recent legal maneuver had been, "overly simplistic" and "analytically unsound." I was so depressed by the judge's words I wanted to run out of the room.

I did receive a small degree of pleasure in knowing Judge Shadur agreed with me regarding Tuite's legal skills, but I also feared what would happen when Shadur got off Tuite's case and onto Richard's. I wasn't the only one in the courtroom who wanted the judge to move on to the actual sentencing because I overheard a man seated behind me mumble under his breath, "Take it to the Bar Association, Judge, and get on with this case, dammit!"

Judge Shadur then began to elaborate about the Sentencing Guidelines, but what he said was so complex and I was so apprehensive about Richard's upcoming sentence, that I didn't grasp most of what he was saying. I only understood two concepts: in direct opposition to what Tuite had claimed, Shadur announced the current Federal Sentencing Guidelines did apply to Richard because he had continued to swindle women until the early 1990s; Shadur also explained that any range set by a Guideline was trumped by what Congress prescribed in the criminal statutes. Shadur noted there were occasions when a judge could ignore the Sentencing Guidelines. What determined those times and how all this applied to Richard I had no idea.

Shadur then said if he sentenced Richard only for the frauds, Richard would be 75-years-old when released and then he would no longer be a threat to American womanhood. There was a gasp in the courtroom after this remark and I, too, was shocked. Shadur's comment was nasty and mean, completely unnecessary.

He then announced his first opinion was proper and that although the statutes did not give him the option of sentencing a man to life in prison, he could sentence him to thirty years. Shadur then added sarcastically that because of his age, such a prison term amounted to life for Richard.

A wave of disbelief rolled through the courtroom and my eyes went to Richard. He didn't even blink and I couldn't imagine what he was thinking. This isn't real, I kept thinking, this isn't real.

Judge Shadur asked Tuite if he wanted to address the million-dollar fine Miller had requested. Tuite said Richard had no money and his brother and I had paid his legal fees. Tuite also pointed out that in the past, Richard had made five figure settlements to many of the women.

Miller leapt up and protested, saying one million dollars was a nominal fee, a conservative fee, and that a defendant need not have a present ability to pay. He further said that Richard looked forward to selling his literary rights, and that the court should and could order a substantial restitution even if Richard were destitute. All of this rhetoric, I realized, was based upon the slim possibility Richard might come into money in the future.

Miller stressed that Richard had admitted to defrauding hundreds of people, but the judge countered with, "Now wait… " Later he referred to that as being a hyperbolic response. But it was as if Miller never heard what the judge said, and the prosecutor repeated that one million dollars was a conservative figure.

I was horrified by what I was witnessing, Richard had been given a veritable life sentence right in front of my eyes, my heart was breaking, and here were these three men, arguing about money, a million dollars to be sure, but money, nevertheless. Even Judge Shadur had to admit the government pulled the figure out of thin air, and it was only based upon income when Richard had money years ago. It was all simply ludicrous.

In the end, Judge Shadur sided with Miller even in this, saying the one-million-dollar figure was indeed the appropriate amount for restitution, and the hearing was over.

Richard would be locked up until he was well into his 90s… he would die alone… in prison… and I was a defeated woman… also alone…still looking for fairness.

Richard was led off between two hulks of marshals, but not before he smiled and blew me one last kiss.

As Richard reached the exit door, I saw the face of David Hamm for a moment and he looked ecstatic, just as he had when Clue Man pointed him out in my dream.

I felt a hand on my arm.

It was Pat Tuite.

"We need to talk," he said. "May I drive you home?"

"No…I'll need some time alone you see."

He nodded and I walked out of the courtroom for the very last time. All during the hearing, I had promised the media I would give them a statement at the end of the hearing, and so I kept my promise, walked outside to where the press was waiting and with the Cyclops eyes of the cameras and a dozen felt-clad microphones shoved in my face, I gave an interview.

I said I didn't believe Richard was guilty of the Brach murder, but found other things he had done in his life very disturbing. I couldn't help but tell them my true feelings about Richard, that he made me feel like I was the only woman in the world and that no other man had treated me like Richard Bailey. The reporters kept asking me what I was going to do in the future, and when I would ordinarily answer my questions straight out, I kept saying, "I don't know. I don't know what I'm going to do." When I finished, I was in tears.

Trevor was mercifully waiting to drive me home, and as soon as I could break away, I hurried to the protection of my car, and we sped off into the overcast Chicago afternoon.

Bali Hai had exploded in my face. I had survived, however, and needed to examine my wounds and think about what my life would be like in the future.

Leaning back against the seat, watching the raindrops drum against the windshield, I prayed silently, "God, I am not a weak, wimpy woman. I want to continue the fight. Please help me find a fair forum."

Chapter 38

In the days after the hearing, I was flooded with poignant memories: Richard's easy laughter and bright flashing eyes that first night at the Waterfront restaurant; Richard in a white tuxedo, holding me close while dancing a tango, whispering, "I love you, beautiful doll," before he spun me away; Richard in the early morning, handing me a breakfast tray with steaming coffee, then the delicious manly scent of his hands tilting my chin up for a long slow kiss.

If this weren't enough, there were also the fantasies I had visualized so many times they seemed real: Richard and I walking barefoot across a pristine white beach in Bali Hai; swimming together in a sparkling jungle pool surrounded by ferns and clusters of orchids; sleeping in Richard's arms under clean starched sheets cooled by ocean breezes, waking to peaceful waves whispering outside our cabana, and a morning topped off with hot banana muffins and endless cups of coffee.

I was soon to discover that the cherished remembrances of what had been real and what I had imagined were luxuries I could ill afford. The more I relived them the more pain I had to fight off. Eventually, I had to put these reflections out of my mind to prevent them from torturing me. Perhaps torture is too strong a word, but it's the only one I can think of that accurately describes what I was feeling.

Only my work promised survival and I threw myself into my medical practice. What I knew best was how to be a caregiver, and in the final analysis, it was ironically my patients who kept me alive.

One day Pat Tuite called out of the blue, saying he had some papers he urgently needed for me to sign and since he was already in my neighborhood to visit his son, he would stop by. Eager to put an end to the mountain of paperwork Pat had burdened me with, I told him yes.

When Pat arrived, he handed me a large manila envelope and we went into the dining room. The minute we sat down at the dining room table, I realized he had tricked me. The first words out of his mouth were that I owed him another $1 million. He went on and on about how I had promised him I would pay him this additional sum.

Promised him?

He had to be kidding!

I looked into Pat's tired eyes, dull in his handsome face, and said, "What do you know about promises, Pat? From the first day I met you in your office, you promised me that Richard would be free in less than four years and you see where that promise got us!"

Pat didn't respond and I realized I had nothing else to say. To have continued to berate him would have been my style and as pointless as Richard's sentencing allocution. Of course, there was the appeal to consider, but that was in the hands of a new lawyer.

Pat then began to badger me for a date. "We really must go to dinner," he said.

I declined.

"Oh well," he said, "if you can't make dinner, then how about lunch or just coffee?"

He had already asked me before to join him and each time I'd refused. I did so again.

In the end, the subject of his "urgent" need to see me never came up. I signed the papers later and sent them to Tuite's law firm by U. S. Mail. Neither did I go to dinner with Pat Tuite…ever.

Nor to lunch… ever.

Nor breakfast… ever.

Nor did I meet Pat Tuite at any time for coffee…ever.

And he tried all of them.

What a shame Pat never understood that my heart belonged to Richard and only to Richard. If Tuite had understood that simple equation, perhaps he would have worked on Richard's case instead of me.

Perhaps Richard would be free today.

I don't know.

I will never know.

All I know for certain is that Pat Tuite really blew it…for Richard…for me…for all-time.

But I knew that While lawyers made mistakes, not…and He never left a man it jail so He could take an early Thanksgiving vacation either. He did not have to because His universe was always unfolding as it should… and my tiny part of that great vastness would not be forgotten. Surely the world would come full circle and the waters of time would rush over me once again.

Chapter 39

"I'm sixty-seven years old. If I knew something, I would have been talking a long time ago." ~ Richard Bailey, *Dateline*

I had refused to go I public with my story during Richard's hearing, but I did meet a television producer one day in the courtroom with whom I had an instant rapport. Her name was Laura Rabhan, and she worked for NBC's popular *Dateline*. Laura was highly professional and extremely intelligent as well as compassionate, not intruding when I was upset, always taking my feelings into consideration. From the first moment I met her, I felt a strong kinship. Laura mentioned she wanted to put a show together about Helen Brach that would not only be intellectually stimulating but would also be fair to Richard. Laura said she wanted to interview a number of the key people involved in the case and get their opinions as to what they thought had happened to the heiress. I was so exhausted by the end of the hearing that if I hadn't had so much respect for Laura, I would not have scheduled a personal interview. I knew all too well the taping would drag up all the pain and memories again, and I had no desire to go on T. V. once more, not after being hounded by reporters for so many months. But Richard's life was at stake. I agreed to do the show.

A short time later, I learned that Jo Anne Wolfson, Richard's former attorney, was not only going to appear on *Dateline*, but she was also going to prepare Richard to be interviewed for the program. I gave her a call and we ended up meeting at Nick's Fish Market.

Jo Anne was angry. Angry at Pat Tuite for stealing her client. Angry she didn't have an opportunity to break down the witnesses' testimony, especially Cathy Olsen. Angry about the outcome of the hearing, saying she could have won the case. I think the only thing she wasn't angry about was the fact that *Dateline* was going forward with the show, and some solid facts would be disclosed for the first time.

I took the entire day off for the *Dateline* interview. I was ready when the crew show up, bringing vanloads of cameras, lights, plugs and extension cords. It took almost the entire day to get everything set up just the way they wanted it, and they ended up filming for about six hours. All that preparation and I was only on camera a few minutes, but I knew the show was a winner and well worth the time spent.

The night of the broadcast, I watched the show alone. It was February 21, 1996. From the moment Helen Brach's beautiful face first appeared on T. V., there was a haunting quality to "The Lady Vanishes" that played up the mystery of Brach's disappearance and gave me chills. The writing was excellent, and the interviews moved seamlessly from one to the next, giving a variety of people a unique opportunity to vocalize their opinions.

Laura had been meticulous in gathering information, and a great deal of attention had been paid to even the smallest details. The music, a mournful saxophone that counterpointed the ghostly image of Brach's face, and a sad little melody in a minor key that ran throughout the program, worked very well with the narrative.

Attorney John Menk started the show off by saying Brach had literally disappeared into thin air and that it all added up to a great tragedy. Jo-Anne then announced, "This is about fraud, fraud and broken hearts."

My old adversary Steven Miller, who was referred to as "Sherlock," said all the familiar things, that Richard was a con man and a swindler, a truly evil man, that it was an overwhelming circumstantial case, and he repeated his now famous motto, "Follow the money, solve the murder."

My segment was next. The crew had interviewed me in my office, seated in such a way that my face was visible through the half-sphere bubble aquarium on the wall. The effect was surreal. I simply told the truth, that I had been smitten by Richard, that I did love him some time ago and that I loved him still.

Dateline then asked a number of very important questions: "Is the wrong man in jail for Helen Brach's murder? Was she done in by Richard Bailey? Or was Helen Brach the victim of a far bigger, far more sinister criminal enterprise?"

Jane Pauley said that Miller had put Richard away for life, but the investigation into Brach's murder had uncovered an extensive network of dangerous men, linked to Richard, men who were still walking free, and they, not Richard, may have plotted to kill the Candy Lady. I agreed, shaking my head up and down until my neck hurt.

Dennis Murphy, the commentator, went into greater detail, explaining that when Richard sold Brach some bum horses, he led her into a very dangerous world… the Horse Mafia. When questioned, Steven Miller had to admit that the stables in Chicago were a "magnet to attract wealthy people for fraud." The lords of this underworld, Murphy said were the Jayne Family.

Cathy Olsen's middle name, Jayne, now took on a different meaning!

Olsen was interviewed in a poolroom, her face even more worn and tired than in Shadur's courtroom. Beer at her side, cigarette in hand, Olsen repeated what she said in court, that Richard had been a participant in the chilling conversations about Brach, but commentator Murphy was quick to point out Olsen had told three different versions of the same story and only the most recent one included Richard; Olsen was also, Murphy said, an alcoholic at the time she claimed she heard the dialogues.

Olsen said her uncle, Silas Jayne, a cold-blooded killer, and head of the Horse Mafia, was a snake and not many people were walking the streets who got in his way.

Dateline then asked, "Did Helen Brach get in his way? Did the Horse Mafia order the hit? Did Richard Bailey take the fall?"

When Dennis Murphy pointed out to Miller that the villains were the Jayne gang and that Richard was perhaps someone they sent out for coffee, Miller disagreed, but once again, he presented no facts.

Plemmons was shown in a barn tending horses and in his high reedy voice, he repeated what he swore to in court, that Richard had solicited him to get rid of Helen Brach. The question was asked, "Was what Plemmons said true?" For fifteen years, the commentator said, he sat on his story until he had reason to say whatever Miller wanted him to say in order to get a reduced sentence.

Jo Anne's next interview went right to the point. She stated that what happened to Richard was a misuse of the justice system, that Miller was no Sherlock Holmes, and that he hadn't solved anything. This, of course, was true. Nobody knew who killed Helen Brach. What Miller did, Jo Anne said, was say Richard was a bad man times ten and, therefore, a killer.

The ladies involved, Jo Anne said, were not buying horses, they were buying Richard. She also said there were women who wanted Richard's attention and they'd buy whatever he had to sell. He wasn't a killer, Jo Ann emphasized, he was a purveyor. All I could think was Jo Ann and Dennis would really get along, they thought alike, and then I had to ask myself why Tuite hadn't brought all those issues up in court.

Jo Ann had a knack for saying a lot in a very little time as she went on to explain it was a long leap from fraud to a murder conspiracy, a theory that relied heavily on the testimony of two dubious witnesses, Plemmons and Olsen, and that Miller had pinned the murder on Richard because his long history of frauds made him an easy target.

Dateline saved Matlick until last.

Murphy introduced Brach's houseman by saying that Matlick didn't fit quite so neatly into the prosecutors' pieces of the puzzle. Private Investigator Ernie Rizzo agreed. "I talked to Matlick for five minutes," he said, "and I knew he killed her. He stole a quarter of a million dollars, he stole her jewelry, he killed her, he got rid of her body, end of story!"

Even ATF agent Jim Delorto admitted it was the end of the gravy train for Matlick because Brach was going to fire him. His comment made me remember Miller saying in court that Matlick had no reason to want to see Brach dead.

Delorto also said that he thought something had happened in a room off the front door of Brach's home, the same room for which Matlick had hired the cleaning crew then redecorated. "I believe she was murdered in her home,"Delorto added.

I couldn't help but put the pieces together… If an ATF agent thinks the murder happened in Brach's home and Matlick was there at the time, then what does that have to say about our system of justice?

But when Dennis Murphy asked Miller about Matlick, pointing out that Matlick's motive was money, and his opportunity was she was coming home and was then leaving for good, Miller replied in a detached precise voice that no one had ever explained to him how Matlick would financially benefit from Brach's demise. He had to be kidding.

I have always thought the American public as far more intelligent than what our government gives us credit for, and I didn't believe that anyone watching the program was buying what Miller was saying. The prosecutor was selling wooden watches to Swiss jewelers, and he knew it.

Richard was next. He finally had a chance to speak out after all those months in jail. *Dateline* interviewed him at the FCI in Marianna, Florida and Richard said very solemnly that the didn't have the slightest idea who had killed Helen Brach, but that somebody out there knew. He said that they had the wrong person in prison for the crime.

With regard to Steven Miller, he said that Miller was out to get him whether he was innocent or guilty, that it made no difference to Miller because all he wanted was to go to the top of the totem pole. I agreed. Miller's motto should have been "Convict at all costs," instead of "Follow the money."

Even incarcerated for a crime he didn't commit and facing a virtual life sentence, Richard was still optimistic. It was amazing to me that he still had faith his government would one day discover that they had locked away the wrong man. Though Richard's statements were brief, what he said was impactive. I was very moved by his honesty and his blind faith in his government.

There was one final shot of me leaving my office, getting into my car, and the commentator said that I planned to stick by Richard, even though I knew he may never be free. The last questions were especially chilling: "Who killed Helen Brach? The Horse Mafia? The houseman? Richard Bailey? Someone knows, but so far, someone may have gotten away with murder."

I hoped that comment gave the American public a lot to think about.

Just as I had expected, Laura had done an excellent job. The facts were presented clearly and in a fascinating way. I especially liked the ghostly way Helen Brach's face kept appearing and disappearing on stable walls and the stone wall in the visiting yard at the prison in Florida where Richard was interviewed. It was almost as if Brach were haunting the sets where people were being taped.

Patrick Tuite?

There were no interviews of Patrick Tuite.

Some lawyers are proud of their work and seek publicity.

The most important thing the program did was to show there were a number of people who had more motive to kill Helen Brach than Richard. If this information had been presented before a jury, Richard might never have been convicted. There would most assuredly have been reasonable doubt, but I was realistic and didn't expect millions of viewers would be writing the Justice Department asking for a retrial. Instead, I consoled myself with the thought that the program was a beginning.

Even though I was sick to death of being questioned by reporters, there was a large group outside my office building waiting to talk to me after the show aired, and so I had to give them a brief interview. I simply said that Richard was not smart enough to have committed Helen Brach's murder, a murder which, after twenty years, had never been solved.

In the days after the *Dateline show*, I kept replaying the interviews in my head. I felt more strongly than ever that Richard was innocent. Yes, he was guilty of fraud, that he admitted, taking full responsibility, but not of murder.

Of course, that didn't mean anything to the Assistant United States Attorneys. Far too late in the game did I come to the realization that our entire system of dispensing justice hinges on the government prosecutors. If they are unethical in any way, such as introducing witnesses who commit perjury, then every person in the United States loses along with the defendant. It's that simple and that complex and that dangerous… to us all.

Chapter 40

Sometime after the *Dateline show* aired, I was sitting alone one night, quietly saying a small prayer for Richard when the phone rang. It was nearly 11:00 P. M. , too late, I thought, for Richard to be calling, and my fear was that one of my children was having a problem. As I reached for the telephone, I chided myself for thinking a negative thought. Little did I know I was about to get some of the most encouraging and yet unsettling news I'd had so far.

"Hey, hey, my beautiful doll," Richard's voice literally sang to me over the miles between us.

"Richard! You sound up, really up! What's going on?"

"Well, it's hard to believe, but I was just talking to one of my many nephews, and you won't believe what he told me... it's incredible!" Richard was so excited his normal measured manner of speaking had gone by the wayside. Now I was really excited!

"Richard, calm down. I can't believe you if you won't tell me. Now, start at the beginning and for goodness sake, slow down."

"Okay, okay. Well, we've solved the mystery..."

"You know who killed Helen Brach?"

"No, but we know why I was set up and who..."

"Richard, will you just spit it out please?" My heart was hammering in my chest. I had no idea what Richard was talking about, but I sensed we had come to another major turning point in the case. "Okay. Years ago, I used to own a fruit stand near where one of my brothers lived. I hired my young nephew to work for me in the summers. He was a bright kid and I really liked him, but I didn't have much cash, so I had to pay him in watermelons."

I could not make heads or tails of what Richard was saying. Watermelons? The only previous connection with watermelons was when Richard told Judge Shadur that he referred to his take in swindles as, "cutting up the watermelons" when he shared the money with a confederate.

"Yes… that's where I picked up the expression, 'cutting up the watermelons.' I used to take the profits from the fruit stand and pay the help with watermelons. They preferred it and I needed to hang on to the cash profits to buy more fruit for the stand. I've been using that expression ever since…"

"Richard, why on earth didn't you tell that to the judge?"

"I told Pat Tuite what it meant, or where the expression came from, and he just gave me one of his looks and told me to keep it to myself." Richard paused for a moment, then said, "But let me get back to the story."

And I did. For the next forty-five minutes (with two breaks from the little beeper that the Bureau of Prisons set off every fifteen minutes to warn you to conclude your conversation), Richard told me everything that was told to him. It was an incredible story, and had it not come from this nephew who I was told was solid, honest, and trustworthy, I would not have believed it, but there it was, all true and the only logical explanation I have ever heard for all of Richard's troubles with the Brach case.

The story began back in the days when Richard was running his fruit stand. There was a young officer on the Illinois State Police named David Hamm (the same David Hamm I quickly realized who had talked Steven Miller into going after Richard and the same Illinois State Police Investigator who had been involved with the "preparation" of the government's witnesses) who was after Richard for something Richard had done. Neither Richard nor his nephew could remember what the supposed crime was, but the tactics used by David Hamm remain indelibly imprinted in the minds of the Bailey family.

Since Hamm could not prove anything against Richard, he got an informant who had a gun charge and schooled the man to give him an affidavit saying the informant had purchased stolen guns from one of the Bailey brothers who ran a motel in nearby Wheaton, Illinois. Once the man had agreed to the deal, Hamm procured a search warrant went with the ATF people and raided the Bailey brother's place of business. They arrested him on the spot and charged him with all sorts of crimes from possession of stolen property to the sale of unregistered firearms to convicted felons.

The ensuing uproar nearly drove the elder Bailey, crazy. He was vilified in the press and publicly embarrassed in his church in Wheaton. One day, David Hamm, who was also a member of that particular church, told the Bailey brother's daughter that he knew the senior Mr. Bailey was not guilty, but that they were after Richard Bailey, and they would get him no matter what or how long it took.

Over the years, his mind and body began to deteriorate and eventually, according to his son, Richard's nephew, the shame and embarrassment of that illegal action by the policeman David Hamm led to the father's mental and physical decline and his death.

The matter remained covered up for years, but David Hamm never let up on Richard Bailey or his quest to find people to help him "get" Richard. There was also a mountain of circumstantial evidence to support the belief that in 1978 it was David Hamm, using the criminal connections he had inside the Silas Jayne gang, who had the messages painted around Chicago that Richard Bailey was responsible for the death of Helen Brach.

It became suddenly obvious to me it was probably David Hamm who had been protecting Jack Matlick all those years because he knew Richard Bailey did not kill Helen Brach Hamm's stunts with the painted messages was another of his schemes to get someone to come forward and lie about Richard or give up some information that would allow him to tie Richard to the crime. Mr. Hamm apparently never cared much whether his information was true or not…as long as he got his conviction.

As a matter of fact, the informant he had used against Richard's brother in his attempt to get at Richard was also the same man who, while working for David Hamm, put several men on Death Row at the Illinois State Prison. This information regarding the false testimony had come to light when the informant had a late life change of heart and confessed that he had repeatedly been a false witness for David Hamm over the years.

As the story unfolded to me, I could not help but think back to those first days in the courtroom when I saw David Hamm's expressions as the witnesses against Richard had stepped up and told their unbelievable stories: Cathy Olsen, Joe Plemmons, Pamela Milner, each of them prepared and prompted by the ubiquitous Lt. David Hamm.

No wonder Hamm had looked terrified when the judge threw out Milner's testimony as an obvious lie! If Richard had had a real attorney right then, he or she would have gone after Lt. Hamm, something I'm sure now that Hamm realized and expected, but then again, maybe he didn't expect it. The prosecution seemed to have a rein on Pat Tuite and every time he got too close to making it over some prosecution hurdle, they pulled on the bit in his mouth, and he refused the jump. There was a horse story I could believe.

Richard also told me that his nephew truly believed his father's death never even phased the irascible Lt. Hamm. Hamm was a dark soul to his core, but the younger Bailey often prayed for him because his father had been unable to forgive his enemy.

After nearly forty-five minutes I had the entire picture.

It was an ugly scene.

There was convincing evidence that David Hamm had been involved in the construction of the case against Richard, and his contribution had been his expertise in the area of conjuring up false images through perjured testimony and sending innocent men to prison. If he had tried it with Richard's brother just to get at Richard, would he try it on Richard himself?

Certainly.

If he sent five different men to prison to die on the strength of testimony he had created and coached a witness into, would he try to send Richard to prison for life without a qualm? Certainly.

Would he brag to Richard's niece that he was going to get Richard any way he could if he did not think he could put Richard in prison and get away with it? My mind was abuzz with the possibilities.

What to do with the information was the first consideration.

Go for a new trial was the first thought.

Get a new trial!

This time let a woman handle the defense!

Someone tough as nails, hard as concrete, who could cut and slash like a street fighter at the women who lied, and she had to be unlike Pat Tuite who had coddled them and helped them limp through their lies, and then even excused one of them by simply allowing her testimony to be stricken!

No!

No more Pat Tuites!

That was the stuff my then vengeful heart wanted to hear.

Thank God for my evening mediation which allowed me to put such thoughts of petty revenge out of my head.

The task was to get Richard out.

I needed a voice to the public.

I needed someone to write a book!

But where to find one?

On that point, Richard had already found one, but I did not know it yet.

And who to trust in the Corps of Tokyo Rose?

Laura Rabhan was the only candidate.

Chapter 41

Months passed after Richard's sentencing without a star of hope shining down on the dreary desert island that had become my life. Oh, there were still those who tried to cheer me, but there was no substance to the encouragement. Of course, Richard's appeal attorney was all smiles and positive words and, in our desperation, Richard's brother Bill and his sister, Faye, laid out another $75, 000, but when we gave the attorney the money, my heart told me the cash would have been better placed in Illinois State lottery tickets.

Maybe I have just become too cynical, but it appears to me that most criminal attorneys are a lot more learned while explaining to you all the positive things they can do for the client. Then they get the money and have to perform.

Here Perry Masons become Elmer Fudds, and when you get fed up and start asking questions, there is another metamorphosis: There is a marked personality change across a brightly delineated line of the same clarity which separated Dr. Jekyll from Mr. Hyde.

I believe that a major part of the problem with the criminal defense system is the money is paid ahead of time for the service. Imagine going into a shop with your car and giving the mechanic the entire amount of his estimate. If you perceive there is any possibility that he might be inclined to do a more workmanlike job when he does not have the customer to please before he's paid, then you are the ideal person to justify the need for a Better Business Bureau, and you are dumber than a box of rocks. But then, lawyers usually make the laws.

When I broached the subject to my friend Dennis, he laughed out loud. "Many criminal defense attorneys are so crooked they have to be screwed into the ground when they die."

I reminded him of his own legal background. "True, but I'm not a member of the bar. I failed the application."

"How on earth does one fail the application?" I asked.

"I stated my parents were married!" Dennis shot back, springing his trap. He paused, and I could hear his thoughts turning somber. "I read the appeal brief. Don't expect any relief for Richard. The argument appears to have been written in the car on the way to the courthouse."

He was right. The Circuit Court denied the issues with little comment and Richard's fate was sealed. The story of our love would have been over except I would not give up in my fight to free this innocent man and find out how the system had failed so miserably.

What I perceived to be the first big break came one evening when Richard called, his voice edged in excitement.

"Hey, hey, my beautiful doll, guess who I have been talking with?"

I knew that *Dateline* had interviewed Richard again, but we still were unaware how he would be characterized next time.

"*Dateline?*" I asked.

"No. Julia, the lady I want to write the book."

"Yes," I said hesitantly," go on…"

"I was talking with her husband the other day and mentioned that the ATF was involved in my case and right away, he said his wife might be interested in doing a book on the ATF's long history of misconduct."

I immediately recognized the initials. ATF stands for Bureau of Alcohol, Tobacco and Firearms, the group which had handled all of the witnesses in Richard's case and are widely known as the bottom of the Federal Law Enforcement Agencies' personnel barrel. (It was, of course, ATF Agents as well who were the architects of the Ruby Ridge, and Waco debacles.

"Who wouldn't want to write about the ATF?" I asked.

"That's not the issue," Richard stated. "As we talked, I was able to get her husband interested in my case, and he thinks she will write the story as a miscarriage of justice."

"What did she think of the David Hamm angle?" I asked at once.

"Blew her away when her husband told her. She was stunned!"

I, too, of course, was stunned by the sordid history of Hamm's vendetta against the Bailey family. My sixth sense had told me repeatedly that Hamm was up to something during the trial, but I had no idea as to the scope of his hatred for the Baileys. But I now had hard evidence that Hamm had a long and well published history of witness tampering and subornation of perjury.

Richard interrupted my thoughts by adding that Julia agreed there might be a vendetta between Hamm and the Baileys!

I was overwhelmed. No wonder Richard was so up! Here was the truth about Hamm and the most logical of explanations for his shenanigans, and though it was mere background on the man, and probably not admissible as evidence, his demonstrated proclivities of the past certainly explained most of my questions about the hearing. Sure, Pamela Milner had known about Joe Plemmons, she had been schooled by David Hamm from Plemmon's testimony. Sure, Plemons knew exactly how to present the lies about the meeting where Richard was supposed to have asked Plemmons to kill Helen Brach. Hamm had met with Plemmons many, many times. And, of course, Cathy Olsen had admitted from the stand that it was David Hamm who had written out the statement she had read to the grand jury!

"And that's not the end of it," Richard added, unable to control the excitement in his voice. "Julia thinks that with Olsen, Plemmons and Milner all tainted by Hamm, we would have only Mr. Katz to contend with, and because the judge had relied so heavily upon his testimony, saying Katz had nothing to gain and was a totally credible witness, if we can find an ulterior motive for his testimony, the case is over!"

"How can we do that? Katz was pure as the driven snow."

"Julia says that when the government is stacking the deck, they pull out all the stops," Richard stated flatly, "and they'll let the witnesses lie when the truth sounds better! She is going with us, after the truth! She's doing background checks on the witnesses already!"

"And she knows how to do all of this?" I asked.

Richard chuckled. "What she can't find, her husband will, he keeps files on government informants, dirty agents, and unethical prosecutors."

"Sounds like a plan to me!"

"Sounds like a team!" Richard said.

We then went over the list of things Richard's nephew had given us, exchanged endearments, and said goodbye.

I was on cloud nine, figuring that at least I could take the David Hamm information and do something with it which would not only help Richard, but also bring more data together for the book.

I called my friend Dennis and the joy of the evening ended in a crash of reality:

"To begin with, Annette, all you have is what everybody in the country knows already. Remember I explained it to you months ago? The witnesses in Richard's case were led to and through their false testimony in a tried-and-true fashion."

"Are you telling me that prosecutors routinely put-on perjured witnesses?" I knew the legal system was flawed; I did not yet believe that it was ethically bankrupt.

"On the contrary," Dennis stated, "they rarely put on testimony they know from firsthand knowledge is false. No, the perjury is a process which begins with a jailhouse rat. He or she is somebody who knows the target and is themselves in trouble with the law. The wanna-be rat contacts the prosecution, trying to resolve his or her legal or financial problems, If the prosecution has a weak case, the potential informer is contacted. But only if the case is this weak because no District Attorney or Assistant United States Attorney would ever put on a felon or drug user unless he had a weak case to begin with. They only use the jailhouse rat or drug addict in an emergency; i. e. , the prosecution is going to lose."

"But how can they do that? Aren't the prosecutors worried about being found out?"

"Nope, the system is designed to protect them from any discovery. Remember the term 'plausible deniability' I from the White House scandals? Same deal. The system works like this: first, one cop goes to the witness and questions him; then, if he had no help to give the prosecution, he is told that 'no, your story is not good enough, we are looking for so and so met with so and so on such and such a date…now, if you had that information, maybe we could do something for you. ' And then the investigator leaves, the informant works up a story and contacts the prosecution again, this time with the new improved version. A second investigator is then sent out and the process is repeated, finally giving the prosecutor something that he can use…a lie…but now a believable one."

"So, the discovery of the Hamm/Bailey vendetta? It's all a candle in the wind? What about truth?"

"Dear lady, you have to remember that we are dealing with the Federal Judicial System and all that counts there is convictions and percentages of convictions. The truth is a foreign land to which these folks do not hold a valid passport."

"But that's not fair!"

Dennis' reaction was a soft sigh. "Annette, we've been down this road before…"

"I know, but I keep hoping…and praying…"

"Do that and see if you can't come up with something concrete."

I accepted that challenge and went to work with Julia on the book, all the while stirring the pots, hoping to make the truth of Richard's case boil up from the mix.

The following is what we came up with, all supported by the documents in the attached appendix:

1. During the course of Richard's case, the Assistant United States Attorney, Steven Miller, was negotiating with various film production companies and publishers for the sale of the rights to portray his role in the

prosecution and conviction of Richard Bailey. These are ethical and legal violations which merit the vacation of Richard Bailey's sentence.

2. During the course of the investigation, an informant wearing a NAGRA wire received information from Ron Cheska that Richard Bailey was not in any way involved in the Helen Brach murder. This information was not turned over to the defense and merits vacation of Richard Bailey's sentence.

3. During the course of the investigation, AUSA Steven Miller attempted by threat, intimidation, and fear, to get Dr. Ross Hugi to commit suborned perjury by lying and saying that he had provided Richard Bailey with illegal medications to dope horses for sale. This sort of prosecutorial misconduct supports the contention that AUSA Miller was not above putting false testimony on the stand.

4. The indictment to which Richard Bailey pleaded guilty was brought outside the statute of limitations, therefore nullifying his guilty plea and judgment of conviction and sentence.

5. Dr. Ross Hugi attempted to give the government documents in his possession which proved that at a date after Helen Brach allegedly told witness Katz that she was going to send Richard Bailey to prison, she set up a date with him to accompany her to the Oakbrook Sale to purchase more horses for her! Such suppression of exculpatory evidence calls for a vacation of Richard Bailey's sentence.

6. In support of Richard's belief that the houseman, Jack Matlick, working in conjunction with the mafia, had set up Helen Brach's home to be burglarized and then when she walked in unexpectedly, they killed her, we found three sources of information (none of whom knew the other), who told the same story supporting Richard's theory that the Spilotro brothers set up the burglary and were then killed by the Chicago mafia for putting too much public scrutiny on the mob. One of these sources was a member of the Spilotro family.

7. That Kenny Hanson, the defense witness who belied the testimony of Joe Plemmons, was not, in fact, a murderer as AUSA Miller had

painted him in order to discredit his testimony in Richard Baileys defense.

8. That Arthur Katz, the man Judge Shadur found totally believable because he had nothing to gain and had come forth as a law-abiding citizen, had, in fact, a criminal record and was then under investigation for extortion when he testified. Failure by the prosecution to divulge this information is grounds for vacation of the judgment of conviction and sentence.

9. Despite the government's portrayal of Helen Brach as an airhead when it came to the horse business, she was, in fact, an accomplished horse trader and licensed owner. In the 20 odd years that Helen Brach bought and sold racehorses and hunter/jumpers, she faired far better than most of her contemporaries. This information came to light when equestrian expert Jill McEwan prepared a case study on Helen Brach's years in the horse business and tracked her sales and purchases and published her margin of profit and loss. Helen Brach was in that elite 4 percent of owners who actually made money on their trades.

10. After a little research, we were able to pinpoint the errors Pat Tuite made in court which incited Judge Shadur to state on the record that the sins of the attorney may be vested upon the client. Not the least of these egregious errors was the fact that Pat Tuite had actually allowed Richard, no, coached Richard into pleading guilty to a fraud that he could not have been indicted on in the first place because no crime had, in fact, happened. Worse, this error occurred with "Victim J" the case AUSA Steven Miller used to bring the racketeering charge which in turn exposed Richard Bailey to a life sentence instead of the thirty-seven to forty-six months Tuite had promised him before Richard Bailey entered the guilty plea. The precise term is Ineffective Assistance of Counsel, and the record is loaded with such acts, each of which will now force Richard Bailey's judgment of conviction and sentence to be vacated as a matter of law.

The investigation continues, the battle goes on, with the eventual victory falling on the side of truth. How much simpler this all would have been if our government had seen through David Hamm and his vendetta against the Bailey family and then acted in a manner commensurate with their sacred oaths of office.

Chapter 42

Nearly two years later I found myself at the Holiday Inn SunSpree, a resort hotel in Hollywood Beach, Florida. I was physically and mentally exhausted and a little depressed.

I had flown in from Chicago the clay before and though the flight itself had been extremely stressful due to terrible weather, I had been able to meet with the writers of this book. The meeting turned into an all-night session, but by dawn, we all agreed that the work was finished, so I faced the day before me with at least one nugget of accomplishment tucked away in my soul.

I walked out onto the balcony and stared out at the world.

High above me, an apricot-yellow sun blazed across a blue sky that went on forever. Gentle waves played tag with one another before splashing lazily onto white sand. Palm trees, tall, regal, so close I could almost touch them, danced merrily to the South Sea rhythms of a warm breeze. Hanging over the balcony's railing were clusters of bougainvillea, their paper-thin petals fluttering like the wings of pink and purple butterflies. From somewhere below, the sweet fragrance of gardenias mixed with that of hundreds of red roses and drifted upwards to where I was standing.

Everything around me seemed to be pulsating slowly, undulating to the magical beat of a South Sea Island breeze.

Scantily clad people paraded up and down the beach, two by two, apparently free from worries, free from care. A pair of barefoot lovers ran playfully into the ocean#, paused, then their lips met in a tender but passionate kiss. Whoever they were, this bit of paradise, this Bali Hai, belonged to them. Not to me and Richard.

Richard was still in prison and the struggle to free him continued without respite.

My eyes drifted to the horizon. I could see exactly where the sea met the sky. There was not a ship in sight. Not a cloud. Not a bird.

I noticed the tide was going out, returning the borrowed sea to a place beyond my view. For a moment, I felt pulled along, and I found peace in the thought that even while I drowned in despair, the, Lord continued to keep things right in the universe. Suddenly, I felt I was being cast into a future beyond the curve of the earth, to a place unknown, but certainly like the distant line where the sky kissed the sea, a life that was bright, clear, and full of promise.

Why was I so sudden confident?

Because I still believed that the truth will prevail.

And I was going to fight.

Richard would one day be free…

MOB

"THE MOB'S NO. 1 HITMAN VICTOR SPILOTRO TOLD BAILEY, 'RETURN JEWELERY OR I WILL KILL YOU.'"

A beautiful lady about forty-five years old came by Bailey's stable looking to buy a horse. I said to her I have just the horse for you. I bring the horse out of his box stall. Take him into the indoor arena and turn him loose. She said that was the type of horse she was looking for. I said perfect. Then I put the horse back in his box stall. Then I said why don't we go to Hackneys and have a hamburger. She agreed. Then after a few drinks, she asked me the price of the horse. I said $125, 000. At that time, she said I am going through a divorce and don't have any money. But my husband owns Peoples Pontiac in Skokie. She said however I have jewelry worth $125, 000. I said that's no problem. However, she said it is in a safe over the kitchen sink and my kids have company. I said that's no problem I have kids of my own. So, we go to the house in Skokie. I keep the kids busy in the living room while she is getting the jewelry out of the safe. Now we go back to the stable. I give her a bill of sale and she gives me the jewelry.

When I looked at the jewelry it looked like the same jewelry Helen Brach was wearing when we were in New York City at Waldorf Astoria. On New Year's Eve in 1976. But I said it can't be. How could she possibly have Helen's jewelry? I couldn't see any connection at that time. Next day I go to Northwestern Stable. There was Frank Jayne, Jack Matlick and Lee Rider. I knew Frank Jayne would know a fence that would buy the jewelry. I got his name and address and left. Next day before I had time to see the fence, Victor Spilotro called me, which never happened before. Victor told me to meet hit at a restaurant in front of the Studio Restaurant in Morton Grove. Which I did. I walked in at the back of the restaurant and in a booth there was Victor and an Italian friend of his. Victor was bouncing a golf ball on the table and drinking a shot of whiskey. I said to Victor what's up. Victor said the jewelry you got for the horse. Has to be returned to her husband. I was a little nervous however I had a smile on my face. I said Victor you have to be kidding. She got a bill of sale for the horse and I got the jewelry. Why don't we split the jewelry three ways? I am not greedy.

The "mob" will kill you guys sooner or later anyway. Victor said he can't do that. I said to myself her husband has to be a front for the "mob." Victor said to meet her husband at the same restaurant in a certain booth at a certain time. Return the jewelry or I will kill you. Victor's partner said I hear you are a pretty good golfer. He said you should come to a certain golf course that was in the Elmhurst area and we play eighteen holes. I told him I would think about it. I didn't tell him I was a scratch golfer. But I had no intention of playing at that golf course. Because In knew that was where the mob hung around.

I went back to the Rest with the jewelry. There was her supposed husband and Victor. Gave them the jewelry and got out of there. Now in 1997 when I was locked up in Marianna FL. I got a letter from my wife Dr. Annette Hoffman. Annette mailed me a Declaration signed by Martin Breiner. Martin Breiner said two of Victor's brothers had met an unfortunate end to their life. Because of a bungled burglary they were involved in at the home of a wealthy heiress living in Glenview, Illinois. (Who later disappeared) This was Helen Brach.

At that time, I got to thinking that jewelry which I thought could have belonged to Helen. Now I know for sure it was. Frank Jayne, Jack Matlick and Lee Rider soon as I left N. W. Stable they had to have tipped Victor off.

Golden Tongue

That Bailey got Helen Brach's jewelry through a horse deal with a lady whose husband owned Peoples Pontiac in Skokie. Right away Victor got into the action. Because they knew this jewelry was taken when they ransacked. Helen Brach's house and killed her.

BURY

Mr. RICHARD BAILEY COERCED BY HAVING HIM TAKE A POLYGRAPH…

Something that investigative reporter; Jim Ylisela, who has been working with STEVE MILLER Prosecutor, against RICHARD BAILEY. Trying to get myself, Richard Bailey, to take a POLYGRAPH for years. My brother, WILLIAM BAILEY and his wife SHIRLEY had always thought Jim Ylisela was a professor of English and they had me believing the same.

JIM YLISELA was an investigative reporter, with Steve Miller as the prosecutor, came up with someone they knew of, thinking Richard Bailey would not pass a POLYGRAPH, with WARREN HOLMES as a polygraph expert. Jim Ylisela flew from Chicago to Miami, and rented a car to drive Warren Holmes to Coleman, Florida Prison, to give me a polygraph. Jim Ylisela sat right there with Holmes interrogating ME with a lot of questions before giving me the polygraph.

Polygraph results were not what Jim Ylisela wanted to hear. WARREN HOLMES, after the test was over, turned around and told my counselor, "Mr. Miro, this man is NOT a criminal."

Before Warren Holmes left for Miami, Holmes said he would mail a copy of the polygraph test results to Richard Bailey. Jim Ylisela had to drive Holmes back to Miami, about four hours away. I waited a few weeks for the polygraph, Holmes was supposed to send it to me. It never showed up. I called Holmes and asked him about it, Holmes said Jim Ylisela told him NOT TO MAIL THE POLYGRAPH TO RICHARD BAILEY. HOLMES told me that he had to do what JIM YLISELA tells him to do…

I had an attorney, Ronald Fox, during the polygraph. I called Ronald Fox and told him what happened. He said Holmes can't do that. "He has to mail a copy to you." Finally, I did get a copy of the polygraph from Holmes.

Attorney Ronald Fox and Warren Holmes told me that Jim Ylisela is not out for Richard Bailey. Ylisela told my brother, WILLIAM BAILEY, that a man named LARRY YELEN, who runs FOX TV in Chicago, use to be one of his "students" and told him, after your brother takes the polygraph, he would do a FULL story about it. But it never happened. Why? Because the polygraph test results came up POSITIVE.

LARRY YELEN, and FOX TV, were hoping for NEGATIVE polygraph results, hoping that I would fail the test, giving them a hot story. Then JIM YLISELA and STEVE MILER, my prosecution, would have had a big celebration on FOX TV, in their compulsion to "BURY RICHARD BAILEY,"but that never happened. In any way whatsoever. Because "MR. RICHARD BAILEY PASSED THE POLYGRAPH WITH FLYING COLORS."

*Note: Here is what the *Chicago Reader Magazine*(October 20, 2011) had to say about Investigative Reporters (like Jim Ylisela):"There is nothing unusual about [Investigative Reporters] working with Prosecutors or Defense Attorneys, for most Investigative Reporters, these are essential relationships for getting the job done. It's part of the GAME; you have to do it."

INVISIBLE MAN

I, Richard Roland Bailey, Jr., am eighty-nine years old and have been locked up for almost twenty-five years. Thursday, March 1, I arrived back at Coleman Low, to begin my next round of torture by a thousand drops of aromatic prayer oil, to which I apparently have developed a powerful allergic reaction. This has occurred in C-3, C-1, and now B-2. I had extensive tests for my heart due to category "ten-plus" chest pains, which as I have explained at great length to Ms. Cook are caused by prayer oil sprayed by inmates. These are violent chest pains! I have taken my cause to my counselor, case manager, unit manager, and the warden. And many other staff members have been made aware. They have tried to help me get relief through medical channels. I have been sent to the local hospital a number of times, but the cardiologists have not been able to connect the prayer oil to my cardiac attacks or to anything else.

In the last five months, I have had four stents put in my circulatory system to help my ailing heart. Before my recent encounters with prayer oil, I had no heart ailments and no stents. All of this has happened in the last year. As long as I am outdoors, I have no problems.

My research has shown that prayer oil works against my nervous system and can cause cancer, as well. It is being heavily used now to cover up various odors… perhaps smoke, or cooking smells.

Richard Bailey

When I arrived back from my most recent hospital trip, I found out that inmates and some staff thought I was dead. All of my property had been stored in two green bags, awaiting shipment of my next of kin. My mattress and locker were gone from my cubicle, there was nothing left of me. The inmates were incredulous to see me alive. Frank, my inmate legal representative had sent materials to be copyrighted before he 'found out that I had died.'

Many years ago, I saw the movie *The Invisible Man*, which came to my mind as part of this fiasco. I began thinking, I am the Invisible Man, supposed to be dead. If I didn't have mind control, this would have driven me crazy. All these years, getting a life sentence. Then, in 2005, informant Joe Plemmons confessed that I was not involved in the murder of Helen Brach, eleven years after I was convicted. He admitted he shot Helen Brach and had the Spilotro Brothers bury her body. Even now that is widely known, even by my judge that I am innocent, I remain in custody for a crime I had no knowledge of.

I am begging you to ship me to Chicago, or somewhere else soon, before I really become invisible, dead from the allergic reactions I keep having to the prayer oil which is so prevalent here at Coleman Low.

Jason Weeks, in B-1, was telling an inmate at Coleman Low in Florida that he Richard Roland Bailey, Jr. when he was an old man. We played a lot of racket ball together. If there was ever an atomic bomb to go off, it would kill everyone except Bailey. Jason said this when he was leaving and going home after many years.

This is just the prime of life, only once I get out of this torture chamber from C3—C1 building and B2. This is unbelievable.

Richard Bailey, 1942

Born: August 9, 1929

The youngest of twelve, six boys and six girls. Mother had German Measles at birth, which paralyzed my eye lids and affected my memory brain. When I was in the first grade, teacher told my mother I should be in a school for retarded kids. Mother did not buy that. So, I remained in a public school.

I joined the 15th Army Air Force at age sixteen with my mother's consent but got out at nineteen after serving three years.

Golden Tongue

When I got out of the Army I found an eye specialist, Dr. Robert Fitzgerald, he connected my eyelids to my eyeball muscle, and it worked.

Mother is on the right, behind me is my sister Linda, to my left is my sister Fay and her boy Ronnie.

One summer I helped my father and brother, Paul, who lived in Kentucky, plowing the fields with one mule, plant tobacco and sucker it. We lived in a shanty of a house, holes in the floor and newspaper print for wallpaper. We slept on the floor. I was so happy when my mother picked me up to bring me back to Bloomington, Illinois.

The photograph is Richard Bailey and older brother Paul J. Bailey to my left. Brother PJ had just come back from San Francisco, California where he became a jockey riding race horses. he had just bout a new four-door black Cadillac with twin spotlights. I asked if it was OK if I drove his car to school the next day. He said, "Any time." I drove around the school a few times to show off my brother's new car. That made my day!

GOLDEN TONGUE

Mind Control Letter

When I was at Coleman-Medium, I had an inmate who was a journalist from college and was working on my autobiography.

After about two weeks, he told me to stop by and pick up my documents. When I stopped to see him, he told me he was returning everything of mine.

He just said that he didn't care to do anymore and that I didn't owe him anything.

Right away, I felt assured that he had something up his sleeve. He had been down for twenty years.

I figured that he had found out what I was locked up for and now he's going to turn in a copout to the Lieutenant's office saying I had threatened him some way.

Two weeks later, I received a call to report to the Lieutenant's office. I reported as requested and sat down.

The Lieutenant was looking at a copout. Before the officer said a word, I told him that whenever he was around the facility, the place runs "smooth as silk."

The Lieutenant reviewed the copout and told me he had a different name on here. He continued, "I am sorry, Mr. Bailey, it was a pleasure meeting you."

I was moved to Coleman-LOW. Had my roommate helping me with a few things on my autobiography. The previous person hadn't finished so I said I'll just leave this with you.

He said he would be finished in one month. I waited 2 months and never heard from him. He knew my autobiography would be priceless.

This was 2005 and Joe Plemmons, an informant, had revealed that Richard Bailey was in no way connected with the disappearance of Helen Brach.

It so happens that a few days later this same Lieutenant was at Coleman-Low. I told him how great it was to have him here.

I had an opportunity to discuss the issues I had with my roommate and the recovery of my autobiography.

The Lieutenant told me to meet him on Thursday at 10:00A. M. at the Recreation Yard and I'll have your autobiography.

I was at the designated location on time, but the Lieutenant was NOT there. However, my autobiography was.

I could write a book on Mind Control that has taken place at all these prisons.

Mind Control! Every inmate I speak with wants to "talk more." That I don't do.

I tell them to be watching for the book *GOLDEN TONGUE VOLUME IV Mind Control* or on television.

Thomas Richardson, good friend of mine, plans on doing an interview with him on mind control or maybe make part of it doing interviews.

CANDY HEIRESS HELEN BRACH FOUNDATION

David Ernie Rizzo, Private Investigator, was compensated with $200,000 to accurately research the sudden disappearance of HELEN BRACH.

Mr. Rizzo sat' through the full court case regarding this untimely occurrence to testify on the behalf of Richard Bailey AND to let the whole world know that Richard Bailey had ABSOLUTELY NOTHING TO DO WITH THE MACBRE EVENTS.

Richard Bailey's wife, Dr. Annette Hoffman, was also in full attendance of the court proceedings with Investigator Rizzo. Both were confident that Bailey would be released.

When the time neared for Mr. Rizzo to testify, Mr. Bailey's attorney, Pat Tuite advised the parties to wait that: "We have the case won. There is no reason for Mr. Rizzo to testify."

As soon as Bailey's attorney, Kathleen Zellner, had time to return to her office, Rizzo notified her that Bailey "got the shaft!" Thirty YEARS.

Attorney Zenner took my case pro-bono in 2005. She advised that her first effort would be check out the modus operandi and details of Attorney Tuite.

Her findings included that he had an insurance policy against malpractice in the amount of $3.5 million in Mr. Tuite's portfolio.

Ms. Zellner's opinion was that the mishandling of my case would cost Lawyer Tuite all of that. Plus, my case would be cleared away completely.

The record would also be expunged regarding a horse fraud' case against me that had been adjudicated in state court twenty years prior.

Pat Tuite was aware of this entire matter and settlement but talked me into saying I had been guilty. Kathleen insisted that my story could become a priceless piece of literature.

Golden Tongue

Mind Control Vol. IV Education of a Lifetime

On my most recent trip to Leesburg General hospital, near the end of February of 2019, I was accompanied by two guards who would be with me at all times. The guards work twelve-hour shifts. On one of the days, a guard and I were engaged in a significant conversation.

This guard had an open mind to learning new things. I encouraged him to pursue the study and application of mind control so that he could be an overcomer of any difficulties that came his way. Everyone has them. I tell people all the time, "It is not what happens to you; it's how you handle it."

I was just laying back in bed sharing principles and stories applying those principles. Imagination, dreams, and visions are more powerful than words.

As the guard got up from his chair and walked to the door shortly after mid-night at the end of his shift, he pointed his finger at me and said, "Mr. Bailey, you just gave me the education of a lifetime!" He had missed many things on his journey through life. He now realizes that he has the ability to control what he thinks about and how he thinks. The same thing can happen for you when you read my book *Mind Control - Volume IV*. My nephew, Herman Bailey says:

Dear Uncle Richard,

You are to be commended for keeping your sanity while in prison, using positive thoughts, without knowing what tomorrow will bring.

You have asked to use my name. Here is my quote about mind control for Herman Bailey: "My mind control conies from a personal relationship with Jesus Christ, daily Bible reading, and prayer. My positive thinking comes from daily meditation on God's Word. I ask daily for God to control my mind, body and soul."

If a professional counselor or pastor/priest/rabbi is working with a mentally handicapped person (what we would call in the old days, retarded) will forget about the patient or counselee's condition momentarily, and wipe any negativity or pre-conceived ideas out of their mind, they can be successful in many ways. Richard Bailey was told that he was 'retarded' as a child and that half of his brain was 'paralyzed' and yet he became successful in business many times over Here is an example from Mr. Bailey.

I got acquainted with an inmate who had half-brain paralyzation like I did. In our first conversation, he told me about his diagnosis. It is a small world to 'think that I would encounter another person with my condition; it is very rare. The inmate told me that, "Once you find your niche, the sky is the limit; there is nothing you can't do." This inmate came up with an idea for a device that K-Mart began using at their checkout counters years ago. He now collects millions of dollars in royalties every year from the use of his idea. Sadly, this inmate was locked up for tax evasion.

There is a second lesson here: When a person is blessed by the revelation of an idea lighting on their mind from our Creator and they are led to develop that idea and are rewarded financially, don't get greedy. Something like this puts a person in the top 1/2 of 1 percent of people in the world in net worth. Do good things with your blessings—bless others as you have been blessed.

Back in 2005, while at Coleman Low the first time, I was in the A-1 dorm. The informant in my case, Joe Plemmons, came forward and confessed that

Mr. Bailey was not involved at all in the death of Helen Brach. When that hit the newspapers and television media, many calls to Coleman were made to reach Mr. Bailey for interviews. People even came to the front gate to get in to see Mr. Bailey so that they could interview him to get his story. It was so problematic that his case manager and counselor met with Mr. Bailey to tell him that the disruption was over the top. The decision was made to send him to Yazoo, Mississippi to the Low Custody prison there.

"There was an outstanding lady warden at the prison in Yazoo. She was in her early 50s I believe. She came to my building one day and gave a fabulous talk to me and the other inmates, sounding like a Harvard graduate. It so happened that on that same day, in front of the dining hall, she was standing by at lunchtime. I had to express to her just what I felt. I asked her if she had ever been a model."

"Oh, Mr. Bailey, why would you say that?"

"The manner in which you talk and move reminds me of a model. I have been out with a few of them myself."

A few days later, the warden came into our building again, inspecting the cubicles that we lived in. One of those was that belonging to Richard Bailey. As she looked around my cubicle, the warden spotted a picture of me with Morgan Fairchild. She queried me, "Who is this lady?" I told her about my dating relationship with Morgan and the trip with her to Maui where that picture was taken. We talked for a while in my cube about life. Meanwhile, I noticed that the captain was standing outside my cubicle, saying nothing, just listening. I got the impression later that the captain must have thought I was quite a guy.

There are thousands of "inmates," both incarcerated and roaming freely with some kind of handicap—negative thinking creeps into their mind. They may be "damaged goods" in their mind. Maybe they have been hurt physically or by words that wounded their spirit. They need to be encouraged to control those negative thoughts; kick them to the curb. These people need to be told and shown who they were made to be by their Creator. They are not to be defined by someone else. Controlling your mind, protecting it from outside influences is a must!

If you look at Mr. Bailey has accomplished, you will see that no medical opinion from childhood held him back. He entered the U. S. Army at the age of sixteen. He succeeded in nearly every business enterprise he undertook. He entered the social lives of people from high society and traveled in those circles.

About a year later, I sold my horse stable and bought Evanston Saddle Stable in Morton Grove, twenty miles from downtown Chicago. It was a perfect location because there were lots of homes nearby. In my new location, I didn't have any concerns about having my barns burned down (at least, not initially). I named my new business Bailey's Riding Academy. It was larger than my previous location; there were sixty stalls, and I built an indoor arena that was 200' x 80'. It was not long before things were popping at the seams, I hired a company with a camera and crew to make a film of my daughter Lisa jumping over three-foot fences on her horse. I wanted to use the film for television commercial, something that had not been done before. Once the commercial aired, the telephone started ringing off the hook and I was able to book 70 percent of the classes we offered. Then Silas Jayne's horse mafia came by.

On several occasions, when Silas came to call, he asked me to step outside to talk to him, which I didn't want to do. One time, he threatened me inside my business. He told me, in no uncertain terms, that if I didn't give him a certain percentage of my horse sales, he was going to poke my eyes out. I did not respond to that threat. Instead, I just went back to my office without saying a word. They never let up and I never gave in.

One nice day, a lady stopped by Bailey's Riding Academy looking to buy a horse. It just so happened that Thad the perfect horse for her, a beautiful seven-year-old gray mare. I helped her get comfortable in the saddle and ride for half an hour. She fell in love with the horse. I said, "Let's go down to Hackney's for a hamburger and talk about your horse." We did. After a couple of drinks, she told me that her deceased husband had been president of a big trucking company. She had a ninety-foot yacht on which he used to take customers out cruising on Lake Michigan.

She said, "I have the yacht; why not trade it for the horse?"

I said, "Let's take a look at your yacht." It was a beauty and even came with a slip to park it in, which was a huge plus in my mind.

All told, I liked all aspects of owning this yacht. We made the deal. The yacht became my party boat and was used on many occasions. And she had a beautiful penthouse at the top of Water Tower Place, one of Chicago's landmarks. We proceeded to get to know each other.

About one month later, I drove down to the yacht and parked my Mercedes in front of the seagoing beauty. I got out and walked around. I was mesmerized by all the sailboats out on Lake Michigan and watched them for quite some time. Then I decided to drive down to the Loop and do a little shopping for a few things. I began walking back to my car. Once I got there, I opened the driver's door and got in and closed the door. I was about to start the engine when a voice hollered, "Bailey, don't start your car!" I recognized the person; he had just gotten out of prison.

The young man came to me and crawled under the car and removed a bomb about twelve inches in length. He confessed to me that after placing the bomb under my car, he had second thoughts about what he had done, and he simply just could not do what he was hired to do. He asked me not to tell anyone because he was afraid that they would kill him. He had lived a hard life so from time to time I had given him a few dollars. I had gotten to know him and liked him. He apparently like me as well, considering the danger he was putting himself in by not doing what he was hired to do. That large bomb would have killed me and some of my yachting neighbors as well as blow my yacht to Kingdom come.

Another time, I had an encounter with Silas Jane of my own making. My brother, P. J. Bailey, was a leading jockey in the horse racing business. He was riding thoroughbred horses at Arlington Race Track. One time when he stopped by my stable, we talked quite a bit about Silas Jayne. P. J. was interested in meeting Silas. So, we took off and went to visit his ranch in Elgin, Illinois. Silas was there, so he invited us to sit down. He and my brother talked. for over an hour. I just sat and listened, not saying a word.

A few days later, I heard that Silas had told his nephew, Frank Jayne, that he should be careful, or Bailey would own his stable, too. Northwestern Stables was a few blocks from my stable. As chance would have it (or divine providence) I did end up owning his stable, but not the way that Silas thought. Frank was caught selling drugs at his stable, which eventually pushed Northwestern Stables into foreclosure, including the five acres it rested upon. I was able to pick it up for $6,000; I sold it some years later for a few million dollars. I am sure if Silas Jayne had heard that, he would have rolled over in his grave, were he able.

Paul Jones, even at the age of seventy, was still president of Glenview National Bank in Glenview Illinois. The bank was only half a mile from Bailey's Horse Stable. I sold Paul a horse referred to as a hunter/jumper, excellent for fox hunting. It was a grey thoroughbred, about seventeen hands high (that is considered a big horse), and perfect for a man six feet in height to use for fox hunting.

Paul Jones had started a 'members only' fox hunting club in Lake Forrest, about forty-five miles north of downtown Chicago. The club was "top drawer," and the area was home to the best fox hunting anywhere near Chicago. They had acquired over one thousand acres for fox hunting. Paul invited me to become a member not long after we met and he learned that I was a top English rider and jumper, able to easily clear six-foot-high fences. I eagerly accepted his offer and joined right away. In the process I met many beautiful ladies, judges, lawyers, and lots of other interesting and important people.

As a newly minted member of this fox hunting club, I began to join in the various hunting events that the club organized for its members. They had about twenty fox hounds and a number of foxes, mostly, provided for the chase. Most of the time, the fox outsmarts the hounds. One day, while on a hunt, a very beautiful lady went galloping by me and my horse. I could not allow that to happen. So, I nudged my horse, and we took off after her and her steed, and quickly caught up and passed her. After the event was over, I congratulated her on her horse-riding ability.

At the gathering in the club after the hunt, a local judge asked me if my name was Bailey. Of course, not being shy, I answered in the affirmative. The judge informed me that I could not be a member of the fox hunting club due to a concern he had after seeing a story about me on television. I informed him that I was ALREADY a member. The judge replied that he would "check that out."

When I told bank president Paul Jones what had transpired with the judge, he felt so strongly about our friendship that he offered to resign if I was re-removed from membership in the club he had started. And that is exactly what he did; Paul stopped hunting at his own club.

I did some checking into some of the best fox hunting in the land. I made plans to go to North Carolina in January where the REAL Elite train and hunt. I found one of the best spots for Paul and me to go to where, incidentally, lots of beautiful ladies are very active members. Shortly after the new year began, I put my horse and Paul's into a two-horse trailer so we could go train them, as well as ourselves, and do a little fox hunting, too. We drove to North Carolina and stayed at a beautiful place. I made sure Paul was taken care of. We stayed in quaint cottages with fireplaces nestled in the Smokey Mountains. They had all the creature comforts one could want. This was so much better than fox hunting in Lake Forrest, Illinois by far!

I later discovered the truth that led to the strange episode with the judge. The beautiful lady who raced by me on horseback at Paul's club was the judge's wife. Apparently, he had heard someone in his courtroom refer to me as the "Galloping Gigolo," and he feared that I was "on the move" after his wife. As I expected, there were plenty of the two-legged kind of foxes on the hunt in North Carolina. And these with a very alluring southern accent.

Paul was one of the greatest people I ever met. He played an important role in my first large real estate transaction. The first building I ever bought was at 5700 Lake Shore Drive, not far from downtown Chicago. Paul provided the financing, a $2.5 million unsecured note. I converted the residence into fifty-seven condominiums and sell everyone. After all was said and done, I had made a $400,000 profit. Glenview National Bank was fully repaid.

A little later, while I was on a trip to Miami, I found a ninety-unit residential building on the Intra-Coastal Waterway, a perfect location.

I telephoned Paul Jones at his bank and requested a loan to buy the property. Paul told me, "No problem," so I flew back to Chicago to discuss the details of the transaction with Paul. We had a productive discussion upon my return, but to my dismay, Paul died of a heart attack before we could effectuate the transaction—he was walking up a flight of stairs and had a massive coronary. I was surprised because Paul seemed to be in excellent physical condition. He showed no signs of weakness or stress during our fox hunting outings. Fox hunting involves a lot of jumping of three-foot high fences and chasing foxes at break-neck speeds. Paul and his horse were able to keep up with all the hunters.

Paul's death ended my condo conversion project in Miami; I could not find another banker who would offer me the type of financing arrangements I required to make the project work.

I was just listening to Elvis; he would be eighty-four years old today. My favorite singer. He died because of his drug addiction. That was caused by a lack of mind control. The world is full of them. Prisons are full of them, too. At least 90 percent of all inmates I have gotten to know are there because they did not know how to control their minds. Control your mind, control your action.

One inmate in particular, Pete, a millionaire, had a business making $200,000 a year. I asked Pete, "What are you locked up for?" He told me he was in the drug business. I told him, "You have no mind control at all." He agreed with me. Just like nearly all of them in prison: doctors, lawyers, policemen, bankers, real estate developers, auto mechanics, even pastors.

Listening to various stories of people not using their own mind. That is hard to believe. Pete will be a guest on my radio and television programs: GOLDEN TONGUE MIND CONTROL—Education of a Lifetime. Mind control is what I have been doing all of my life. I was not even fully aware of it until I was talking to my nephew, Herman Bailey. Herman has been in the television business for thirty-nine years. He has his own cable television network. He travels all over the world.

I was talking to another inmate who is twenty-six years old and all excited that he is getting out of prison in two weeks. Then I told him my life's story: I joined the army at age sixteen and became part of the 15th U. S. Army Air Base. I got out of the Army at age nineteen and hitchhiked to Chicago. I did not go back to my old environment. Most young inmates go back to the old neighborhood, the old friends, where they were, 'led into trouble' before. I told him of many of my successes in Chicago.

A week later, this same young man comes to me and tells me, "I have decided to move and live with my uncle in Las Vegas." I reinforced his decision, telling him that will help him avoid temptation while he gets a new life, and he strengthens his mind. I explained this story to my nephew, Herman. He said, "Uncle Richard, you have been doing that all your life. You should have a T. V. program and write a book on mind control."

I am working on plans for both of those ideas now and this will take place as soon as I am acquitted in the Chicago federal court. Here is just a start on Mind Control. Something you may want to read. I will be seeing you in a few months.

"Richard Bailey just finished having lunch in the dining hall. It so happened that the warden, Miss Lane, and the assistant warden, Miss Strasburg, were standing outside in front of the dining hall talking with inmates as they passed by after eating. Once it was Richard Bailey's turn, he said to Miss Lane and Miss Strasburg, 'You have Coleman Low running as smooth as silk. The two of you are the best I have been around. ' A compliment goes a long way because all they hear complaints and negativity from inmates."

This case of success and many others will be a part of *Mind Control Volume IV*, a page book. Everything will be copyrighted. In the meanwhile, please don't send any copies of my writing to anyone. These are for your eyes only. Especially not for those two that made sure that I got a life sentence. You know who they are. Brother used to tell me he wasn't the one.

Have great day and a better tomorrow.

Uncle Richard Bailey, Jr.

MOB HITMAN VICTOR SPILATRO THREATENS BAILEY'S LIFE

One day, a beautiful lady in her late forties came by Bailey's Stable looking to buy a horse. I said to her, "I have just the horse for you." I brought the horse out of his stall. I had one of my trainers take the horse into the indoor arena and turn him loose. The lady told me that was the type of horse she was looking for. I replied, "Perfect." When the trainer brought the horse back to me, I put him back in his stall. I then said to her, "Why don't we go down to Hackney's and have a hamburger?" She agreed.

After a few drinks, she asked me for the price of the horse. I gave her a price of $125, 000. She told me she was going through a divorce. "I don't have any money, but my husband owns People's Pontiac in Skokie (Illinois). I have jewelry worth that much."

I said, "That is not a problem; I can take the jewelry in exchange for the horse."

"My jewelry is at home in a safe over the kitchen, and at the moment my children are there and have friends over," she posed.

I said, "I don't see that as a problem, I have kids of my own, I can keep them entertained." So, I pulled the kids into the living room and kept them busy while she got the jewelry out of the safe. We went back to Bailey's Stables so we could finish our business. I gave her a receipt, a bill of sale, and she gave me the jewelry. The young lady left, and I began to think.

When I looked closely at the jewelry, I noticed that the pieces looked very familiar to me. In fact, it looked like the same jewelry that Helen Brach was wearing on New Year's Eve in 1976 when we were together in New York at the Waldorf Astoria. I said to myself, this can't be Helen's jewelry. How could this lady be in possession of Helen's things? I saw no connection at the time.

The next day I went to Northwestern Stable looking for Frank Jayne, Silas Jayne's brother, knowing he could connect me to a fence who would buy the jewelry. Sure enough, Frank was there with his pals, Jack Matlick and Lee Rider. I got his name and address and left and went home.

The day after all of this transpired, and before I had time to see the fence, mobster Victor Spilotro called me at the stables. We were not friends; he had never called me before. Victor told me to meet him at the Studio Restaurant in Morton Grove, which I agreed to. I went to meet him at lunch time; he was sitting near the back with an Italian friend of his. Victor was bouncing a golf ball on the table and drinking a shot of whiskey. I asked Victor, "What's up?"

He replied, "The jewelry you got for the horse has to be returned to the husband." I was nervous, but I did not show it. With a smile on my face, I said, "Victor, you have got to be kidding. She got a bill of sale, and I got the jewelry. Why don't we split the jewelry? I am not greedy?"

Victor replied, "I can't do that." Victor told me which booth to meet the booth in the same restaurant to meet the husband and gave me a time. He insisted, "Return the jewelry, or I will kill you." (I thought to myself, "The mob will kill you two sooner or later. Her husband has to be a front man for the mob.")

Victor's partner offered, "I hear you are a pretty good golfer. Why don't you join us for a round of golf with us at a club over in the Elmhurst area?" I told him I would think about; I didn't tell him I was a scratch golfer. I had no intention of playing that golf course with him. I knew the course he was alluding to; it was a club almost exclusively for mob people, much too dangerous for me.

Later that day, I returned to the restaurant at the appointed time with the jewelry. I found Victor and the supposed husband sitting at the designated table as expected. I gave them the jewelry and got out of there quickly.

Years later, in 1997, when I was locked up in FCI Marianna (Florida), I got a letter from my then wife, Dr. Annette Hoffman. She included a declaration signed by Martin Breiner stating that two of Victor's brothers had come to an unfortunate end to their lives due to a bungled burglary. This had taken place at the home of wealthy heiress, Helen Brach, of the Brach Candy family, in Glenview, Illinois. She later disappeared.

When I got that letter, I began to think that the jewelry that I had bought could have belonged to Helen. Now I know for sure that it did. After I left Northwestern Stables, one of the three men who I talked with, Frank Jayne, Jack Matlick, or Lee Rider must have tipped Victor off. That explains why Victor called me before I got time to call the fence about the jewelry. It bothered them that Richard Bailey had acquired Helen Brach's jewelry through a lady whose husband owned People's Pontiac in Skokie, Illinois. Victor acted because he knew that this jewelry was taken when Helen Brach's house was ransacked, and she was killed.

"Chicago Horse Mafia" leader, Silas Jayne, had mob connections through the Spilotro brothers. Silas had one of his brothers killed. This goes back about sixty years, to the mid-1950s. I decided to get into the horse business. Dundee bought eighty acres about forty-five miles west of Chicago. It included an indoor arena that was 60' x 80' with forty, 10' x 10' horse stalls. Those would be used to board horses both for sale and breeding. Silas Jayne told the horse community, "Richard Bailey will go broke; he doesn't know anything about horses."

I hired a trainer, then started buying horses for a few thousand apiece. I started working with them by training them to jump three to six feet high. I sponsored some television specials by advertising Bailey's Horse Business. The advertising put the business in high gear! Then one of the Horse Mafia's men, a six-foot, 250-pound enforcer in a big cowboy hat appeared in front of my academy. He had been driving his brand-new Cadillac Sedan de Ville like a bat, out of hell, raising a Texas-sized dust storm. I happened to be standing out near the entrance. He asked, "Are you Bailey?"

I replied, "Yep, that's me." He cut loose by threatening my life, and ad. , vised me that the best thing I could do was to get out of the horse business. I listened and just smiled. I told that big cowboy, "You do your thing, and I'll do mine," whereupon he left in a huff and in a hurry. He went straight to the local police department and swore out a peace bond against me by name, Richard Bailey. It is all about MIND CONTROL. It's what you say, how you say it and, of course, the big smile.

A few weeks later, I found out that if the Horse Mafia could not get a piece of your profits, they would burn your barn down. That, indeed, had been the fate of a few barns in the area surrounding Chicago. It so happened that I didn't subscribe to that school of thought. I wasn't interested in giving anyone a piece of anything to do with my business.

CASE OF SUCCESS

To become a success in the business world, you have to be well rounded in many different enterprises. When you combine that balance with knowledge, gumption, and the right amount of influence, you get called genius.

From the humblest of beginnings, born into the Great Depression in 1929, and with nothing more than a ninth-grade education, I joined the Army as part of the 15th Airborne. After an honorable discharge, I came home armed with a desire and, as it would turn out, a knack for entrepreneurship. From a driving school to medical clinics to real estate to franchising, I've started and built more than just a business, I've built success.

Many—if not most—people I come across that have their own businesses have followed a traditional path. They went to school, got a degree, got a job, became a specialist, then took that specialty and went out on their own. Now, there's nothing wrong with that, but despite their GPA or MBA, they'll probably never be called genius. They've become too specialized. They're not well-rounded. Much of my success has come from hiring the right people and giving them thorough training, such as how to answer and close a sale over the phone. Either you have it, or you don't, and if you don't, you don't work for Richard Bailey. Hire and associate with the best, give them the best, and you'll get the best in return, with dividends.

My next venture will be "THE PARTY OF THE CENTURY," which will be the best thing to happen to the band(s) or artist(s) I choose. Details are still being worked out, but I guarantee that, like everything else I got after, it'll be the best.

In the meantime, here's a "taste" of how I work....

One of my ex-girlfriends, by the name of Criss Kabot, brought a friend of hers by my stable, Bailey's Stable. His name was Fred Bernstein. Criss had bought a horse from me and recommended Bailey's Stable to Fred for the purchase of his horse.

As it happens, I didn't sell Fred a horse4 His purpose for the visit was to introduce himself as an investor with whom I might like to deal with. Despite the name, Fred came from Italy and was then living in Melrose Park. He was looking for someone to open a pasta franchise in West Palm Beach, Florida. Fred had access to excellent authentic ingredients, as well as a $100, 000 to invest. He wanted me to be in charge of everything. I told him "no problem," and assured him I knew just how to put together a franchise.

Well, the first thing I did was to check the Yellow Pages for an attorney experienced in franchising matters. I found one on Michigan Avenue in Chicago. I set up a meeting.

The first thing out of his mouth was that he was a Harvard graduate. He asked for $75, 000 up front. "No problem," I said, "but first, just how will you go about putting this franchise together?"

This had been my plan all along, and the Harvard attorney played right into it. To make a long story short, he told me everything I needed to know in one meeting. By the end of the meeting, I knew more about franchising than McDonalds!

So, Fred, his investor, and I headed south for Florida. We found a nice location in a West Palm shopping mall, as well as office space for the company's headquarters. The investor had ordered in a special pasta sauce from Italy. In fact, it was ready to be unloaded. I had the advertising all set and before you could say Mamma Mia, the business was bursting at the seams. We were about to open our second location in Miami when, all of a sudden, Fred's father shows up from Ohio. We were introduced. Afterward, he began spending more and more time around the office until Fred eventually wanted him to be managing partner.

"No problem," I told Fred, and I genuinely liked the idea of hit4 bringing in his father. "I'll just need X amount of money." I walked away with a nice settlement.

On the drive back to Chicago, I stopped for lunch in Atlanta. I saw a sign for Spud World. I went in and saw that all they served was potatoes and toppings. I ordered one with everything on it: a steaming baked potato with all the goodies, something I'd never had—or even heard of—before.

I approached the employee who made my spud and asked for the owner. The poor guy got worried and wanted to know why. When I told him that I thought Spud World had great franchise potential, he relaxed. His job was safe and suddenly I had the owner's name and number in my pocket.

We talked by phone, and I explained some of what I had in mind. Naturally, he was overjoyed. I told him I'd fly back to Atlanta within a few weeks, and we could work out the details then.

My first spud and pasta restaurant was opened in a neat little part of Atlanta they call Underground, a collection of shops, clubs, and restaurants literally under the streets of Atlanta. I decided we would call it Down Under Spot and Pasta World. Business was more than booming. We were excited to open our second location when tragedy struck. One day, while driving back to the airport, the owner broke the news that he'd just been indicted for having his wife killed. I didn't say anything right away, but on my return to Atlanta, I asked to be bought out. He was such an excellent partner and didn't seem the type to be involved in such a thing, but I couldn't see being partnered with him; not with murder hanging over him like that. I wished him well and though I never got a chance to make money off it, it was a valuable education. I got to set up a restaurant and I now knew I could do it with anything.

As fate would have it, I found out about a place called One Potato Two Potato. They were all over the world, the BIGGEST spud franchise out there. I was confident I could take over and double their existing business. I set up a meeting at their Minneapolis headquarters. When I walked in, I got quite a shock. There was a big conference table set up with no less than thirty suit and tie executives sitting around it. I instinctively knew where it was headed, with so many head honchos tuning in. I gave it my best shot anyway.

I opened with how impressed I was with their first-class operation. Even so, I could double their earnings with my expertise in sales and marketing. Next, I talked about compensation. I wasn't after a salary, but a mere 2 percent of the gross increase on total revenue. I cited my experience in setting up Down Under and the plans to take it worldwide, along with the possibilities of adding the pasta sauce from Italy.

With that, I thanked them for their time, and told them I'd rather join than compete with them. I presented my business card and said I looked forward to being associated with their company.

I received a letter from them, telling me what I already knew: They thanked me for my ideas, and although they decided not to move forward at that time, they may want to speak again later.

There were just too many executives in the room. I guarantee if there had been five or less, I could've closed the deal on the spot. Just like I have done with 90 percent of my closings!

PRINCESS FROM EGYPT

In 1978, I was offering for sale a two-hundred-acre tract of land near Antioch, IL. Applicable signs were posted announcing this availability.

An Egyptian doctor stopped by to check out the prospects of the premises and possible uses.

He first noticed a broodmare cavorting in a pasture. He inquired about the asking price. I had just sold the broodmare for $250,000.

Dr. was undaunted and indicated that we should get acquainted. He said that he owned fifty Arabian horses that he wanted to sell and that we could discuss possible mutually agreeable transactions.

In the past I had owned Blue Ribbon Stables in Northbrook, IL. This facility included an indoor show arena larger than Madison Square Garden in New York, City.

Auctions of a variety of horse breeds were auctioned. The last, just coincidentally, were Arabians. The last had been sold two years prior and the least paid for an animal was $200,000. Since that time, the market for Arabians had bottomed out. I reminded the price was since that sale. I did promise him that I would see what I could do with his animals.

The doctor and I continued to chat and get to know each other. I inquired of the doctor what his medical specialty included.

He reported that he had formerly been a bone specialist in a hospital setting. However, he had decided to open a conclave of Chelation Clinics.

I was curious about his operation. He advised he already had facilities just outside of Antioch, IL and on the west side of Chicago.

I suggested that "we" could possibly set up a franchise operation for the clinics with operations worldwide.

The doctor was impressed with the possibilities. I already had a primary location in mind. Specifically, the office building where my fiancé, Dr. Annette Hoffman, had her medical practice located. Actually, wanted him to meet Dr. Hoffman!

The Egyptian doctor looked at the available space, but decided it was too small for how he had envisioned his facilities. He alternately leased a ten-thousand-square-foot space at Union Station in downtown Chicago.

Doctor already had established a clientele and felt that the more central location in the city and access to major transportation facilities were in his best interest. There was even a local train between Where airport and Union Station for the convenience of remote clients.

His medical expertise coming from a different country, I investigate the treatment offerings. I was completely "sold" on his practice when I read a biography of a girl of about ten years who had been confined to a wheelchair and, following the effects of the doctor's treatments, she was able to move about no longer requiring the handicap's aide.

I had already executed many business agreements through Attorney Gus Kangles. He was the best in the business when it came to insuring that Richard Bailey still had the control to call the shots on the total enterprise.

Before the Egyptian doctor's decision on the alternate location, I was prepared to sign on to an agreement of 10 percent of the two medical clinics he already had operational and we would split, equally, all the profits from any franchise operations for as long as the franchises were producing revenue.

This arrangement would have produced a gross revenue of billions of dollars annually.

The doctor was also discussing a personal friend who would be arriving from Egypt that he wished to introduce. I was looking forward to that.

The "friend" was a princess, which explains, in part, the exhilaration I was feeling toward meeting her.

Without a doubt, I am positive I could have taken over "Egypt!" I could have been her "Consultant."

Unfortunately, other nemesis were at work against the fruition of any working arrangements with the Egyptian entourage.

The Doctor and his intimates saw the malicious reporting about my much erroneously and maliciously "publicized" involvement in the death of Helen Brach.

A SMOOTH SUCCESS

Some years back, this polished country Jewish boy with Harvard smarts met a lady and business was the name of the game. I never revealed to her that I was. Jewish. That factor was revealed by my mother, Margaret Self Bailey and only after I had sold a horse to the lady.

The lady, Kit Moss, an up-and-coming entrepreneur and Harvard Business Graduate had sales and marketing businesses who employed a thousand staff members.

(She and I dated for a few years. During that time, she ventured to Peoria, Illinois on the prospect of purchasing a cosmetic manufacturer whose product was a female depilatory for legs. It had a primary outlet in Las Vegas.

She offered $250,000 plus royalties of 10 percent to the current owner. He refused the offer, so negotiations were terminated. When Kit explained the full story to me, I asked her to provide me with a bottle of the product which I would proffer to a chemist to investigate the possibility of our producing a competitive product.

I scoured the Yellow Pages searching for a laboratory willing to invest a time to develop a new product with the same resulting properties. I found Irving Domesky, president, of Allied Laboratory in Elmhurst, IL.

Mr. Domesky said, "No problem," and a product called Satin Leg Shaving Solution was born.

I took Kit in as a partner and went to Las Vegas to a Franchise Show event where one could rent booth spaces (10' x 10') to set up a display of one's product(s).

I displayed signs indicating: "MASTER EXCLUSIVE FRANCHISE OPPORTUNITY AVAILABLE." Several potential customers made inquiries. The terms of such a relationship was an initial investment of $250,000. One particular potential investor and was from Japan and was curious to see a close up of our operation at Northbrook, IL.

He was impressed! He offered that he had his own private plane with him, and he and I could leave Sunday to visit our operation in Northbrook, IL.

I called Kit to advise what was happening and to be ready to meet with him upon our arrival.

Upon our arrival at our facility, I introduced Kit to our guest and gave him a tour of our operation.

Kit listened to every word of our partnership arrangements which took only about fifteen to twenty minutes. Our new business partner sat across form me during the conversation.

Kit had a large, private office at her disposal. After the primary discussion, Kit left the meeting and recessed into her office to type up the agreement.

When she returned to the conference area, she presented the client with a final copy of an agreement of our agreement which the client enthusiastically signed.

Terms were $25,000 down and the balance when the product was delivered to his facility in Japan. Further, he was locked into a five-year minimum time frame providing he lived up to the provisions of the contract.

This is just an example of many such business deals that I engineered over the years. The story goes on and on.

Kit used to tell me that she had never met another man like myself. She had been married and divorced on multiple occasions. One of her eses was a president of Walgreens.

Kit wanted to get married again in a few years after selling her business.

Only because of the negative publicity I was getting on the news media at the time. Once that turmoil settled, we would move to New Mexico and purchase an eighteen-hole golf course. She knew that I loved to play golf. She said I was one of the best golfers she had ever seen.

Unfortunately, those hope and dreams never came to fruition.

Later in history, I was having a glass of wine in a Rush Street bistro in Chicago, IL. A classy place, to be sure.

In walks a beautiful lady looking like a model; diamonds in the ears, and all the other fine features and accoutrements of class. She seated herself.

I signaled the bartender and told him to put her beverage on my tab. This vision of society ordered a glass of wine. She turned to thank me. I decided to join her for lunch.

We chatted over our drinks, and she introduced. herself as Dr. Annette Hoffman. We dated for two weeks and departed to Las Vegas to be married.

As great as a major portion of my life has been, the greatest is yet to come. Hollywood, here I come. LOOK OUT!

I was a "Millionaire Richard Bailey" long before meeting the "Candy Heiress" Helen Brach. My millions were made not from laziness and chicanery, but from working six and seven days a week utilizing wisdom and keen business sense. I was always a smooth and intuitive businessman and knew the right times to best capitalize on my moves.

Having a ninth-grade education never stopped me, because I knew how to find or hire the right person to handle each facet of an operation. I did my own marketing, and I was so accomplished that many entrepreneurs—such as Kit Moss, while I was dating her would seek out my advice. A few were even fortunate enough to sit in, and be educated, during some of my clever and original dealings.

It is both foolish and specious to believe that I was incapable of doing anymore with my life than to wait for an unlucky and unsuspecting "pigeon" to leech off of. I was not only able to succeed on my own I already had!

Helen Brach, more than anything in the world I would like to find out what really happened to her.

Steve Miller set me up as a Scape Goat and he knows it, so does my lawyer Pat Tuite.

In 1996, NBC *Dateline* came to the federal prison in Marion, Florida with Joanne Wolfson, an Attorney I had known for years. The purpose of the visit was to conduct a one-hour taping. Prosecutor Steve Miller was to be in this same taped segment. The producer, a Mr. Murphy, asked Mr. Miller if he had paid to have Joe Plemmons and his girlfriend released from prison. Miller was asked if this could be considered "bribery." he choked and said this was the way they did business. I have a copy of this taped segment if you would like to see it.

While Joanne Wolfson was here during the taping she told me that "invitations" had been sent out to certain Judges and attorneys. The purpose of the invitations was to celebrate the conviction of Richard Bailey in the Helen Brach case! It just so happened that a friend of Joanne was at the celebration. According to the friend once the attorneys and judges present heard the comment about "bribery," and Miller's statement of "that is how we do business," the television was immediately shut off.

HELEN BRACH and RICHARD BAILEY

"**B**RACH CANDY HEIRESS and Richard Bailey" (at a spectacular black tie affair in New York)

"Waldorf Astoria was romantically enduring, dancing to Guy Lombardo's band."

The Year was 1976, the "LOVE OF MY LIFE" was in my arms…

We as a couple were on Top of the World.

"Treat a lady like a Queen and she will love you forever…"

Before he succumbed to leukemia on July 13, 1987, Si apparently laid the groundwork for one last scheme—one that sent Hamm on a wild goose chase through Minnesota looking for the body of Helen Brach. A former cellmate of Si's, Morris Ferguson, told investigators that he had been paid by Si Jayne in 1979 to remove Brach's body from Bailey's stable in Morton Grove and rebury it in a cemetery in the Twin Cities. The story turned out to be false. FBI agents learned later that Si had concocted the scheme to throw off the investigation into the disappearance of Helen Brach. Hamm remains convinced that Si played a significant role in the presumed demise of Brach.

Richard Bailey

Hamm and inmate Morris Ferguson were flown from the penitentiary in Parchman, Mississippi, in a helicopter for days. This was all on the T. V. networks around the country. I am sure Hamm and Si Jayne laid out this scheme together. There has been a family vendetta with Hamm for years.

Today, the fiefdoms of the Jayne family have largely faded from the landscape. The site of Si's Idle Hour stable is now the parking lot for an office building located across Higgins Road from the. O'Hare Marriott. George's first stable, Happy Day, is a parking lot for a Baskin-Robbins store. The pain and disruption caused by Si and the brother's feud can't be erased so easily.

When I, Richard Bailey, first got into the horse business, my brother P. J. who used to be a jockey, and I, decided to go out to Elgin, Ill, where Silas had his stable of horses. Nothing much was said, P. J. did most of the talking, I just LISTENED. When we left, I told brother P. J. , "That GUY is a SNAKE. I want no part of Silas Jayne."

A few weeks went by, then Silas told his nephew, Frank Jayne, "Be careful with P. J. 's brother, Richard Bailey, or he will wind up with your horse stable." Which did HAPPEN.

Lt. David Hamm
and Family Vendetta with Bailey
Brothers Richard Jr. , and Herman Sr. for years:

The Death of Dr. Annette M. Hoffman

Annette M. Hoffman, M. D. died January 4, 2014, twenty-six days short of her seventy-second birthday. My beautiful wife, Dr. Hoffman was finally killed by the horrors and never-ending delays of the U. S. federal justice system. After so many years of waiting she was finally overwhelmed by the crushing immensity of the system. I will never forget the frustration and pain suffered by Annette while she waited in Chicago in 2005 alongside William and Shirley Bailey and their family. She had hopes that the time had arrived, finally her husband would be released. She and Richard would return to her native South Africa where they would be married for the third time and remain there for the rest of their lives.

Dr. Hoffman's hopes seemed justified by the facts. Any reasonable person would have agreed with her reasoning. Joe Plemmons had finally confessed to killing Helen Brach. He openly admitted to shooting Helen and placing her body in an industrial furnace at Inland Steel in Indiana. Plemmons had said that Bailey was not involved in the murder in any manner or form. Surely Judge Shadur would do the right thing now. Surely he would not continue to keep Richard incarcerated for a crime he did not commit. Justice would be late in coming for Richard and Annette, but it would finally come. It was not meant to be, Judge Shadur would not listen to the evidence. Dr. Hoffman would return to South Africa, Richard would return to prison. Annette would linger on for several more years, filled with sadness she would die on January 4, 2014. She was tired, she could not hold on any longer. She would never see Richard again. WILLIAM BAILEY made sure of that.

By insuring that Attorney Zellner could not get Richard Bailey into court for a hearing, there was NO POSSIBILITY of an Acquittal for Richard Roland Bailey Jr.

Full details will be revealed in Vol. II of the autobiographical trilogy of *GOLDEN TONGUE*, Richard Roland Bailey, Jr.

STATEMENT OF FACTS

UNDER THE PENALTY OF PERJURY, THIS DOCUMENT IS AN AFFIDAVIT OF THE FACTS, TO THE BEST OF MY KNOWLEDGE, AND AS I REMEMBER THE ACTIONS OF THE NAMED PARTIES, TO HAVE BEEN.

By signature to this Statement of Facts, as held within this document, I, RICHARD BAILEY, states the statements to be the truth and nothing but the truth; X. _____ Dated; _____ 2010.

"FRANK JAYNE, insisted that I, RICHARD BAILEY, purchase "his" 'one way' ticket, for $20.00, to Palm Beach Florida." "I used his ticket for my travel to Palm Beach, FRANK, insisted on it. I never understood why, until later."

This transaction took place at the same as the issues with the threat on my life. The immediate question that comes to my mind now is "WHY", would he even have a need for a 'one-way' ticket to 'PALM BEACH FLORIDA'???

It is 'obvious' now...why "FRANK JAYNE", was so insistant that I buy his 'one-way' ticket to 'PALM BEACH, FLORIDA'. I finally figured things out. He had to have, everything all set, to conduct the murder of 'HELEN BRACH'...... The 'ticket' would show FRANK went to 'PALM BEACH', if there would have been a problem???

① 5-18-20

The Love of my Life, Helen Brach was worth more DEAD than alive. It was all about 287 million dollars a year. Helen Brach Candy heir, she was the richest woman in the world at that time. "Love of my Life" If you saw the movie "Casino" The one right after Richard Bailey was convicted for "life". It states that Two Spillatro Brothers were murdered due to scams in Los Vegas. That was a lie as you can see coming from Dr. Mike Spillatro's brother Victor Spillatro in the letter. I do meditation often and I was thinking about the lady who testified in court that Helen Brach was a good friend of hers. She drove over to see Helen one day, she was met by a strange man she had never seen before. He stopped her and said that no one was allowed there and told her to leave and before she rolled the window up she heard a lady screaming from the house. This all fits right into my story coming straight from Dr. Michel Spillatro's brother in the Declaration of Martin M. Breiner an Attorney.

The story about the two Spillatro Brothers murdered due to scams in Los Vegas was a lie and a cover-up as you can see

②

Did you know that the Busch Estate pays them (MOB) 287 million dollars a year. Before her death Helen was donating one million dollars a year to the Animal Foundation. It doesn't take a Rocket Scientist to figure this one out, and to think I got a life sentence for a crime I did not commit is horribly wrong. I want the world to know the truth and I am ready to testify in Court or take any Poly-Graph test. I am Innocent and I deserve justice!

The last time I was with Helen Busch was New Years Eve of 1976 at the Waldorf Astoria in New York City. The Mob made sure of that! After dating Helen Busch for four years we were planning on getting married on a large yacht which Helen was planning on buying. We were going to invite our friends and family for a romantic wedding cruise.

So you see I have spent the last 30 years of my life thinking of this horrible act of injustice to the only woman I ever truly loved. As for me I had to serve the ultimate punishment of a life sentence and a broken

③

heart for something I couldn't even fathom or think of doing. So in my last years I would like to get closure and justice. I believe I deserve at least that much. Sincerely: Richard Bailey Jr

It is very obvious Helen Brach was screaming, because "The Mob" had to have been Torturing Helen Brach until she signed the Documents stating all of the Brach "Estate" will be turned over to the Animal Foundation. She was donating One Million per year which was Controlled by "The Mob" then the Mob "Killed Helen". I have no doubt in my mind this is what took place. Helen's Lady friend who stopped by to see Helen. "The Mob" stopped her and told her to drive away and told her no one was about here. The Lady heard the woman screaming and it was coming from the Brach Estate. It was a white car the window was down and a stranger she had never seen before said turn around and leave. She had no choice.

Richard Bailey Jr.

DECLARATION OF
MARTIN M BREINER

Approximately eight years ago, I was in Northfield, Illinois on an Easter Sunday and stopped by to visit a friend of mine, Dr. Michael Spillatro. Dr. Michael Spillatro is a very nice human being with a family of twelve. He is an excellent dentist. I had tutored several of his children on past occasions, and had used his professional services to remove two impacted wisdom teeth. He had removed these two teeth painlessly and expeditiously. I had always enjoyed being invited to his house to meet his charming wife and engaging family.

While I was there that afternoon, two of Dr. Mike Spillatro's older brothers came over to visit with him. One of them was named Victor. Dr. Mike Spillatro introduced me, and then we had a very brief conversation. I marveled at how large a family Dr. Mike Spillatro had, and asked Victor if he had also come from a large family. He then told me that he had five brothers and two sisters. Then, suddenly, he stopped. He then said that he had three brothers. He added that two of his brothers had met an unfortunate end because of a bungled burglary they were involved in at the home of a wealthy heiress living in Glenview, Illinois (who later disappeared). Then he became completely silent. No further conversation ensued between Victor and me.

I didn't make any connection between these comments and past events until three days later. At that time, an acquaintance of mine informed me that Victor Spillatro's two brothers were those killed whose dismembered bodies were found in a cornfield in Indiana. This acquaintance also told me that the wealthy heiress whose house they were accused of burglarizing was probably Helen Brach. I filed this information away for several years.

This past June 1997, I was tutoring Dr. Annette Hoffman's daughter, Julia, when she mentioned that she had been involved with Richard Bailey, the man convicted of planning Helen Brach's murder. I mentioned my conversation many years earlier with Victor Spillatro at his brother's home in Northfield, Illinois; and Dr. Hoffman asked me if I would mind submitting my statements in writing since Richard Bailey was attempting to overturn his conviction in the Helen Brach murder case (1994) by submitting a Post Conviction form 2255. I stated that I would be very receptive to helping Mr. Bailey in any way that I could.

I have never met Mr. Richard Bailey, am not conversant with the events preceding his trial and conviction in federal court three years earlier, and have no personal interest or agenda in the success or failure of his Post Conviction Appeal 2255.

I hereby declare, pursuant to Title 28, United States Code, § 1746, under full penalty of perjury that all of the above is true and correct.

Executed on this 28th day of August, 1997

Martin M. Breiner, Declarant

I, RICHARD BAILEY, DECLARE UNDER PENALTY OF PERJURY THAT THE FOREGOING IS TRUE AND CORRECT. X. Richard Bailey .

EXECUTED ON Monday May 11 , 2009

Helen Brach murder mystery: Mob hoodlums carried out crime

By Chuck Goudie

January 6, 2005 — Sources close to the investigation into heiress Helen Brach's disappearance said one of Chicago's most notorious organized crime families is linked to the case. The ABC 7 I-Team has learned that a member of the infamous Spilotro family allegedly helped carry out the 1977 murder.

When your nickname is "The Candy Lady" and your reputation is that of a sweet suburban socialite, one of the last persons you'd expect to be connected with would be an outfit enforcer and hit man. For Helen Brach, such a hoodlum was among the last people she saw on earth. He was a member of the infamous Spilotro family and Thursday afternoon, federal law enforcement sources say he made Mrs. Brach's final arrangements.

Which Spilotro was involved? It wasn't Tony Spilotro, the unforgiving Chicago mobster who ran Las Vegas rackets until he and his brother, Michael, were buried alive in a cornfield. It was another Spilotro brother -- Victor -- who was recruited to dispose of Helen Brach's body. Victor Spilotro was perhaps the most vicious of the Spilotro hoodlums. Mrs. Brach was one of at least a dozen people whose lives were ended with the help of Victor, according to law enforcement sources.

Tony and Michael Spilotro

A well-placed informant has told agents from the U.S. Alcohol, Tobacco and Firearms Bureau that in 1977 Victor Spilotro made arrangements to sneak Helen Brach's corpse into the Inland Steel plant in East Chicago, Indiana. Authorities say Mrs. Brach was thrown into a blast oven and cremated.

Inland Steel plant in East Chicago, Indiana

Officials say that the mob connection to the Brach case also included a man named Curtis Hansen, who worked with Victor Spilotro to get rid of the body. Hansen was part of the Jesse Jayne gang of horse swindlers. He was also a feared hit man for the outfit crew of Jimmy "The Bomber" Catura and a suspect in seven mob murders. His family also had a reputation. His brother, Kenneth Hansen, is a convicted killer.

Both Victor Spilotro and Hansen have died of natural causes. But the alleged mastermind behind the Brach murder is still alive. Frank Jayne Jr., 70, is currently serving time in a state prison for setting his horse stables on fire.

Federal authorities said they have solid evidence that Jayne orchestrated the Brach disappearance to prevent her from exposing his crooked horse business. They said that Jayne hired the two mobsters to carry it out and incinerate the evidence.

Frank Jayne Jr.

Lee Reiter, a former Skokie police sergeant, allegedly worked as a lookout during the murder. Reiter now lives in a beachside condominium in Mexico.

Reiter and Jayne have consistently denied having any role in the demise of Helen Brach.

Helen Brach

You can see the ABC7 report by clicking on the video icon above. You will need Windows Media Player 9 or higher to view this video. You can get it FREE by clicking here. NOTE: Video clips will only be available for 6-days from the date they were created. ALSO: Video clips will play in a separate window on Mac OS X machines, you may also see a video help screen.

Spilotro family and Thursday afternoon, federal law enforcement sources say he made Mrs. Brach's final arrangements.

Which Spilotro was involved? It wasn't Tony Spilotro, the unforgiving Chicago mobster who ran Las Vegas rackets until he and his brother, Michael, were buried alive in a cornfield. It was another Spilotro brother -- Victor -- who was recruited to dispose of Helen Brach's body. Victor Spilotro was perhaps the most vicious of the Spilotro hoodlums. Mrs. Brach was one of at least a dozen people whose lives were ended with the help of Victor, according to law enforcement sources.

Tony and Michael Spilotro

A well-placed informant has told agents from the U.S. Alcohol, Tobacco and Firearms Bureau that in 1977 Victor Spilotro made arrangements to sneak Helen Brach's corpse into the Inland Steel plant in East Chicago, Indiana. Authorities say Mrs. Brach was thrown into a blast oven and cremated.

Inland Steel plant in East Chicago, Indiana

Officials say that the mob connection to the Brach case also included a man named Curtis Hansen, who worked with Victor Spilotro to get rid of the body. Hansen was part of the Jesse Jayne gang of horse swindlers. He was also a feared hit man for the outfit crew of Jimmy "The Bomber" Catura and a suspect in seven mob murders. His family also had a reputation. His brother, Kenneth Hansen, is a convicted killer.

Both Victor Spilotro and Hansen have died of natural causes. But the alleged mastermind behind the Brach murder is still alive. Frank Jayne Jr., 70, is currently serving time in a state prison for setting his horse stables on fire.

Federal authorities said they have solid evidence that Jayne orchestrated the Brach disappearance to prevent her from exposing his crooked horse business. They said that Jayne hired the two mobsters to carry it out and incinerate the evidence.

Frank Jayne Jr.

Lee Reiter, a former Skokie police sergeant, allegedly worked as a lookout during the murder. Reiter now lives in a beachside condominium in Mexico.

Reiter and Jayne have consistently denied having any role in the demise of Helen Brach.

Helen Brach

You can see the ABC7 report by clicking on the video icon above. You will need Windows Media Player 9 or higher to view this video. You can get it FREE by clicking here. NOTE: Video clips will only be available for 5-days from the date they were created. ALSO: Video clips will play in a separate window on Mac OS X machines, you may also see a video help screen.

Print story

M Gmail

Kathleen Zellner <kathleen.zellner@gmail.com>

97cv7665 USA v. Bailey

Gloria_Lewis@ilnd.uscourts.gov <Gloria_Lewis@ilnd.uscourts.gov> Thu, Apr 5, 2018 at 8:39 AM
To: Andrew.Erskine@usdoj.gov, kathleenzellner@gmail.com, dhjohnson43@aol.com

Counsel-

Judge Blakey wanted me to forward a copy of this letter that was sent to the Court and ultimately filed under seal.

Click HERE to take our customer service survey

Mrs. Gloria Lewis
Court Room Deputy to the Honorable John R. Blakey
US District Court for the Northern District of Illinois
219 S. Dearborn Street
Chicago, IL 60604
312-818-6699

Bailey Sealed Letter.pdf
705K

Indian Creek Veterinary Clinic
Ross E. Hugi, D.V.M.
Equine Veterinary Medicine and Chiropractics

25147 N. Garner Road
Mundelein, IL 60060
(847) 949-0055 office
(847) 949-0154 fax
(847) 707-1720 cell
Email: [illegible]

March 12, 2018

Honorable Judge John Robert Blakey
Everett Mc Kinley Dirksen Building
United States Court House
219 South Dearborn Street
Chicago IL. 60604

RE: Richard Bailey Case Number 97 C 7665

Dear Honorable Judge Blakey,

I am writing this letter on behalf of Richard Bailey, not because I am trying to defend him, but to clear my own conscience. I made the biggest mistake of my life when I got involved with Richard Bailey in a horse sale transaction in 1989. To start making amends, I immediately began to cooperate with the United States District Attorney and his investigators in 1990. As part of this cooperation, I wore a recording device several times. On February 22, 1991 I recorded Robert Cheska and others (see enclosed Exhibit A). After the recording was transcribed, I was given a copy to review. I made a copy of this transcript. During this conversation Robert Cheska made a very fanatic statement about Richard Bailey NOT being involved in the disappearance of Helen Brach (enclosed Exhibit B). This evidence was never made available to Richard Bailey or the Court.

I have a lot of respect for your deceased colleague - the Honorable Judge Milton Shadur and was aware that he was not a fan of using the civil sentencing scale in a criminal trial. I can not help but think that this evidence and witness might have tipped the scale in the other direction. There are several reasons that I did not present this information to this Court before today - I was married a second time in 1996 and started a second family in 2000 and was afraid to expose them to any retaliations or notoriety, I truly wish I would have sooner.

I realize that Richard Bailey was denied his motion and his case is on Appeal. I have no idea what you can do with the evidence I have brought to your attention today or even if you will care, but I had to tell the Court so that I may finally move past the second biggest mistake I ever made... helping the truth become what prosecutors get a judge or jury to believe.

If I can be of further assistance, please don't hesitate to contact me.

Sincerely,

Ross E. Hugi, D.V.M.

EXHIBIT A

1DATE:	FEBRUARY 22, 1991
CG FILE:	196B-75683
CONSENSUAL:	NAGRA
PARTICIPANTS:	ROSS HUGI; ROBERT CHESKA; BILLY LIGGET

SA JAMES P. REILLY:	This is SA JAMES REILLY the date is 2/22/91, we're at the ROSS HUGI residence in Gilmer...
HUGI:	Mundelein.
SA REILLY:	Mundelein, Illinois. ROSS HUGI is...has a recording device on his person in anticipation of conversations he may have with ROBERT CHESKA later this morning.
HUGI:	Washroom — Hug. We've just been sitting here, you're ears must of been ringing like crazy cause we've been sittin here....BILLY's been here an hour.
CHESKA:	I know where we can buy a great stable. Cheap. I bet Equestrian Oaks is really getting cheaper everyday.
HUGI:	Well I don't know, I don't know ya know. I don't want to know. (Laughs). I wouldn't buy it. There ain't a way in the world I'd buy it.
CHESKA:	(Garble)
HUGI:	Not me.
CHESKA:	I guarantee that old man will.
HUGI:	Ya know I had (IA) telling him...I had a long conversation with MICHAEL, MICHAEL's ah....shipped her to and from ledgers or helped and he got in a long conversation with DON and DON claims he knew nothing about BURNS' history, knew nothing about nothing....and I suppose then if that's the case you can probably feel sorry for him.

- 1 -

	said to the best of my knowledge I really don't know how that went down.
HUGI:	Nooooo.
CHESKA:	Make the deal, make the deal and then let 'em just go along with it. (Laughing) Hey I didn't see nothing...I don't know....
HUGI:	Yeah but they start to get close, they start to get....
CHESKA:	They're gonna come....I'm serious. March.
HUGI:	That's what you heard to huh?
CHESKA:	March indictments here. Oh they're gonna have indictments though...but things that happened three/four years ago they're talking....
HUGI:	I just told him...the one time they come and talk to me....they wanted to start 1977-78 BRACH.
CHESKA:	(IA) poor you and BAILEY, I will promise you I know for a proven fact...BAILEY...RICHARD BAILEY had nothing to do with BRACH. He did not put her in the ground, he did not have nothing to do with it...other than he was doing her, selling her some expensive cheap cheapen race horses and everything else, and jumpers and everything else. The only thing he did was con her out of some money. He had nothing to do with her getting killed....and he had to take the rap for it because he was.
HUGI:	Well because the only other way was to fess up to...well I mean he, he fessed up to selling horses to her and I mean...ya know they were junk. He's told me the same story. I mean the first thing he ever said to me about that was why the hell would I kill the golden goose

INDIAN CREEK EQUINE CLINIC
25167 N. GILMER ROAD
MUNDELEIN, IL 60060
(847) 949-0055

Honorable Judge John Robert Blakey
Everett McKinley Dirksen Bldg.
United States Courthouse
219 South Dearborn St.
Chicago, IL 60604

MOB
"MOB" NO. 1 HITMAN VICTOR SPILLATRO TOLD BAILEY RETURN JEWELERY OR I WILL KILL YOU

A beautiful lady about 45 years old came by Bailey's stable looking to buy a horse. I said to her I have just the horse for you. I bring the horse out of his box stall. Take him into the indoor arena and turn him loose. She said that was the type of horse she was looking for. I said perfect. Then I put the horse back in his box stall. Then I said why don't we go to Hackneys and have a hamburger. She agreed. Then after a few drinks, she asked me the price of the horse. I said one hundred twenty five thousand. At that time she said I am going thru a divorce and don't have any money. But my husband owns Peoples Pontiac in Skokie. She said however I have jewelry worth one hundred twenty five thousand. I said that's no problem. However she said it is in a safe over the kitchen sink and my kids have company. I said that's no problem I have kids of my own. So we go to the house in Skokie. I keep the kids busy in the living room while she is getting the jewelry out of the safe. Now we go back to the stable. I give her a bill of sale and she gives me the jewelry.

When I looked at the jewelry it looked like the same jewelry Helen Brach was wearing when we were in new York City at Waldorf Astoria. On New Years Eve in 1976. But I said it can't be. How could she possibly have Helen's jewelry? I couldn't see any connection at that time. Next day I go to Northwestern Stable. There was Frank jayne, Jack Matlick and Lee Rider. I knew Frank Jayne would know a fence that would buy the jewelry. I got his name and address and left. Next day before I had time to see the fence, Victor Spillatro called me, which never happened before. Victor told me to meet him at a restaurant in front of the Studio Restaurant in Morton Grove. Which I did. I walked in at the back of the restaurant and in a booth there was Victor and an Italian friend of his. Victor was bouncing a golf ball on the table and drinking a shot of whiskey. I said to Victor what's up, Victor said the jewelry you got for the horse. Has to be returned to her husband. I was a little nervous however I had a smile on my face. I said Victor you have to be kidding. She got a bill of sale for the horse and I got the jewelry. Why don't we split the

MOB

jewelry three ways? I am not greedy.

The "mob" will kill you guys sooner or later anyway. Victor said he can't do that. I said to myself her husband has to be a front for the "mob". Victor said to meet her husband at the same restaurant in a certain booth at a certain time. Return the jewelry or I will kill you. Victor's partner said I hear you are a pretty good golfer. He said you should come to a certain golf course that was in the Elmhurst area and we play 18 holes. I told him I would think about it. I didn't tell him I was a scratch golfer. But I had no intention of playing at that golf course. Because In knew that was where the mob hung around.

I went back to the Rest with the jewelry. There was her supposedly husband and Victor. Gave them the jewelry and got out of there. Now in 1997 when I was locked up in Marianna FL. I got a letter from my wife Dr. Annette Hoffman. Annette mailed me a Declaration signed by Martin Breiner. Martin Breiner said two of Victor's brothers had met an unfortunate end to their life. Because of a bungled burglary they were involved in at the home of a wealthy heiress living in Glenview, Illinois. (Who later disappeared) This was Helen Brach.

At that time I got to thinking that jewelry which I thought could have belonged to Helen. Now I know for sure it was. Frank Jayne, Jack Matlick and Lee Rider soon as I left N.W. Stable they had to have tipped Victor off.

That Bailey got Helen Brach's jewelry thru a horse deal with a lady whose husband owned Peoples Pontiac in Skokie. Right away Victor got into the action. Because they knew this jewelry was taken when they ransacked Helen Brach's house and killed her.

March 11, 2005

NEWS

MICHAEL SNEED
e-mail
sneed@suntimes.com

The Brad case...

Sneed's sources: Investigators are still looking for "shopping bags of bearer bonds" reportedly taken with millions missing from the estate of heiress Helen Brach — which they believe could finally connect the case against whoever killed her in 1977.

"Brach's husband reportedly bought shopping bags full of bearer bonds from a Glenview bank which the couple hid in their home," he said. "Some of it has been found," he said.

▲ Investigators are trying to determine if someone cashed them in — or are holding them in safety deposit boxes.

Sneed hears search warrants are imminent.

The LeFlore case...

The White Supremacist Connection: Sneed hears the Chicago Police crew responsible for putting
 together against white

EXHIBIT A

LIFE
MEMBER

HOLMES POLYGRAPH SERVICE, INC.
6210 WEST FLAGLER STREET
MIAMI, FLORIDA 33184

Confidential Polygraph Examinations
Personnel Screening
Internal Security Consultants

TELEPHONE 44

WARREN D. HOLMES

1. Former Detective Sergeant in charge of the Lie Detection Bureau of the Miami Police Department, 1955-1963.

2. Self employed, Holmes Polygraph Service, Inc., Miami Florida, 1963 to present.

3. Graduate Keeler Polygraph Institute Chicago, Illinois.

4. Former President of the Florida Polygraph Association.

5. Former President of the Academy for Scientific Interrogation (predecessor name of the American Polygraph Association.)

6. Charter and Life Member of the American Polygraph Association and the Florida Polygraph Association.

7. Mr. Holmes has been a regular guest lecturer for the FBI, the CIA, the Secret Police, The Canadian Police College, the Singapore Police Force and many other U.S. federal agencies.

8. Mr. Holmes has written numerous articles on criminal interrogation for various police journals.

9. Mr. Holmes has administered polygraph examinations in many national cases, including the following: The John F. Kennedy Assassination, The murder of Martin Luther King, Watergate, The Robert Vesco case, Philadelphia Major Frank Rizzo, The Pitts/Lee case and the William Kennedy Smith rape case.

10. Mr. Holmes has administered polygraph examinations, nationwide in 922 separate murder cases.

11. Mr. Holmes was the lead investigator in five separate murder cases that led to the exoneration of Joe Shea, Mary K. Hampton, Freddy Pitts, Wilbert Lee and Joe Spaziano, who were wrongly convicted and incarcerated for first degree murder.

www.TheInnocentRichardBailey.com

"BURY"
MR. RICHARD BAILEY
COERCED BY HAVING HIM TAKE A
POLYGRAPH...

Something that investigative reporter; Jim Ylisela, who has been working with "STEVE MILLER" Prosecutor, against RICHARD BAILEY. Trying to get myself, Richard Bailey, to take a POLYGRAPH for years. My brother, WILLIAM BAILEY and his wife SHIRLEY had always thought Jim Ylisela was a professor of English, and they had me believing the same.

JIM YLISELA was an investigative reporter, with Steve Miller as the prosecutor, came up with someone they knew of, thinking Richard Bailey would not pass a POLYGRAPH, with WARREN HOLMES as a polygraph expert. Jim Yleisela flew from Chicago to Miami, and rented a car to drive Warren Holmes to Coleman, Florida Prison, to give me a polygraph. Jim Ylisela sat right there with Holmes interrogating ME with a lot of questions before giving me the polygraph.

"Polygraph" results, were not what Jim Ylisela wanted to hear. WARREN HOLMES, after the test was over, turned around and told my counselor, "Mr. Miro, this man is NOT a criminal."

Before Warren Holmes left for Miami, Holmes said he would mail a copy of the polygraph test results to Richard Bailey. Jim Ylisela had to drive Holmes back to Miami, about four hours away. I waited a few weeks for the polygraph, Holmes was supposed to send it to me. It never showed up. I called Holmes and asked him about it, Holmes said Jim Ylisela told him NOT TO MAIL THE POLY-GRAPH TO RICHARD BAILEY. HOLMES told me that he had to do what JIM YLISELA tells him to do...

I had an attorney, Ronald Fox, during the polygraph. I called Ronald Fox and told him what happened. He said Holmes can't do that. "He has to mail a copy to you." Finally, I did get a copy of the polygraph from Holmes.

Attorney Ronald Fox and Warren Holmes told me that Jim Ylisela is not out for Richard Bailey. Ylisela told my brother, WILLIAM BAILEY, that a man named LARRY YELEN, who runs FOX TV in Chicago, use to be one of his "students" and told him, after your brother takes the polygraph, he would do a FULL story about it. But it never happened. Why? Because the polygraph test results came up POSITIVE.

LARRY YELEN, and FOX TV, were hoping for NEGATIVE polygraph results, hoping that I would fail the test, giving them a hot story. Then JIM YLISELA and STEVE MILLER would have had a big celebration on FOX TV, in their compulsion to "B U R Y" RICHARD BAILEY... but that never happened. In any way whatsoever. Because, "MR. RICHARD BAILEY PASSED THE POLYGRAPH WITH FLYING COLORS."

*Note: Here is what the Chicago Reader Magazine had to say about Investigative Reporters (like Jim Ylisela);

October 20th, 2011:

"There is nothing unusual about [Investigative Reporters] working with 'Prosecutors' or Defense Attorneys, for most Investigative Reporters, these are 'essential relationships' for getting the job done.
It's part of the GAME, you have to do it."

Richard Bailey

INVISIBLE MAN

I, Richard Rolad Bailey, Jr., am 89 years old and have been locked up for almost 25 years. Thursday, March   , I arrived back at Coleman Low, to begin my next round of torture by a thousand drops of aromatic prayer oil, to which I apparently have developed a powerful allergic reaction. This has occurred in C-3, C-1, and now B-2. I had extensive tests for my heart due to category "ten plus" chest pains, which as I have explained at great length to Ms. Cook are caused by prayer oil sprayed by inmates. These are violent chest pains! I have taken my cause to my counselor, case manager, unit manager, and the warden. And many other staff members have been made aware. They have tried to help me get relief through medical channels. I have been sent to the local hospital a number of times but the cardiologists have not been able to connect the prayer oil to my cardiac attacks or to anything else.

In the last five months, I have had four stents put in my circulatory system to help my ailing heart. Before my recent encounters with prayer oil, I had no heart ailments and no stents. All of this has happened in the last year. As long as I am outdoors, I have no problems.

My research has shown that prayer oil works against my nervous system and can cause cancer as well. It is being heavily used now to cover up various odors ... perhaps smoke, or cooking smells.

When I arrived back from my most recent hospital trip, I found out that inmates and some staff thought I was dead. All of my property had been stored in two green bags, awaiting shipment ot my next of kin. My mattress and locker were gone from my cubicle, there was nothing left of me. The inmates were incredulous to see me alive. Frank, my inmate legal representative had sent materials to be copyrighted before he 'found out that I had died.'

On my first visit bacj to the rec yard, Mr. McCook put his hand on my shoulder and said, "Mr. Bailey, you are living!" He had heard of my demise also.

Many years ago I saw the movie The Invisible Man, which came to my mind as part of this fiasco. I began thinking, I am the Invisible Man, supposed to be dead. If I didn't have mind control, this would have driven me crazy. All these years, getting a life sentence. Then, in 2005, informant Joe Plemmons confessed that I was not involved in the murder of Helen Brach, eleven years after I was convicted. He admitted he shot Helen Brach, and had the Spillastros Brothers bury her body. Even now that is widely known, even by my judge that I am innocent, I remain in custody for a crime I had no knowledge of.

I am begging you to ship me to Chicago, or somewhere else soon, before I really become invisible, dead from the allergic reactions I keep having to the prayer oil which is so prevalent here at Coleman Low.

Jason Weeks, in B-1, was telling an inmate at Coleman Low in Florida that he Richard Roland Bailey, Jr. when he was an old man. We played a lot of racket ball together. If there was ever an atomic bomb to go off, it would kill everyone except Bailey. Jason said this when he was leaving and going home after many years.

Richard Roland Bailey, Jr.
Richard Roland Bailey Jr.
90 years old

This is just the prime of life, only once I get out of this torture chamber from C3-C1 building and B2. This is unbelievable.

Fairchild AFB
Strategic Air Command
Spokane, WA

1942.

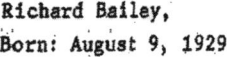

Richard Bailey,
Born: August 9, 1929

    The youngest of twelve, 6 boys and 6 girls. Mother had german measels at birth, which paralyzed my eye lids and affected my memory brain. When I was in the first grade, teacher told my mother I should be in a school for retarded kids. Mother did not buy that. So I remained in a public school.

    I joined the 15th Army Air Force at age 16 with my mother's consent, but got out at 19 after serving three years.

    When I got out of the Army I found an eye specialist, Dr. Robert Fitzgerald, he connected my eyelids to my eyeball muscle and it worked.

    Mother is on the right, behind me is my sister Linda, to my left is my sister Fay and her boy Ronnie.

Paul Bailey, jockey, dead at 79

Paul J. Bailey, a popular jockey who rode from 1944 to 1968, died Thursday morning of a malignant brain tumor at his home in Florida, a family friend said. Bailey was 79.

A native of Kentucky, Bailey rode his first winner at Mission Park in Oregon. He retired 24 years later with $5.9 million in career earnings and 1,788 victories.

Among his most memorable races, Bailey won the Travers Stakes in 1955 aboard Thinking Cap and the 1958 Gardenia Handicap on the champion filly Quill. He was also second in the 1951 Kentucky Derby aboard Royal Mustang, a 53-1 shot.

— *Matt Hegarty*

One summer I helped my father and brother, Paul, who lived in Kentucky, plowing the fields with one mule, plant tobacco and sucker it. We lived in a shanty of a house, holes in the floor and newspaper print for wallpaper. We slept on the floor. I was so happy when my mother picked me up to bring me back to Bloomington, Illinois.

The photograph is Richard Bailey and older brother Paul J. Bailey to my left. Brother PJ had just come back from San Francisco, California where he became a jockey riding race horses. he had just bout a new 4 door black Cadillac with twin spotlights. I asked if it was OK if I drove his car to school the next day. He said "Any time." I drove around the school a few times to show off my brother's new car. That made my day!

Product description

Product Description

Golden Tongue: Helen Brach "Candy" Heiress and "The innocent man that killed her?"

On January 1, 1977, Richard's Life changed forever...

Imagine, experiencing the enormity of emotional extremes from spending New Year's Eve, dancing with the 'Lady of his Dreams' to a wonderful night of romance at the Waldoff Astoria. Then her 'no-show' on February 19, 1977, in Florida, the devastation of her disappearance, inconceivable, that 20 years later, being accused of the Murder of HELEN BRACH, "insanity!"

Helen Voorhees Brach, was known as the "Candy Heiress," who lived a life of Luxury and prestige. Her mansion in the northern suburbs of Chicago was staffed with butlers and housekeepers, but all of that couldn't compete with her love of horses. Brach, the wealthiest woman to ever disappear, disappeared without a trace in 1977. Her disappearance sparked national attention and her male suitor Richard Bailey was swept into the limelight of this enduring murder mystery. There were several suspects, but never a conviction, at least until federal prosecutors came after Richard, a Chicago area stable owner.

RICHARD was involved in Murder... invented by David Hamm, Illinois State Police. Fueled by an old vendetta, with Richard's Family, convincing Steven Miller (AUSA), that RICHARD BAILEY, a 'womanizer' was the main suspect in "Candy Heiress," HELEN BRACH... "RICHARD's HEART WAS CRUSHED."

Richard went from Dance & Driving Instructor, and Horse Entrepreneur, to a "COLD-HEARTED MURDERER," of a "lady that brought only pleasure into Richard's Life."

Golden Tongue: Volume I tells the story through the eyes of Dr. Annette Hoffman, a plastic surgeon who fell madly in love with a stranger, Richard Bailey. Will Dr. Hoffman believe in Richard's innocence or guilt? Dr. Hoffman is slung into the drama and sensationalism of who killed the "Candy Heiress" Helen Brach. This is the story of a search for Truth, Love, Lies, Murder, the Mafia, a Rogue Prosecutor and Detective, and a justice system that isn't very just!

THE INNOCENT MAN THAT KILLED HER?

The story is also being told by the man that has been sentenced to a death penalty by his age and his health... a man that has proven the "facts" that should have released him and the facts could only be told after LOVING this LADY.

Golden Tongue

Volume 1

Picture taken Marianna Fl-Prison '95

Richard Bailey with his newlywed Dr Annette Hoffman. Only person ever locked up for Helen Brach. Brach Candy heiress mysterious disappearance. Treats a lady like The Queen of Shuba. Married to a murderer - or was I?

Annette Hoffman was a successful Gold Coast plastic surgeon when a silken Romeo named Richard Bailey stole her heart. Seven years later, Bailey sits in prison, convicted of conspiring to murder the candy heiress Helen Brach. But Hoffman stands by her man. "He knew how to treat a lady," she says

Love with the Improper Stranger

by Dennis Rodkin

When she met him, she was a 52-year-old plastic surgeon, practicing out of a Gold Coast townhouse and raising the younger of her two daughters in a new home on one of Lincoln Park's best streets. Dr. Annette Hoffman's practice billed about a million dollars a year, and she dressed in boutique clothing and drove a black Mercedes—"the only color I ever drive," she says. "I think it's just elegant." Sometimes she thought about how far she had come since her lonely childhood as a ballet prodigy from an emotionally cold middle-class family in South Africa.

One Friday in April 1994, as she often did at the end of the workweek, Hoffman went by herself to The Waterfront, her favorite Rush Street seafood place, for lobster and a glass of wine. She had been seeing patients all day, so she was dressed to the hilt, she says, "in my designer stuff, with eight or nine bangles on one arm."

Richard Bailey spotted her right away. "When she walked in, the way she was dressed and the way she carried herself, she was a knockout," he says today. "It was love at first sight. That was the first time I ever felt that way in my life." Bailey sent over a glass of wine, and she looked over to thank him.

"He was fairly handsome," recalls Hoffman, "but he had bad eyelids. I thought, He should see me for his eyelids." They started talking and wound up extending the conversation at her house later.

So started a whirlwind romance, soon to be interrupted by a storm of a very different kind. Eight days and two dates after meeting, the couple flew to Las Vegas and got married, but 13 days later Hoffman had the marriage annulled and told Bailey to move out of her house, although they continued to see each other. That July, she was surprised when he didn't show up for their date at a Rosemont restaurant. She soon found out why.

Richard Bailey, her smooth-voiced, tango-dancing Romeo, was being charged with soliciting the murder of the Chicago candy heiress Helen Brach, who had disappeared 17 years before. Investigators made the case that Bailey—who did admit that he had helped several other people dupe wealthy women into investing in worthless racehorses—suspected that Brach had figured out his scam and was about to turn him in. Although Bailey claimed, and still claims, that he had nothing to do with Brach's disappearance, U.S. district judge Milton Shadur concluded in June 1995 that Bailey had conspired to have Brach murdered, and sentenced him to 30 years in prison—the equivalent of a "life sentence," acknowledged the judge, for the 62-year-old con man.

By the time of Bailey's arrest, Hoffman already had ample evidence that there was more to his silken persona than he let on: When they met, he had lied to her about his age; full of Champagne on their wedding night, he got so sick, she says, that "he couldn't consummate the marriage, if you don't mind my putting it that way"; and he had no credit cards or even a wallet, just a wad of papers held together by a rubber band. Still, Hoffman stood by Bailey throughout his trial and today claims to love him more than she has ever loved anyone except her two daughters. She even married him briefly a second time, in a meeting room at the Metropolitan Correctional Center downtown, when it appeared he might be released from custody if he had a home to go to.

If Bailey is ever released from prison, says Hoffman, "I will marry him again—I just won't buy a horse from him." Bailey, too, says he hopes they will be together again. He misses her "kiss of fire," he says in a phone interview from the Florida prison where he is serving out his sentence. "It was a fabulous relationship, and every time I see her it starts all over. I'll go anywhere she goes."

▲ Hoffman today: a "kiss of fire"

That could be difficult: This summer, Hoffman moved back to South Africa, where she hadn't lived in more than three decades, since coming to Chicago with her first husband, fresh out of medical school. Hoffman closed her practice two years ago, sold her $1.2-million house and her $860,000 office building, and has accepted a teaching job in Durban. With no grandchildren and none promised, she wants to live again near her only brother. But she also says a big reason for leaving Chicago is her frustration with the legal system that "set Richard up." The stress of the experience also contributed, she says, to debilitating back pain that now has her wearing a weighted harness to correct her posture.

To further vent her frustration, Hoffman has written a book she calls *Married to a Murderer—or Was I?* that her agent, Sharon Kissane of South Barrington, says has had nibbles from major publishers, though Kissane declined to identify any by name. She is at the moment beefing up Hoffman's manuscript, "putting in more of the courtroom story," Kissane says, "which readers always want."

Hoffman's older daughter, Yvette Gordon, a 31-year-old obstetrician and gynecologist in Houston, says that the past seven years of her mother's life are fertile literary material, though she may not have in mind the same book her mother has written. "It's like a Danielle Steel novel or something," Gordon said recently, while in town to buy one of her mother's two Mercedes. "She comes from nothing and builds herself up to the top, but she kind of destroys it herself."

Gordon, the only child from Hoffman's first marriage, says that her mother has been lonely all her life, but that Bailey relieved the loneliness somewhat. "She seemed happier with him," Gordon says. Gordon met Bailey twice. The first time was right after the wedding, when Gordon was a student at Southern Illinois University School of Medicine in Springfield and her mother and Bailey drove down to introduce him over dinner. Their second meeting occurred at a holiday dinner. Gordon also attended a day of Bailey's trial, at her mother's request. Having seen so little of him, she says, she has no solid impression of Bailey, only of the way her mother felt about him. "She believed he loved her more than anyone since my father had loved her," Gordon says.

"I don't think my mother has ever really been happy," Gordon continues. "She didn't have an easy childhood. Her parents were kind of distant and they had no money, and she was driven to succeed because the money and the success would kind of replace the loneliness. But I don't think it ever worked." Hoffman herself acknowledges much of this, telling rueful stories about her isolated childhood, when she spent hours alone practicing ballet and studying. "In South Africa," she says, "parents didn't really speak to their children."

Born Annette Lotter in Pretoria in 1942, Hoffman is a petite woman with short dark hair, high round cheekbones, and distinctly feline, diamond-shaped brown eyes. She says she had plastic surgery to repair a broken nose while in medical school and to lift her upper eyelids when she was 38. Despite having lived in Chicago since the mid-1960s, she still has a strong South African accent, and she speaks so intently that the accent becomes very fetching. She smokes nonstop and sits with the restrained energy of a coiled spring while we talk in a half-packed office on the third floor of her former practice.

"I was born very hyperactive, so my parents were told when I was three to put me into high-intensity physical activity," she says. They chose dance and gymnastics, and by the time she was four, Annette had begun a long streak of winning medals and trophies. She also excelled in her studies, and emphasizes that she was not only first in her class but first in her entire school of 1,500 girls. At 14, she turned down a prestigious dance scholarship to London in order to pursue a medical career. She started medical school at 17. "My problem was that I was too smart," she says.

Right out of medical school, at age 23, she followed her first husband, a fellow South African doctor named François Booyse, to Chicago, where he had a postgraduate research post. Her first job was at the University of Illinois hospital, with the pediatric cancer department. She soon moved to Northwestern Memorial Hospital's ear, nose, and throat department, where she specialized in head and neck surgery. In 1973, she set up her own private practice in plastic surgery.

By the time she met Bailey in April 1994, Hoffman had been divorced twice and widowed once, in 1986. Her first divorce had resulted from conflicting career paths: Hoffman had a flourishing career here, but Booyse wanted to move on to a post in another city, she says (Booyse is now at the University of Alabama). Her second husband, an older doctor at Northwestern, left his wife for her but made her agree to have no children with him. The third husband, William Hoffman, lost his business, a Maywood Pontiac dealership, over tax problems weeks into their marriage, so she helped him finance a luxury imports dealership. When he died of hepatitis B in 1986, their daughter, Julia, was five years old.

Annette Hoffman says she dated a lot after William Hoffman's death, but gradually got fed up with men. "I couldn't find one that interested me at all, because like Elizabeth Taylor, I always had more than the men I met," she says. "I had more money, I had more brains and education, and a nicer home. I would buy them cars and everything, and that's my fault. You can't buy love. It's either there or it isn't."

Hoffman claims to have been surprised by her head-over-heels fall for Bailey; as they tell it, both fell fast and hard. Following their chance meeting at The Waterfront, they had two more dates that first week, one of them at the fabled Pump Room, where he had called ahead to reserve a prime booth and a bottle of Dom Pérignon. He held her hand lightly throughout the meal, and they danced waltzes and tangos. "He knew how to treat a lady," she says. "His manners were Victorian, Old World, and he was funny, funny, funny." Bailey told Hoffman that he owned two stables and sold horses and gave some lessons. He even boasted that he had once sold Helen Brach some horses. "But I'm not a horse person," Hoffman says, "so I had just listened superficially to be polite."

A few days later, he called to say he wanted to take his "beautiful doll"—he had taken to calling her that—to Las Vegas. She

platinum card," she says. He spent the afternoon sick—"not from the Champagne, I don't think, but from the excitement and his age," she says—and their planned dinner at Caesars Palace was ruined when he spent a long time in the men's room vomiting. She hauled him back to their suite, and while he slept, she took some identification information from his driver's license, then sat up all night watching him and worrying.

At work, Hoffman was accustomed to running background checks on employees, so she was already plugged in to a private investigator, Nancy Lewis, who worked for the well-known Chicago detective Ernie Rizzo. Hoffman says she told Lewis (who could not be reached for comment on this story) that she had just done something wild—married a man she had known only a week. "How wonderful!" responded Lewis. "Who is he?" When Hoffman said the name Richard Bailey, there was a very long pause, and then Lewis said, "You don't mean Richard Bailey, the horse man?"

A man in uniform: two versions of Bailey

If Bailey ever gets out of prison, "I will marry him again," Hoffman says. "I just won't buy a horse from him."

The investigator told Hoffman that Bailey was widely known for fleecing rich women with horse sales. Hoffman called a close friend and told her all this, and the woman advised her to act nice to Bailey but get an annulment right away. So when they got back to Chicago, Hoffman started the process of an annulment. Meanwhile, Bailey moved into her home—he had been living with another woman in the far north suburbs, but says the woman understood that their relationship was not exclusive—and took up driving Julia, 12 years old at the time, to school and friends' houses and making dinner for the three of them.

When Nancy Lewis told Ernie Rizzo about the call from Hoffman, he thought, "Holy Christ, he got another one," Rizzo recalls. "I had been watching Bailey's gigolo act for years, since before Helen Brach disappeared, because he'd been involved with other women who had called me." Rizzo says he told Hoffman she had made a mistake.

Thirteen days after the wedding, Bailey came home with a surprise, not knowing that Hoffman had one of her own. His was a wedding band he had bought at Marshall Field's. Hers was an annulment. She had packed all his things, and she told him to move out. He says he replied, "'No problem.' I didn't marry Annette to give her problems, but unfortunately these things

(continued on page 190)

says she told him that there would be "no hanky-panky, and we'd have two rooms, and I would pay for my own. He said, 'I'll be a very good boy.'" Off they went on a Saturday morning, just eight days after meeting each other.

Hoffman calls herself "a smart professional woman who's had to take care of herself," but no alarms went off when the rose-filled limo that picked them up at the Vegas airport took them straight to the courthouse, where they filled out papers for a marriage license. "I thought this was a funny joke I would play along with," says Hoffman. She noted, however, that although Bailey had told her he was in his early 50s, he indicated on the form that he was 61. Today he says he hadn't discussed the wedding idea with her. "I was in love and I could see that she was," he says. "There was no reason to get into a conversation."

Next stop was a wedding chapel where they sealed her fourth and his second marriage—she in a silver jumpsuit and he in lime green slacks. On the way to the hotel, they polished off a bottle of Dom Pérignon, but then when they got to the front desk, she finally started to wonder about this guy. "He had no credit cards,

LOVE WITH THE IMPROPER STRANGER
continued from page 147

of the woman he had left for Hoffman.

Bailey says today that it wasn't just Rizzo who tried to sour Hoffman on him. He says that a few days before she threw him out, Hoffman had heard from a man who told her Bailey was trouble. "[The caller] was one of my investors who put up a $100,000 investment in Blue Ribbon Stables and lost his money," says Bailey. "He evidently had a chip on his shoulder about me, and [when] the grapevine told him about Dr. Hoffman marrying me, he called her several times and told her, 'Richard Bailey will poison you. You might not wake up.'"

Richard Bailey was the youngest of 12 children, and spent an impoverished childhood in Illinois and Kentucky. As a boy, his older brother Bill recalls, Richard was a caddy at a golf club in Bloomington, Illinois, and he loved to dance. As Gretchen Reynolds reported in Chicago in 1994, after leaving home Bailey bounced around Texas, Kentucky, and California before landing with his first wife in St. Louis, where he ran a driving school. Most of his customers were older women, many of them widows. Even after months of Bailey's supposed instructions, some of them were still unable to drive. When a Missouri regulatory board shut him down in 1970, Bailey and his wife moved to Chicago. Eventually the couple divorced.

Bailey met Helen Vorhees Brach on a blind date in 1973. She was the 61-year-old widow of Frank Brach and an heir to his Chicago candy empire. She was worth about $30 million and living on a country estate in Glenview. She and Bailey became close, and he sold her horses. Four years later, on the eve of a vacation in Florida, Brach disappeared. She is presumed dead, and her body has never been found. When the disappearance was first investigated, Bailey's alibi was solid: He demonstrated that he had already been in Florida waiting for her when she disappeared. It wasn't until 1994 that the FBI pulled together a complete case, which involved an elaborate scheme of horse killings, insurance fraud, and corruption among a web of horse industry figures, including Bailey and the prominent stable owners Silas and Frank Jayne. The FBI claimed that Brach might have been on to Bailey's tricks, and that a witness had heard Bailey say she had to be gotten rid of.

The case attracted national attention, and 18 different people pleaded guilty to corruption charges. The big catch, though, was Bailey, who pleaded guilty to 16 counts of racketeering, conspiracy, money laundering, and mail and wire fraud in the horse-trading scheme before Judge Shadur decided that Bailey had also conspired to murder Helen Brach.

"They've got the wrong guy locked up," Rizzo says. "He's not a murderer. He's a gigolo." Rizzo is well acquainted with Bailey, having investigated him for several women clients over the years; after his arrest, Bailey recruited Rizzo for his defense team. Rizzo says Bailey wouldn't have wanted to lose Brach—his goose that laid the golden egg—and that Brach didn't mind the horse-dealing. The tax write-offs on the losing horse investments were bigger than the cost of the horses, he says. Rizzo believes that Brach's houseman, Jack Matlick—a long-time employee with a grudge over a recent firing and rehiring—was the killer. (Matlick has always maintained that he is innocent of any involvement in the Brach disappearance.)

Bailey's brother Bill is convinced that Richard was railroaded. Now 81 and living in Palatine, Bill Bailey raised some of the money that went to defending Richard. He says Brach had become a friend of the family, and that another sibling, Faye Hanley (now deceased), used to welcome Brach to her home in Sarasota and to her downstate farm. His brother Richard was "a businessman," says Bill. "He had had a driving school and a meat-smoking business and he was rehabbing condos in the city. He loved to dance, and women like Helen Brach loved to dance. Those women went to him to have a good time, and they were happy to be with him. He didn't make a hell of a living on those women."

Nevertheless, Bailey received a 30-year jail term, blowing Annette Hoffman a kiss as U.S. marshals led him from the courtroom following the sentencing. Since then, Hoffman has stood by him, certain that Bailey's romance with her was different from his mercenary relationships with other women. "He paid me back for everything I put on my credit card in Las Vegas," she says, "and he never asked me for a penny." (Rizzo, though, says that following the 1994 annulment, Bailey's attorney was close to requesting alimony from Hoffman when he had to back off to handle the more serious federal charges instead.) She even shot off the best zinger of the whole sordid saga: Shortly after his arrest, when a judge labeled Bailey a flight risk and was hesitant to free him, Hoffman offered to let Bailey stay with her. "He could stay in the guest room, which will really aggravate my current boyfriend," she told a Tribune reporter at the time.

Later Hoffman married Bailey a second time, at the Metropolitan Correctional Center, in an effort to get him released into a stable home setting, because the judge had suggested Bailey had no ties in Chicago and might flee if released. Bailey was never released, and Hoffman later got a divorce on the advice of her attorney. (Hoffman says her younger daughter, Julia, was so disturbed by the jailhouse wedding that she told her mother, "The best thing you could do for this family is kill yourself.") Hoffman spoke with Bailey by phone twice a week for a few years, but has let that taper off because, she says, it bothers her daughters. She has visited him at the Florida prison—the last time was about 20 months ago—and even got to know one of his prison buddies, who was the first to encourage her to write a book.

"Annette is a very fine lady who stuck by Richard, and when you stick with somebody through that, you must be pretty good," Bill Bailey says.

Rizzo suggests that even though Bailey appears not to have swindled her, Hoffman is just like Helen Brach and others he did con. "They didn't have a problem with giving him money," he speculates. "They had a problem with him leaving. Annette Hoffman was the same way. Lonely. She wanted the love and loyalty. She was a good score for him. She would have kept him in fine jewelry and clothes. He wasn't looking for sex with her. Living well was his sex."

Bailey continues to pursue appeals, but Hoffman quietly acknowledges that he will almost certainly die in jail. If he were released, she says, she would set him up in an apartment separate from hers and, while her attorneys drew up a prenuptial contract, spend a few years getting to know him better before marrying him again. Though she knows that a third marriage to Bailey is unlikely, and that his messy life spilled all over hers, Hoffman keeps the candle burning anyway. "[Richard Bailey] treated me like I was the only woman on earth," she says, "like I was the Queen of Sheba."

Golden Tongue
Volume II

"R I C H A R D   R O L A N D   B A I L E Y"
"AUTO BIOGRAPH"
FROM CHILDHOOD UNTIL TODAY - 1929-2012...
"Treat a Lady like a Queen...and she will Love You, forever..."

The history of grandeur "BAILEY'S HORSE FACILITY" acquisitions, of a World rated fabulous running horse, which was claimed by the 'eye of the owner'. Mr. Bailey, was known for his "horse sence", not only with the horses but, the business of horses, as well. This Rulers Ile, was claimed by the corporate acquisition, for the ridiculous price of $10,000.00.....

Rulers Ile, won it's first five races after a trimming of the horse's talents, by the personal direction of Mr. Bailey. Mr. Bailey's stable's view was always, the best for the horse, is the best for the rider. Rulers Ile, became very accustom to the rides that would be taken through the riding trails in Tryon, North Carolina.

Rules Ile, would enjoy the trail rides so much that he never denied a jump that I ask of him...

A 17-year-old murder mystery may be solved

RAKISH ROMEO

Stable owner Richard Bailey (left) was married when he dated candy heiress Helen Brach (above, in a 1952 painting).

WHEN CANDY HEIRESS HELEN Vorhees Brach vanished 17 years ago, there were few clues but plenty of speculation about her fate. Did the shy, 65-year-old widow—worth an estimated $20 million—go into hiding after a botched facelift? Was she killed by the caretaker of her 18-room mansion in the Chicago suburb of Glenview? Was she buried beneath a fireplace in a nearby stable? "Everyone had a theory," says Ernie Rizzo, a private detective hired after her disappearance in February 1977. "None of them panned out."

Until now, perhaps. On July 27 federal authorities announced sweeping indictments against 23 people in the clubby world of race and show horses —owners, trainers, veterinarians—for various fraud and racketeering schemes. One of those charged was Richard Bailey, a former Chicago-area stable owner who authorities say had been romancing Brach at the time of about to report his little scam," says Henderson. "I said, 'Helen, you should not have told him. You should have just gone to the authorities.'"

In February 1977, Brach entered the Mayo Clinic in Rochester, Minn., to have a general checkup. Returning home a few days later, she was met at Chicago's O'Hare airport by her houseman, Jack Matlick. He later told police that he spent much of the weekend with her at her Glenview mansion and then drove her back to O'Hare to catch a Monday morning flight to Fort Lauderdale, where she was buying a condo. Brach never arrived.

Matlick, who had been the Brachs' caretaker for 18 years, was originally a prime suspect in the case. "He had the easiest access to her and the opportunity to destroy physical evidence," says Pat Colander, author of *Thin Air*, a 1982 book about Brach's disappearance. But with no body and very little evidence, local police never even officially classified the case as a homicide.

Then in 1979, two years after the disappearance, a spray-painted message appeared on the road near Brach's house: Richard Bailey Knows Where Mrs. Brach's Body Is. Stop Him! Please! When Bailey was called in for questioning, recalls former Glenview police sergeant Joseph Baumann, "he never said anything."

Brach was finally declared dead in 1984, and the bulk of her estate—now valued at $70 million—was used to set up a foundation to support animal causes. Then in 1989 a wealthy widow from another well-to-do Chicago suburb came forward with claims that she too had been fleeced by Bailey. Similarities between her allegations and long-standing questions about Bailey's relationship with Brach prompted the federal investigators to launch a racketeering probe.

Investigators have yet to reveal any details of how they believe Brach was murdered but are keeping Bailey in a Chicago jail while he awaits trial. Meanwhile an ornate family cemetery plot that she had built in Unionport, Ohio, tells a sad tale. Her husband is already buried there, along with her dogs Sugar and Candy. But a marker Brach had placed next to her own gravesite reads, "Father, I pray I may be worthy to be near my loved ones who are with thee." That grave remains empty.

▪ DAVID GROGAN
▪ BARBARA SANDLER and ALYSIA TATE in Chicago and CINDY DAMPIER in Miami

Keep burglars and muggers away from your home, with...

BodyGuard 2000 Infrared Security Alarm still only $49.95*

But read this ad for an even better deal!

Unsavory characters roam the streets. They are eyeing your property, waiting for their chance, and have only one thing in mind: how to get into your home and how to burglarize it. It's difficult to defend yourself against these determined criminals. Until now, there was only one way, and that was to protect yourself with a central security system. Those systems are indeed effective, but they are very expensive. Installation can cost more than $1,000, and there is also a stiff rental fee every month. But the battery-operated *BodyGuard 2000 Infrared Security Alarm* can replace such an expensive system. You install it yourself in a matter of minutes. You arm and disarm it with your personal security code. It detects movement in a 90° arc up to 30 feet distance. If the infrared field is invaded, it emits a piercing siren tone that will scare the daylights out of even the most hardened and experienced burglar.

We are one of the largest importers of this advanced security device and can bring it to you at the unbeatable price of just $49.95. But we have an even better deal: *Buy two for $99.90, and we'll send you a third one, with our compliments—absolutely FREE!* Protect yourself and your family. Get the advanced and sophisticated *BodyGuard 2000 Infrared Security Alarm* system today!

*The BodyGuard 2000 Infrared Security Alarm is more than just a sophisticated alarm system. In its "ding-dong" mode, you can also use it as an announcer of visitors, for your home, for your store or for your office. Each system comes with two stickers announcing that your property is protected with this sophisticated system.

FOR FASTEST SERVICE, ORDER TOLL FREE (800) 797-7367
8 a.m. to 6 p.m., 7 days a week

For quantity orders (100+), call Peaches Jeffries, our Wholesale/Premium Manager at (415) 543-6675 or write her at the address below.

Please give order Code #1010A310. If you prefer, mail check or card authorization and expiration. We need daytime phone # for all orders and issuing bank for charge orders. Add $4.95 standard shipping/insurance charge (plus sales tax for CA delivery). You have 30-day return and one-year warranty. We do not refund shipping charges.

since 1967

185 Berry St., San Francisco, CA 94107

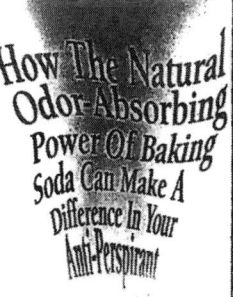

What Makes ARM & HAMMER® Baking Soda Such A Great Deodorant?

Baking Soda (Sodium Bicarbonate) is one of nature's building blocks refined from a mineral called "Trona."

Found in all living things, baking soda is a natural buffer, which means it neutralizes acids and bases to help keep pH as close to neutral as possible.

That's why baking soda is such a powerful deodorant. Unpleasant odors are technically acids (like sour milk) or basic compounds (like fish). They evaporate into the air and can then be smelled.

Baking soda, as a buffer, targets odors, absorbing and neutralizing them before they can evaporate and be smelled.

Why Is ARM & HAMMER® Deodorant Anti-Perspirant The Natural Choice?

It's the first brand that combines the natural deodorizing power of genuine ARM & HAMMER® baking soda with a powerful anti-perspirant to keep you dry.

Perfumey cover-ups work differently. They use fragrance to blend with unpleasant odor. The odor is still there—but it's masked.

With Baking Soda, The Absorbed Odor Is Eliminated Effectively And Naturally.

It's A Different Kind Of Odor Protection You Can Trust.

▲ Helen and Frank Brach wed in 1951.

her disappearance. Among other things, Bailey, 65, is accused of conspiring to cause Brach's murder after she threatened to turn him in for duping her into buying virtually worthless horses at vastly inflated prices. She lost hundreds of thousands of dollars. Bailey is also charged with defrauding 12 other women of more than half a million dollars in bogus horse deals.

"He wined these women, took them to the fanciest restaurants and professed his love for them," says Assistant U.S. Attorney Ron Safer. "It was a classic confidence game." For his part, Bailey insists that he is innocent. "My client is a charming guy who women fall in love with," says his attorney Patrick Tuite. "But that is not a crime."

Friends say Brach's naïveté made her susceptible to Bailey's charms. She had been living alone since the 1970 death of her husband, Frank, a cofounder of the Brach candy company, keeping mostly to herself, consulting a psychic by phone almost daily and sending donations to animal welfare organizations. "She was a dignified, soft-hearted woman—a quiet Doris Day," says former actress Robyn Douglass, who also kept her horses at Bailey's stable. "But she was a poor judge of character."

Nor was she a woman of great sophistication. The daughter of an Ohio coalfield engineer, Helen Vorhees was a pretty, 38-year-old redhead working as a coat-check girl at Miami Beach's Indian Creek Country Club in 1950 when she met Frank Brach, 22 years her senior. Married a year later, they had no children. Bailey says he met Brach at a car wash five years after Frank's death and soon she began boarding horses at his stables. Described by one investigator as "a Cary Grant type who could take you to the cleaners with his charm," Bailey went riding with Brach, wooed her at candlelit dinners and, a few weeks before her disappearance, escorted her to New York City to ring in the New Year dancing to the music of Guy Lombardo.

Soon after, Brach began complaining about her companion. She told her cousin Edelene Henderson that he had swindled her by selling her second-class show horses. "When the horses came up lame, she told me she had told Bailey she was

▼ Jo-Anne Wolfson, Bailey's lawyer and riding mate in the 1970s, says he is innocent.

MEMORIAL TO HELEN BRACH;
(Proceeds from these literary effort will help support these such Memorials,)
(This is what 'The Love of My Life', would of wanted...)

THIS IS AT THE:

LINCOLN PARK ZOO,

IN

CHICAGO ILLINOIS.

It's Time for Herman & Sharron

June 11, 2015

Barack H. Obama
Executive Office of the President
1600 Pennsylvania Ave
Washington, D.C. 20500
202-395-3000

Dear Mr. President,

Approximately 2 to 3 weeks ago, Richard Bailey, who is 85-years of age, and also my uncle, submitted a petition for commutation of sentence. Bailey was sentenced to 30-years imprisonment in the year 1995. Approximately 222-months of Bailey's sentence was based on his alleged involvement or participation in the murder or disappearance of Ms. Helen Vorhees Brach, the Brach Candy heiress. Recently, another man has admitted that he and two other men committed the murder of Ms. Brach and also disposed of her body. Also, Bailey was recently given a polygraph examination and questioned about his knowledge and involvement in Ms. Brach's murder and disappearance. Bailey denied that he had any knowledge or involvement in the murder and disappearance, and the polygraph examination showed no signs of deception. In light of the above, I respectfully request you to strongly consider and grant my 85-year old uncle a sentence commutation.

Sincerely,

Herman Bailey
Executive Television Producer
Christian Television Network
6922 142nd Avenue
Largo, Fl 33771
727-535-5622

A Ministry of CTN WCLF TV22, P.O. Box 6922 Clearwater, FL 33758

U.S. Department of Justice

Office of the Pardon Attorney

Washington, D.C. 20530

July 15, 2015

Mr. Herman Bailey
Christian Television Network
6922 142nd Avenue
Largo, FL 33771-4725

Dear Mr. Bailey:

  Thank you for your letter to the Attorney General of June 11, 2015, requesting that the petition for commutation of sentence for your uncle, Mr. Richard Bailey, be granted.

  I wanted to confirm for you that Mr. Bailey's petition for clemency has been received, and we have added your letter to his clemency file. His application is under consideration. While we cannot predict when a decision will be reached, he will be notified promptly once final action has been taken on his application.

  Thank you for sharing your thoughts with the Attorney General.

Sincerely,

Deborah Leff
Pardon Attorney

In Loving Memory
of
ANNETTE MARIE HOFFMAN

Date of Birth: 30 JANUARY 1942
Date of Rest: 04 JANUARY 2014

GOD SAW YOU GETTING TIRED

God saw you getting tired,
When a cure was not to be.
So he wrapped his arms around you and whispered ,
"come to me ."

You didn't deserve what you went through,
So he gave you rest.
God's garden must be beautiful.
He only takes the best.

And when I saw you sleeping,
So peaceful and free from pain.
I could not wish you back,
To suffer that again

Giving comfort. Taking care.
24 Hour Helpline . 24-uur Hulplyn
0860 025 500
www.doves.co.za

31 01 2013

14a Edge of the Sea
24 Lagoon Drive
Umhlanga Rocks, 4320
South Africa

My Dear Richard,

I am dictating this letter since my right arm is still a bit weak following the stroke I had last February. In general though I am doing fine and hope to be fully recovered by the time that you complete your retrial.

I am still hoping that you will take me up on my invitation and move to South Africa so that we can be together again.

I have a very lovely 3-bedroomed condo — gated and situated right on the waters edge here in Umhlanga Rocks.

* Please note the correct address above

I am very thankfull and filled with joy that you and I are in touch again. I received the file that you sent me during late December and the letter with photographs two weeks ago. You look just wonderfull in your photo! I am so pleased to see you have not gained weight.

I am not sure I quite understand what the next step in your life is. My current understanding is that you are to have a retrial infront of Judge Shadur. If this is true, I hope that you will conduct yourself with extreme humility. We all know that your somewhat "cocky" behaviour during the original trial resulted in the judge giving you a maximum sentence. What is important right now, is your freedom only. Any financial gain that you may think may or may not be on the cards — is of such secondary importance!

ANNETTE M. HOFFMAN.MD.,FICS.(USA)
Mb.ChB(Pret).,M.Med.(USA)
Diplomate: American Board of Otolaryngology
Diplomate: American Board of Cosmetic Surgery

Facial Cosmetic and Corrective Surgery
'edico-Legal Consultant

A-14 Edge of the Sea
24 Lagoon Drive, Umhlanga Rocks 4320
South Africa
PH: + 27 31 561 7960
FAX: + 27 31 561 7990
E-mail: ahoffman@lantic.net.

31/07/13

My dear Richard,

I apologize for not writing to you sooner, but as you can see it is still very hard for me to write since my stroke affected my right side.

Time goes by so quickly, I had so much hoped that your new trial would be coming up now. I guess all you can do is to wait one day at a time and make sure that your new lawyer is prepared. I assume you will still be guilty of racketeering charge under RICO but hopefully you will get a shortened sentence on the Brady issue.

I trust that you are still in excellent shape physically. I am looking good myself but I just still have trouble moving about freely as well as writing. It is slowly getting better. Thank you for your last two letters which arrived safely. I hope to hear from you again very shortly. Your letters always cheer me up.

Well, that's all I can handle right now.

Best wishes & all my love,
Annette
XXOO

It's Time for Herman & Sharron

June 19, 2018

Donald J. Trump
Executive Office of the President
1600 Pennsylvania Ave.
Washington, D.C. 20500
202-395-3000

Dear Mr. President,

Richard Bailey, who is 89 years of age, and also my uncle, submitted a petition for commutation of sentence.

Richard Bailey was sentenced to 30 years imprisonment in the year 1995. Approximately 222 months of Richard's sentence was based on his alleged involvement or participation in the murder or disappearance of Ms. Helen Vorhees Brach, the Brach Candy heiress. Since then, another man has admitted that he and two other men committed the murder of Ms. Brach and also disposed of her body. Richard Bailey was given a polygraph examination and questioned about his knowledge and involvement in Ms. Brach's murder and disappearance. Richard denied that he had any knowledge or involvement in the murder and disappearance, and the polygraph examination showed no signs of deception.

In light of the above information, I respectfully request you consider and grant my 89 year old uncle a sentence commutation.

Sincerely,

Herman Bailey
Executive Television Producer
Christian Television Network
6922 142nd Avenue
Largo, Fl 33771
727-535-5622

A Ministry of CTN WCLF TV22, P.O. Box 6922 Clearwater, FL 33758

It's Time for Herman & Sharron

Richard Bailey
FID 08727-424
Federal Correctional Complex – Coleman LOW C1
P.O. Box 1031
Coleman, FL 33521-1031

August 27, 2018

Dear Uncle Richard,

You are to be commended for keeping your sanity while in prison, using positive thoughts, without knowing what tomorrow will bring.

You have asked to use my name. Here is my quote about mind control for Herman Bailey: "My mind control comes from a personal relationship with Jesus Christ, daily Bible reading, and prayer. My positive thinking comes from daily meditation on God's Word. I ask daily for God to control my mind, body and soul."

<u>You have permission to use my words only.</u>

Sincerely,

Herman Bailey
Executive Television Producer
Christian Television Network
6922 142nd Avenue
Largo, Fl 33771
727-535-5622

A Ministry of CTN WCLF TV22, P.O. Box 6922 Clearwater, FL 33758

▼ Jo-Anne Wolfson, Bailey's lawyer and riding mate in the 1970s, says he is innocent.

In 1996 NBC Dateline came to the federal prison in Marrean, Florida with Joanne Wolfson, an Attorney I had known for years. The purpose of the visit was to conduct a one hour taping. Prosecutor Steve Miller was to be in this same taped segment. The Producer, a Mr. Murphy, asked Mr. Miller if he had paid to have Joe Plemmons and his girlfriend released from prison. Miller was asked if this could be considered "bribery". he choked and said this was the way they did business. I have a copy of this taped segment if you would like to see it.

While Joanne Wofson was there during the taping she told me that "invitations" had been sent out to certain Judges and attorneys. The purpose of the invitations was to celebrate the conviction of Richard Bailey in the Helen Brach case! It just so happened that a friend of Joanne was at the celebration. According to the friend once the attorneys and judges present heard the comment about "bribery", and Miller's statement of "that is how we do business", the television was immediately shut off.

The Scent of Danger

Manufacturers use fragrance to sell, but it can hurt your health. BY JORG MARDIAN

YOUR FACULTY OF SMELL IS probably your most underrated sense. You can detect at least 1 trillion distinct scents. Your memories and emotions linked to smells can be stronger than those associated with sight or sound.

Manufacturers have tapped into this powerful emotional consumer response, adding artificial scents to many household products. And this has brought about some serious health concerns.

A Fragrance by Any Other Name

In the commercial industry, a fragrance is anything that adds a smell to something else. Manufacturers of products like shampoos, air fresheners, house cleaners, candles and dryer sheets re-create inviting scents in products. Some grocery stores artificially pump in aromas of chocolate and baked bread; car dealerships spray artificial "new car smell" inside vehicles; perfume manufacturers create "scent logos" to elevate a brand's appeal. A study by Nike showed that adding scents to their stores increased intent to purchase by 80 percent.

The public generally perceives scented products as pleasant and harmless. But these fragrances often contain chemicals that can be dangerous when inhaled or touches the skin. Many are listed on the Environmental Protection Agency's (EPA) Hazardous Waste List. They include numerous carcinogens, neurotoxins, respiratory irritants, solvents, aldehydes, petro-chemicals, phthalates, narcotics and more (Connie Pitts, *Get a Whiff of This*).

There are many clinical accounts of fragranced products causing, triggering and exacerbating an increasing number of health conditions. People with multiple chemical sensitivities experience excessive reactivity to a wide range of chemicals and can develop dysfunction in organ systems that baffle physicians.

It increasingly appears that chemical sensitivity comes from the body's detoxification systems suffering from accumulated chemical exposure. This can result in strange forms of cancer, neurological, autoimmune or genetic disorders, and a widening array of allergies, says the Arizona Center for Advanced Medicine.

Consider this stunning fact: When you see the word "fragrance" on the label of a product, that scent will typically contain a blend of 100 to 350 ingredients. About 5,000 fragrance ingredients are used in heavy rotation, and the Food and Drug Administration gives them a free pass from being revealed to consumers, even when products have caused serious health problems.

But the fragrance industry is facing a real problem: About 30 percent of U.S. citizens (98 million people) now exhibit serious symptoms to the toxic chemicals in their products, according to the *Journal of Environmental Health*. Some experts believe chemical fragrances may be causing many modern diseases. This concern is slowly seeping into public consciousness as the new "second-hand smoke."

Hazardous Household Products

If you have not given this subject much thought, you should start examining some of the products you use.

The EPA reveals that potent carcinogens are present in your fabric softeners and dryer sheets. Benzyl acetate is linked to pancreatic cancer; limonene is a known lung irritant; dichlorobenzene, a carcinogenic solvent, causes respiratory distress and heart attacks. Fabric softeners and dryer sheets are specifically designed to transfer their scent onto clothing, which means these chemicals stay close to your body.

Laundry detergent is no better. It may contain nonylphenol, shown in studies to cause reproductive and developmental problems. The carcinogen formaldehyde has also been added to fragrance formulas, as have phthalates, causing hormone disruptions, cancer, birth defects and fertility problems, according to the Natural Resources Defense Council.

Everyone has favorite hair products, but shampoos and moisturizers may contain paraben preservatives that tamper with hormone function, perfumes that cause allergic reactions, and even lead, which can lead to cancer.

Air fresheners also poison the very air you're trying to enliven. The Environmental Working Group says they include the known carcinogen 1,4-Dichlorobenzene, a dangerous chemical found in the blood of 96 percent of Americans, as well as other volatile organic compounds that can cause headaches, breathing difficulties, depression, irregular heartbeats and other health challenges.

Do you want to create some ambiance with scented candles? Many of these contain acetone, benzene, lead, carbon monoxide, toluene and more. The lead comes from metal wicks that release particles, and these have been found in the human brain where they are associated with Alzheimer's Disease, as well as birth defects in babies, according to National Air Quality Testing Services.

Go Fragrance Free

Chemical fragrances are invisible and often pleasant, but most are deceitfully dangerous. Look for products that are free of fragrances. Check ingredient lists. Avoid any product with one of these as an ingredient: fragrance, parfum, phthalate, DEP, DBP, DEHP, limonene or linalool. And note: Some products labeled "fragrance free" still contain fragrance ingredients to mask unpleasant chemical smells.

If you want a scented product, look for one that uses essential oils instead of chemical artificial fragrance. You can use essential oils (in a diffuser) as an excellent, safe way to freshen up a room, and you can dab a drop or two of essential oil onto a washcloth and put it in the dryer with your laundry to freshen your clothes.

For a list of safer cleaning products and recipes for making your own, visit Less-ToxicGuide.ca. You can also search the Skin Deep database at ewg.org/skindeep, a comprehensive list of safe products for cleaning and personal care. ■

1942.

Richard Bailey,
Born: August 9, 1929

The youngest of twelve, 6 boys and 6 girls. Mother had german measels at birth, which paralyzed my eye lids and affected my memory brain. When I was in the first grade, teacher told my mother I should be in a school for retarded kids. Mother did not buy that. So I remained in a public school.

I joined the 15th Army Air Force at age 16 with my mother's consent, but got out at 19 after serving three years.

When I got out of the Army I found an eye specialist, Dr. Robert Fitzgerald, he connected my eyelids to my eyeball muscle and it worked.

Mother is on the right, behind me is my sister Linda, to my left is my sister Fay and her boy Ronnie.

RICHARD ROLAND BAILEY- From Childhood Until Today- 1929-2012....

- CADDIED at Bloomington Country Club, made enough money to buy a bicycle and sell newspapers.

- SOLD 'LOOK' Magazine door to door after school.

- RAISED PIGEONS and sold babies (scabs) to Mr. Goodspeed

- SOLD SNAKES to a scientist. My dog Bob and I would hunt garter snakes water moccasins in a special pasture with a creek.

- WORKED ON PIG FARM, chicken farm, and dairy farm.

- PASSED OUT PAMPHLETS and collected alms for brother Tom, a preacher, for his tabernacle.

- WENT INTO PRODUCE BUSINESS after the Air Force.

- GOT INTO COSMETICS BUSINESS with a product known as 'Satin Leg Shaving Solution'. At a franchise show in Las Vegas, sold business to customer for $250,000.

- STARTED A BALLOON GIFT WRAPPING BUSINESS.

- OPENED DRIVER EDUCATION SCHOOLS in Illinois and California with over 70 instructors. Built from the ground up in California on a choice piece of property.

- TOOK OVER MEDICAL CLINICS at 500 North Michigan Avenue and the Oak Brook Professional Building in Chicago.

- BOUGHT A 57 UNIT APARTMENT BUILDING on a $3,000,000 unsecured note. All condos sold out within a few weeks.

- HAD A LEASE OPTION ON A 207 ACRE FARM in Antioch, Illinois.

- PROVIDED WORLD CLASS SALES AND MARKETING to independent inventors and entrepreneurs, trademarking or patenting their ideas.

- TAKING OVER BUSINESSES FOR 20 YEARS, such as Allied Labratory, World Class Sales and Marketing for 10% of the gross on a five-year agreement.

The List Goes On And On

Regards,

Richard Roland Bailey
The Golden Tongue

Golden Tongue

There has been volumes of news media including television, radio, books, magazines and other print media about **Richard Bailey** recently.

GOLDEN TONGUE. Prosecutors used tis term to imply that I was very persuasive and convincing in what I would tell people, particularly ladies.

GALLOPING GIGILO was used by the neational news media based on comments by a person in the courtroom told saying that he saw Helen Brach and myself riding the horse trails.

RAKISH ROMEO was the Brainchild of People Magazine's "Romance" Editor.

NUMBER ONE CON-MAN IN THE WORLD was the input from World News.

SILKEN ROMEO was the creation of the noted Chicago Magazine.

NATURAL BORN CON-MAN is attributable to author Ken Glade in his book titled HOT BLOD.

POLISHED COUNTRY BOY came into being after I sold a horse to Kit Moss, a Harvard Business Graduate who employs a thousand in her sales and marketing business. She even dated that "polished country boy for a few years........Hmmmmmmmmm?????.

THE GENIUS...this Richard Bailey comments Perry Snyderman, a top real estate attorney at Rudnick & Wolf Law Firm in Chicago, to this day at the successful conclusion of negotiations to purchase a $3,000,000 condominium property (55 units) on Lake Shore Drive in Chicago. Funding was guaranteed to **RICHARD BAILEY** on an unsecured NOTE through Paul Jones, through GLENVIEW BANK.

Both Mr. Snyderman and Mr. Jones boarded horses at Bailey's Stables and were considered Mr. Bailey's good friends.

Further, Mr. Jones and Mr. Bailey went fox hunting together in Trion, North Carolina each January.

Kitt Moss, Perry Snyderman, and Paul Jones are only a very few of the myriad friends of **Richard Bailey.**

Richard's first grade teacher told his mother, Margaret Self Bailey, Jewish, that she believed Richard belonged in a school for "retarded youngsters".

Other hand, Richard's Mother believed in her son and knew he would become a polished, suave entrepreneur.

WORLD NEWS and **KEN GLAD** will both be proven that I am NOT a "CONMAN from CHILDHOOD....

A CASE OF SUCCESS

will be the

AUTOBIOGRAPHY in FOUR VOLUMES

o f

GOLDEN TONGUE
Richard Roland Bailey, Jr.

****

Volume I

Introduce Dr. Annette Hoffman

****

Volume II

Illuminates the Life of the

G O L D E N   T O N G U E

Richard Roland Bailey, Jr.

****

Volume III

Concludes the tale with Candy Heiress Helen Brach

****

Volume IV

Golden Tongue "MIND CONTROL"

****

Books will be written by one of the world's top authors

and

will be the best books and movies ever presented.

Once one has developed a rounded sense in the business world, there is nothing you can't do.

Even run for PRESIDENT!